DogLife ❧ Lifelong Care for Your Dog®

DACHSHUND

tfh

Susan McCullough

DACHSHUND

Project Team
Editor: Stephanie Fornino
Indexer: Ann W. Truesdale
Designer: Patricia Escabi
Series Designers: Mary Ann Kahn, Angela Stanford

TFH Publications®
President/CEO: Glen S. Axelrod
Executive Vice President: Mark E. Johnson
Publisher: Christopher T. Reggio
Production Manager: Kathy Bontz

TFH Publications, Inc.®
One TFH Plaza
Third and Union Avenues
Neptune City, NJ 07753

Printed and bound in China

11 12 13 14 15   1 3 5 7 9 8 6 4 2

Library of Congress Cataloging-in-Publication Data
McCullough, Susan.
  Dachshund / Susan McCullough.
    p. cm. -- (Doglife)
  Includes index.
  ISBN 978-0-7938-3613-0 (alk. paper)
  1. Dachshunds. I. Title.
  SF429.D25M326 2011
  636.753'8--dc22
                    2010034080

This book has been published with the intent to provide accurate and authoritative information in regard to the subject matter within. While every reasonable precaution has been taken in preparation of this book, the author and publisher expressly disclaim responsibility for any errors, omissions, or adverse effects arising from the use or application of the information contained herein. The techniques and suggestions are used at the reader's discretion and are not to be considered a substitute for veterinary care. If you suspect a medical problem consult your veterinarian.

Note: In the interest of concise writing, "he" is used when referring to puppies and dogs unless the text is specifically referring to females or males. "She" is used when referring to people. However, the information contained herein is equally applicable to both sexes.

The Leader In Responsible Animal Care for Over 50 Years!®
www.tfh.com

CONTENTS

INTRODUCTION

INTRODUCING THE DACHSHUND

Most people can't help smiling when they see a Dachshund. To those who aren't accustomed to living with this breed, that long body and stubby legs look a little comical, especially when compared with the way most other dogs look. Unfortunately, the Dachshund's unique appearance has led to nicknames such as "wiener dog," "sausage hound," and other equally derisive monikers.

But those who love the Dachshund know better. They understand that inside that comical-looking body beats the heart of a dog who's loyal, loving, courageous, independent, and totally unafraid to show a little attitude when he believes the occasion calls for such. That said, you don't need to be on a first-name basis with a Dachshund to appreciate this breed in its totality. You simply need to know about his roots and understand how he came to be—from his frankfurter-like appearance to his big-dog temperament.

HOW DOGS BECAME DOMESTICATED

We know that the Dachshund's history began many centuries before the breed itself actually came into being, but we don't know exactly how many of those centuries preceded the development of this long-bodied, short-legged little dog. In fact, there's no scientific consensus as to when or where wild canids began to evolve into domestic dogs. The one idea upon which experts do appear to agree is that today's canine companions—whether those dogs are Dachshunds, Dandie Dinmont Terriers, Doberman Pinschers, or any other breed or breed combo—are all descended from wolves.

Until recently, scientists did agree on where the domestic dog originated: They thought that point of origin was in eastern Asia. However, in the summer of 2009, that consensus was called into question when two anthropologists from the University of California at Davis and a biologist from Cornell University collected and analyzed blood samples from village dogs in Egypt, Namibia, and Uganda. The samples revealed that the African dogs have just as much genetic diversity as the East Asian dogs do. That doesn't mean that domestic dogs originated in Africa—for one thing, there are no wolves there—but scientists are now wondering whether the domestic dog's beginnings were somewhere in between east Asia and east Africa, such as the Caucasus mountains.

Scientists also aren't certain when the process that transformed the wild wolf into the domestic

The Dachshund is loyal, loving, courageous, and independent.

dog began. Various theories posit the start of domestication anywhere between 15,000 and 40,000 years ago. Determining a more precise figure will probably require considerably more scientific study and testing.

But although scientists are a long way from figuring out exactly when wolves began to attach themselves to human beings, they've not been shy about suggesting how the domestication process might have started. They—that is, the scientists—theorize that the wolves began to hang out on the outskirts of human villages to eat the bones, skin, and other leftovers from human hunts of other animals. And while the free goodies clearly benefitted the canine hangers-on, the human villagers also benefitted—at least according to psychologist Stanley Coren. In his classic book *The Pawprints of History*, Coren speculates

that people came to realize that canine consumption of leftover human food not only cut down on odors and insects but also kept predatory animals away from the village. Enterprising villagers might have capitalized on these benefits by taking some of the dogs' puppies, raising them within their own homes, and breeding subsequent generations for desired traits such as friendliness to people, willingness to learn, hunting skill, and herding ability.

EARLY DEVELOPMENT OF THE DACHSHUND

Although the Dachshund is considered a German breed, his earliest roots may lie outside Germany's borders. Some experts believe that the Dachshund really began in ancient Egypt. They base this belief not only on findings of mummified dogs who look like Dachshunds but also on an inscription of the word *teka* (similar to the German word *teckel*, which is another name for the Dachshund) on a monument to an Egyptian pharaoh. Other experts speculate that Dachshund-like dogs may also have existed in China and even South America.

That said, experts agree that the modern Dachshund did indeed begin in Germany, probably in the 15th century. German foresters wanted to breed a dog to help them control badgers, which were predators that landowners considered to be a pest. Because badgers burrow underground, the foresters needed a dog with a build that enabled him to follow a badger into a burrow. The dog also needed to be courageous and tenacious enough to hold the badger at bay until a forester arrived. Through selective breeding, the foresters developed a long-bodied, short-legged dog with a big-dog attitude. The foresters dubbed these dogs "Dachshunds"—two German words that together mean "badger dogs." Other names for these dogs were *erdhundle* (earth dog) and *teckel*. (And even though the Dachshund's name denotes his primary hunting quarry, he's not limited to chasing badgers. Individual Dachshunds can also hunt rabbits and foxes and track deer; in packs, they've been known to hunt wild boar as well.)

Initially, Dachshunds were bred with either the very short coats of the Smooth Dachshunds or the longer, Irish Setter-like coats of the Longhaired Dachshund. The third Dachshund variety—the Wirehaired Dachshund, whose coat resembles that of a Schnauzer—did not appear until the late 19th century. Breeders also developed two different Dachshund sizes: a larger dog who weighed up to 35 pounds (16 kg) to pursue badgers and boar and a smaller dog of up to 22 pounds (10 kg) to

hunt foxes and rabbits. In addition, over time, Dachshunds began to sport a wide variety of coat colors; those colors include red, cream, black and tan, black and cream, chocolate and tan, blue and tan, and fawn and tan. In some Dachshunds, these solid colors are overlaid with patterns such as dapple, double dapple, brindle, sable, and piebald.

THE DACHSHUND IN EUROPE

Records of the modern Dachshund began appearing in Germany in the 19th century. A German hound studbook of 1840 included a number of Dachshunds, and German hunting clubs also recorded those dogs who had exceptional hunting ability. By 1888,

Although the Dachshund is considered a German breed, his earliest roots may actually lie in ancient Egypt.

Dachshund devotees had established a breed standard—a written blueprint that specifies what a perfect Dachshund should look and act like—and had established the Berlin Teckelclub, which was the first Dachshund club in the breed's native Germany.

Meanwhile, in England, Queen Victoria's consort, Prince Albert, was presented with several Smooth Dachshunds by a German cousin around 1840. The Queen took to the long-bodied, short-legged dogs and kept them at Windsor Castle. Monuments to at least one of those Dachshunds were built on the castle grounds after the dog passed away. The Queen's interest in the breed helped build momentum for the first dog show featuring Dachshunds in England, which was held in 1859.

The breed's popularity took a nosedive during World War I, when anything having to do with Germany became unpopular in Great Britain. Anti-German propaganda pieces featured Dachshunds to depict Germany—in effect, demonizing the breed. Dachshund owners were branded as traitors, and Dachshund kennels were forced to close. The Dachshund Club of America (DCA) reports that in England, some Dachshunds were stoned to death. After the war, however, the breed began to regain its popularity—due in some measure to the efforts of a German Dachshund fancier and dog show judge named Gustav Alisch, who exported Dachshunds from Germany to other countries to build the breed outside German borders, including in the United States.

THE DACHSHUND IN THE UNITED STATES

Not surprisingly, the Dachshund made its way across the Atlantic but got off to a somewhat slow start in the United States. According to the Dachshund Club of America, between 1879 and 1885 only 11 Dachshunds were registered with the American Kennel Club (AKC). However, that state of affairs changed rapidly; by the end of the century, Dachshunds were among the most popular breeds in the United States.

The start of World War I in 1914 resulted in the same unfortunate anti-German targeting of Dachshunds in the United States that was also occurring in Europe. The anti-German fervor actually prompted the American Kennel Club (AKC) to rename the breed "Badger Dog" in an effort to give the breed a more neutral-sounding name. But the public was not fooled; only 26 dogs were registered that year.

The name "Dachshund" actually means "badger dog," derived from the fact that Dachshunds excel at hunting badgers.

Fortunately, however, the breed was not allowed to become extinct. The efforts of Gustav Alisch to export Dachshunds from Germany to other countries, including the United States, enabled the gene pool to be rebuilt, albeit slowly. By 1938, more than 3,200 Dachshunds were registered with the AKC. That growth has continued; while there was some backlash against the breed in World War II, it was much less intense than during the previous war. Today the Dachshund is consistently among the most popular breeds in the United States, ranking 8th in registrations to the AKC in 2009, the most recent year in which such data was available when this book was written.

RECOGNITION BY MAJOR CLUBS

By 1879, the AKC had registered its first Dachshund, signifying its official recognition

By 1938, more than 3,200 Dachshunds were registered with the American Kennel Club (AKC).

The Wirehaired Dachshund, whose coat resembles that of a Schnauzer, did not appear until the late 19th century.

of the breed. Enthusiasts in the United States formed the Dachshund Club of America in 1895. This formation was a significant development for the breed in the land of Old Glory.

Formation of the DCA gave enthusiasts a platform upon which to educate the American public about Dachshunds and to hold events that would showcase not only the breed's distinctive looks but also its versatility. To that end, the DCA holds an annual national specialty show that includes not only conformation (show) events but also agility trials, competitive obedience trials, rally obedience trials, tracking, field trials, and a special event called earthdog, at which Dachshunds excel. More information about all of these events appears in Chapter 11. In addition, regional clubs hold their own

Breed enthusiasts in the United States formed the Dachshund Club of America (DCA) in 1895.

specialty events, giving Dachshund devotees lots of opportunities to develop and exhibit the versatility of their breed.

Finally, the DCA confers special recognition upon highly accomplished Dachshunds. Dogs who produce many breed champions can qualify for Register of Merit (ROM) certification. The club also offers a Versatility Certificate for Dachshunds who excel in conformation, field trials, and obedience.

INFLUENTIAL DACHSHUND PEOPLE

The Dachshund is one of the oldest breeds recognized by the AKC, and its origins extend back centuries. As such, compiling an exhaustive list of influential people in the breed is difficult. Here is a partial list of those individuals who have had an impact on the breed:

- **Prince Albert:** The consort of Queen Victoria, Prince Albert brought the first Dachshunds out of Germany to England and presented one of those dogs to his wife.
- **Queen Victoria:** The longest-reigning monarch in British history, Queen Victoria clearly appreciated her husband's gesture. She owned several Dachshunds among her many dogs, and her appreciation of the breed helped fuel its growth in England.
- **Gustav Alisch:** This gentleman was an influential Dachshund enthusiast and dog show judge. After World War I, he made

it a point to export Dachshunds to other countries to rebuild the breed's gene pool, which had been severely reduced due to anti-German sentiment in World War I. By the 1930s, he was Executive Vice President of the German Dachshund Club.

- **Iris Love:** Love was an archaeologist, socialite, and Dachshund enthusiast in New York City. For many years, Ms. Love gave an annual party honoring her Dachshunds at Tavern on the Green in New York City at around the time of the annual Westminster Kennel Club Dog Show. The event was considered one of the highlights of a very crowded social calendar surrounding the show, which is the second-oldest sporting event in the United States. (The Kentucky Derby is the oldest.)
- **Dorothy O. (Dee) Hutchinson:** A noted American Dachshund breeder, author of a book about Dachshunds, and AKC show judge whose many assignments included six at the annual Westminster Kennel Club Dog Show in New York's Madison Square Garden. Mrs. Hutchinson passed away in May 2010.

MEMORABLE DACHSHUNDS

Some of the Dachshunds listed in this section are famous in their own right, while others acquire their fame from being owned by famous or otherwise notable people. And while some are (or were) real individuals, others are the stuff of fiction. These memorable Dachshunds include:

- **Lump:** A Dachshund who lived for several years with artist Pablo Picasso and appears in some of the artist's work. The relationship between dog and artist is chronicled in *Picasso and Lump: A Dachshund's Odyssey*, by David Douglas Duncan (Bulfinch Press).

- **Ryan:** A Wirehaired Dachshund who was a canine companion of General George S. Patton in World War II and is featured in a photograph in which General Patton is conversing with the Supreme Allied Commander and future president Dwight D. Eisenhower. Patton's German counterpart, General Erwin Rommel, also enjoyed the companionship of Dachshunds.
- **Archie and Amos:** Two Dachshunds owned by Andy Warhol in the 1970s. Both dogs appear in some of Warhol's work and traveled with him extensively.

The Dachshund is one of the oldest breeds recognized by the American Kennel Club (AKC), and its origins extend back centuries.

PART I

PUPPYHOOD

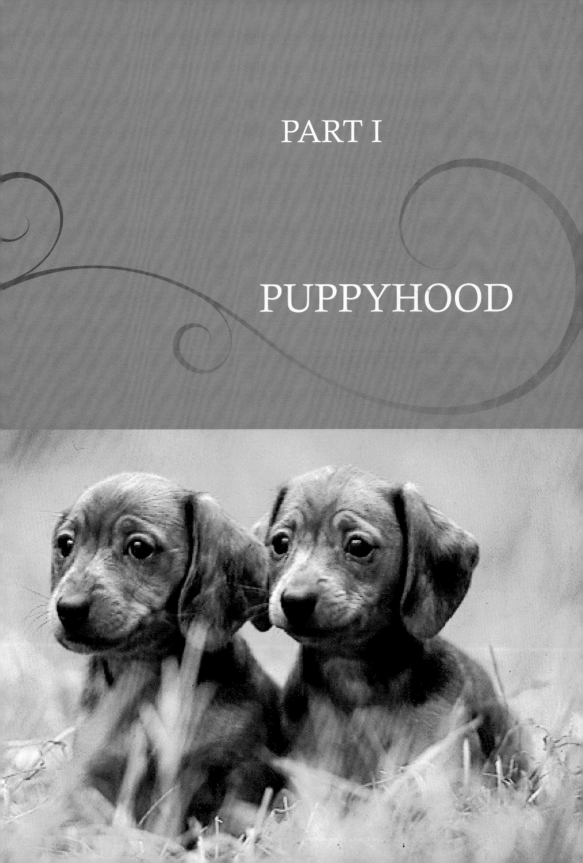

CHAPTER 1

IS THE DACHSHUND RIGHT FOR YOU?

The Dachshund's diminutive stature, big-dog personality and comedic flair captivate many people—including, perhaps, you. And like many other people you may think that raising a Dachshund from puppyhood will not only maximize the amount of time you have with him but also allow you to have a dog with whom you can build a bond from almost the very start of his life.

However, enchantment with a breed and being able to live successfully with an individual dog of that breed are two entirely different propositions. That's just as true with a Dachshund as it is with any other dog. And while a Dachshund's puppyhood generally lasts about a year, that year can seem awfully long when you're grappling with the mischief-making and individual quirks of any juvenile Dachshund.

This chapter will help ensure that, as you consider whether to add a Dachshund puppy to your life, your fantasies will not collide with reality.

BREED CHARACTERISTICS

The Dachshund may have a comical appearance, but don't view him as a dog to be laughed at. This is a dog with dignity to spare.

That's not to say that he can't be clownish, but the clownishness will be on his terms, not yours.

The Dachshund Club of America (DCA), like all other breed clubs, maintains a detailed written description of how the ideal Dachshund should act and look. This description is called a breed standard. Very few (if any) Dachshunds totally conform to this standard, but it does provide a blueprint for recognizing a healthy, well-bred representative of the breed.

Temperament and Common Personality Traits

The breed standard states that the Dachshund is "clever, lively, and courageous to the point of rashness." These characteristics make him well suited to do what no other dog breed can do: hunt both above and below the ground. As such, according to the DCA, a shy Dachshund is a big no-no.

Of course, every Dachshund is an individual, but these dogs do have some traits in common. These can include:

Deviousness
A Dachshund can show considerable cunning, particularly when he wants to score an

the simple, sometimes slavish devotion of other breeds. He'll want to know where you are, but he's often perfectly happy to know that you're in the next room as opposed to being next to him. That same independence, plus his unique appearance, can lead the Dachshund into comical waters (figuratively); these dogs are just naturally funny, even when they're not trying to be.

Barkiness

The hunters who developed the Dachshund wanted a dog who would bark to alert his owners to the proximity of prey. You may not need such notifications, but your Dachshund will probably not hesitate to alert you to other developments, such as perceived intruders. As a hound, the Dachshund has a vocal repertoire that extends beyond barking to howling and yodeling—and the Dachshund's song is a mournful song indeed.

Scent Oriented

Being a hound, your Dachshund lives to sniff. His super-developed nose and olfactory center in his brain enable him to pick up scents that others, particularly human beings, cannot. This type of nosiness—really more like a

The breed standard states that the Dachshund is "clever, lively, and courageous to the point of rashness."

unauthorized goodie or do something he's not supposed to do. But while a Dachshund can be devious, don't expect to get away with any corresponding deviousness on your part. Your Dachsie will want to know everything that's going on in your life—and if he needs to be with you 24/7 to provide you with adequate supervision, he'll be there.

Independence

While the Dachshund is devoted to his people, such devotion may be difficult for the casual observer to discern. This dog rarely exhibits

By the Numbers

Dachshunds begin resembling their adult selves in early adolescence—around six months of age—but don't achieve full physical and emotional maturity until they reach their first birthdays.

Because he's a hound, the Dachshund loves to sniff; he has a super-developed nose that enables him to pick up a variety of scents.

nose for news—can get him into trouble. That's because, like most other hounds, a Dachshund is apt to wander off in pursuit of an interesting scent. A secure fence is a must if you plan to let your Dachshund spend time in your backyard.

Inquisitiveness

The Dachshund needs to know about anything and everything that goes on in your home, and he will take it upon himself to stay up to date on the latest developments in his household. This behavior by no means runs counter to his sense of independence, though—because the Dachshund chooses where he wants to be and when. If something interesting is going on, though, count on your four-legged friend to be right where those goings-on are.

Tenacity

A dog who was bred to hold a badger or other quarry—which often would be nearly the same size as the Dachshund himself—at bay until the hunter arrived needed to have plenty of courage and tenacity to do his job. Your Dachshund probably won't be hunting badgers, but chances are good that he's held onto the courage and tenacity of his forebears. Those traits exhibit themselves in interesting ways. For example, if you've hidden a cherished dog toy somewhere in your house, your Dachsie won't give up the search for that toy until he finds it.

Physical Appearance

Here, in layman's terms, is what the DCA specifies that the perfect Dachshund should look like.

General Appearance

The Dachshund is low to the ground, with a long body and short legs. He should look very muscular and have skin that's pliable but not too wrinkled. His demeanor should look bold and confident, and his face should have an alert, intelligent expression.

General Body Structure

The trunk of the Dachshund's body should be long and fully muscled. When viewed in profile, the back lies in the straightest possible line between the shoulders and the short, very slightly arched loin. The abdomen should have a slight upward tuck when viewed in profile.

The front of the body is strong and deep and long and cleanly muscled. The breastbone is strongly prominent in front so that on either side a depression or dimple appears. When viewed from the front, the thorax appears oval and extends downward to the midpoint of the forearm. The enclosing structure of the well-sprung ribs appears full and oval to allow, by its ample capacity, complete development of the heart and lungs. The keel merges gradually into the line of the abdomen and extends well beyond the front legs. Viewed in profile, the lowest point of the breast line is covered by the front leg.

The shoulder blades should be long, broad, well laid back, and firmly placed upon the fully developed thorax, closely fitted at the shoulders. The shoulder muscles should be hard but also pliable.

The upper arm should be the same length as the shoulder blade and sit at a right angle

The Dachshund is low to the ground, with a long body and short legs.

to the shoulder blade, with strong bones and hard muscles. The elbows should lie close to the body but be structured to move freely. The lower arm (the forearm) should be short, supplied with hard but pliable muscles on the front and outside, and have tightly stretched tendons on the inside and at the back, slightly curved inward. The joints between the forearms and the feet (the wrists) are closer together than the shoulder joints so that the front of the dog does not appear absolutely straight. The inclined shoulder blades, upper arms, and curved forearms form parentheses that enclose the ribcage, creating the correct "wraparound front." The front paws are full but compact, with well-arched toes and tough, thick pads. There are five toes, four in use, close together with a pronounced arch and strong, short nails. The front dewclaws are located on the inside of the front legs above the wrists.

The Dachshund's hindquarters should also be strong and cleanly muscled. The pelvis, rear thighs, and rear pasterns (the area where the foot blends into the leg) are the same length and give the appearance of a series of right angles. The legs are straight; they turn neither in nor out.

The hind paws are smaller than the front paws and have four compactly closed and arched toes with tough, thick pads. The entire foot points straight ahead and is balanced equally on the ball and toes and not merely on the toes. The rear dewclaws should be removed. The croup (the highest part of the rump) should be long, rounded, and full and sink slightly toward the tail. The tail should extend as a continuation of the spine without kinks, twists, or pronounced curves.

The Dachshund should have a fluid, smooth gait. The forelegs should reach well forward, without much lift, in unison with the driving action of the hind legs. Viewed from the front,

The Dachsie's eyes are of medium size and almond shaped.

the legs do not move in exact parallel planes but incline slightly inward. The hind legs drive on a line with the forelegs, with the hock joints and rear pasterns turning neither in nor out. Viewed in profile, the forward reach of the hind leg equals the rear extension. The feet must travel parallel to the line of motion with no tendency to swing out, cross over, or interfere with each other.

Size

Today's Dachshund is bred in two sizes. Miniatures weigh 11 pounds (5 kg) or less.

Training Tidbit

Like any other dog, a Dachshund is far easier to train when he gets sufficient exercise. And his small stature makes exercise easy—what for you is a moderately paced walk around the block constitutes a full-fledged aerobic workout for a Dachshund.

Standards usually weigh between 16 and 32 pounds (7.5 and 14.5 kg).

Head and Neck

When viewed from above or from the side, the head tapers uniformly from the top of the skull to the tip of the nose. The area between the eyes, where the muzzle meets the forehead (in breeder parlance, the stop) is very slightly defined. The muzzle should be slightly arched, with the nostrils well open. The lips are tightly stretched, well covering the lower jaw. The jaws should open wide, with the hinges well back of the eyes. The teeth should fit closely together in a scissors bite. The skull is slightly arched, neither too broad nor too narrow.

The neck is long, muscular, and clean cut, with no loose skin under the throat. The nape of the neck should be slightly arched and flow gracefully into the shoulders without creating the impression of a right angle.

Eyes

The eyes are of medium size, almond shaped, dark in color and dark rimmed, with a pleasantly alert expression.

Ears

The ears are set near the top of the head but not too far forward and should be rounded at the bottoms. When the dog is animated, the ears should

The Dachshund is bred with three coat varieties: Smooth (far right), Wirehaired (center), and Longhaired (far left).

be long enough for the forward edges to just touch the cheeks so that the ears frame the face.

Coat

The Dachshund is bred with three varieties of coat: Smooth, Wirehaired, and Longhaired. The breed is also shown in two sizes: standard and miniature. All three varieties and both sizes must conform to the characteristics already specified. In addition, each variety must also conform to other specific standards. The following features are applicable for each variety:

Smooth Dachshunds

The Smooth Dachshund should have a short, smooth, and shining coat. The coat may be one-colored, two-colored, or patterned. One-colored Dachshunds include red and cream, with or without a shading of interspersed dark hairs. Two-colored Dachshunds include black, chocolate, wild boar, gray (blue), and fawn (Isabella), each with deep, rich tan or cream markings over the eyes, on the sides of the jaw and underlip, on the inner edge of the ear, front, breast, sometimes on the throat, inside and behind the front legs, on the paws and around the anus, and from there to about one-third to one-half of the length of the tail on the underside.

Dappled Dachshunds have colored areas that contrast with the darker base color, which may be any acceptable color. Neither the light nor the dark color should predominate. Unlike the other varieties, a dappled Dachshund's eyes may be partially or completely blue. Some Smooth Dachshunds exhibit patterns rather than single colors on their base coats. For example, brindle is a pattern in which black or dark stripes occur over the entire body, although in some specimens the brindle pattern may be visible only in the tan points. The sable pattern consists of a uniform dark overlay on red dogs. The overlay hairs are double pigmented, with the tip of each hair much darker than the base color. The pattern usually displays a widow's peak on the head.

Wirehaired Dachshunds
The Wirehaired Dachshund's coat is tight, short, thick, rough, and hard on top, with a softer undercoat beneath. Longer, softer hair appears on the jaw and eyebrows. The ear hair is shorter than on the rest of the body and is almost smooth.

The most common coat colors for Wirehaired Dachshunds are wild boar, black and tan, and various shades of red. All colors and patterns listed earlier are admissible. The wild boar color, which appears at the banding of the individual hairs and imparts an overall grizzled effect, is what's most often seen on this variety. Tan points may or may not be evident.

Dachsies will fit into almost any living environment, but owners should be aware that they tend to be noisier than some other breeds.

Variations include red boar and chocolate-and-tan boar.

Longhaired Dachshunds
The Longhaired Dachshund's coat consists of sleek, glistening, often slightly wavy hair that is longer under the neck and on the forechest, the underside of the body, the ears, and behind the legs. Coat colors are the same as those of the Smooth Dachshund.

CAN A DACHSHUND FIT INTO YOUR LIFE?
The Dachshund can adjust to life with almost any type of human or in any type of household. However, just like with any other breed of dog, some of those humans

Multi-Dog Tip

Do you already have a dog? Think carefully before you add a Dachshund to your pack. Dachsies can get along with other dogs, but you need to consider whether your particular dog will interact well with a Dachsie.

The Dachshund is an active dog who needs plenty of exercise, both physical and mental.

and households suit him better than others do. This section describes the sorts of environments in which a Dachshund is most likely to thrive—and in which, consequently, his people are most likely to thrive as well.

Environment

Because these dogs come in two sizes with three types of coats, there's really a Dachshund to please just about anyone. People who reside in tight quarters can live happily with a miniature Dachshund, while people who have larger digs can share their space with a standard. Those who love long-tressed dogs can tend to their Longhaired Dachshunds' coiffures as much as they and the dog will permit; those who want a wash-and-wear hound can stick with the Smooth Dachshund. Those who like

mustaches, beards, and eyebrows on their dogs can opt for the Wirehaired Dachshund.

That said, certain environments are not as good as for Dachshunds as others. For example, a person who lives in an apartment should think very carefully about welcoming a Dachshund. Although these dogs are small enough to fit comfortably in an apartment, they tend to be noisier than some other breeds. Thus, if you have a Dachshund who vocalizes frequently, you might not be very popular with your neighbors. However, with consistent training, a Dachshund can learn to turn his barking off as well as turn it on. Chapter 10 explains how.

A person who has difficulty picking up a dog of up to 30 pounds (13.5 kg) should probably opt for a miniature Dachshund. Because these dogs tend to have back problems, they should be given assistance when going up to and down from furniture and other areas where they might want to recline. Fortunately, special pet steps and ramps can help a Dachshund get off and on furniture and beds without his person needing to lift him.

Someone who takes great pride in her landscaping and who doesn't want to have to supervise the dog's outdoor activities should reconsider adding a Dachshund to the family. That's because Dachshunds love to dig—and an unsupervised dog could redesign landscaping in a way that would not please the original landscaper. However, it's possible to train a Dachshund or any other dog not to dig in a garden by providing him with a digging area of his own.

The ideal environment for a Dachshund, then, is probably a single-family home, townhome, or very large apartment (think penthouse) in which his person or people can manage him appropriately, train him patiently, and have realistic expectations. Such households can be in the city, country, or suburbs—it doesn't matter at all.

Exercise

Dachshunds were bred to engage in active pursuits—chiefly hunting aboveground and underground—so they need to be active. That means that they need plenty of exercise, both physical and mental.

But here's the thing: Just because the Dachshund needs plenty of exercise doesn't mean that you necessarily have to exert yourself all that much, especially on the physical side. Think about it. Human legs are relatively long, and

Dachshund legs are quite short. Consequently, a slow saunter for a human can be a brisk walk for a Dachshund because he needs to take several steps to keep up with just one of yours—and many more such steps if you pick up the pace. So when it comes to physical exercise, a couple of steady 15-minute walks per day will give your Dachshund the level of exertion he needs to reap significant aerobic benefits.

Moreover, such exercise will also help your Dachshund in the behavior department. Wise trainers tell their human clients that a tired dog is a good dog, and they are absolutely right. A Dachshund who's exercised regularly not only benefits physically but is also likely to be more cooperative and just generally better behaved than a Dachshund who is a couch potato.

Happily, frightful weather outside doesn't preclude a good physical workout for your Dachshund; all you have to do is move the action indoors. Short sessions of tug-of-war (played by certain rules that give the person, not the dog, control over the game most of the time) and fetch sessions that require the dog to use the stairs can help siphon off the energy and boredom that build up when a Dachshund develops cabin fever.

In addition to physical exercise, a Dachshund needs mental exercise to be truly healthy. Regular positive training sessions can help keep that Dachshund brain nimble; so too can indoor games such as hide-and-seek and hide the toy. Another mental exercise option is to give your dog an interactive treat-dispensing toy that requires him to think to figure out how to get the toy to dispense the treat.

Want to Know More?

For more information on Dachshund grooming, check out Chapter 6.

Grooming Needs

All Dachshunds require their people

Like most other purebred dogs, Dachshunds have their share of health concerns.

to perform certain grooming tasks for them, such as dental care, ear cleanings, and nail trimmings. Beyond those basics, the breed's grooming needs range from minimal to fairly high maintenance, depending on the type of coat the dog has.

The Smooth Dachshund is your basic wash-and-wear dog. Twice-weekly sessions with a damp cloth and a slicker brush, along with an occasional bath, should be all that's needed to keep this dog's coat and skin healthy.

The Longhaired Dachshund requires considerably more tending to keep his tresses looking their best. Thrice-weekly sessions with a slicker brush and comb are necessary to keep the coat healthy and tangle-free. This dog also needs periodic clipping of the hair between his paw pads to keep debris from accumulating and causing foot problems. A monthly shampoo will help keep the coat and skin clean and healthy.

The Wirehaired Dachshund requires daily to thrice-weekly brushings with a hard bristle brush and periodic trims to his eyebrows, mustache, and beard. He should also receive monthly baths. In addition, this variety requires the services of a professional dog groomer to strip the coat twice a year.

Health Issues

Like most other purebred dogs, Dachshunds have their share of health concerns. Among the health issues that would-be Dachshunds owners need to be aware of are:

Want to Know More?

For more information on breed-specific diseases, consult Chapter 8.

Acanthosis Nigricans

This condition causes hair loss and a darkening and thickening of the skin. One rare form of this condition is an inherited illness that's limited to Dachshunds and shows up before the affected dog's first birthday. A second, much more common form, results from other causes such as allergies, hypothyroidism (insufficient production of hormones by the thyroid gland), and friction of the skin due to obesity. Treatment of the more common form depends on the underlying cause. To relieve the skin problems, veterinarians may prescribe a low-level steroid or recommend that vitamin E supplements be added to the dog's food.

Diabetes

A diabetic Dachshund is a dog whose pancreas fails to produce sufficient insulin. Symptoms include increased appetite and thirst, weight loss, increased urination, and a sudden appearance of cataracts. Treatment includes adjusting the dog's diet and beginning insulin therapy.

Elbow Dysplasia

This condition, which is often genetic in origin, occurs when the dog's elbow joint develops in an abnormal manner, resulting in an improper fit of the two bones that form the joint. An affected dog may exhibit lameness in his front legs, swelling of the joint, and pain, and may be reluctant to exercise. Treatment options include weight reduction (if the dog is overweight), controlling the dog's level of exercise, medication to relieve pain, and surgery to repair the joint.

Epilepsy

There are many possible causes of epilepsy, which is a nervous disorder that results in behaviors ranging from a brief jerking of the

Want to Know More?

More information on developing your Dachshund's sociability appears in Chapter 4.

muscles to full-blown seizures that result in losses of consciousness in the affected dog. Although any dog of any breed can get epilepsy, a genetic cause of a rare form of canine epilepsy has been found in miniature Wirehaired Dachshunds. Anti-seizure drugs such as phenobarbital, potassium bromide, and diazepam can help reduce if not eliminate seizures. If an underlying cause for the epilepsy is found, additional treatment aimed at alleviating that condition can help eliminate the epilepsy as well.

Eye Problems

Dachshunds can suffer from a number of eye problems, including cataracts (a cloudiness or film over the lens of the eye); progressive retinal atrophy (a group of inherited disorders that cause the retina to deteriorate over time); and glaucoma (an increase of fluid pressure within the eye), among others. All of these problems can result in impaired vision or total blindness. Treatment options are limited.

Intervertebral Disk Disease (IDD)

The long-bodied, short-legged Dachshund is particularly vulnerable to this condition, which occurs when one of the gelatinous disks that lie between the vertebrae either ruptures or becomes displaced, resulting in considerable pain, and all too often, paralysis. Mild cases may respond to several weeks of rest in a crate, but moderate to severe cases may require surgery.

Patellar Luxation

The breed's extremely short leg bones may cause some Dachshunds' kneecaps to move out of their positions to the inside of the leg. An affected dog may stop suddenly while running and cry out in pain. Surgery is usually required to return the kneecap to its proper position.

Sociability

A sociable dog is a dog who enjoys being around people and other dogs. He just generally likes having company and meets new individuals with ease and aplomb. Dachshunds can certainly fit that definition if they are introduced to new people and pets with care and with an understanding of the dogs' basic nature.

With Kids

Got kids? A Dachshund can make a great family pet but not always. For example, a family with very young children (aged six or under) should think twice about adding a Dachshund to the household, particularly a mini. A child could inadvertently injure a little dog by playing too roughly. Moreover, Dachshunds are not always as patient with misbehaving children as other breeds are. Many experts agree that a Dachshund will be quicker to snap or otherwise use his teeth to express his displeasure at behavior he considers inappropriate, such as being picked up or teased. However, well-socialized Dachshunds can be fine companions to well-behaved older children, not to mention their parents.

Many Dachshunds live peacefully with other dogs.

With Company

Got company? Your Dachshund has the potential to be a sedate, mannerly canine host—and if the dog is a mini, to warm some of those guests' laps. One of the Dachshunds to whom this book is dedicated happily served as a lap warmer to the members of her owner's bridge club whenever the club met at the owner's house. Training and early socialization are the key to cultivating a welcoming attitude in the Dachshund, who may be initially wary of strangers.

With Other Pets

Got other dogs or pets? Many Dachshunds live peacefully with other dogs—but other pets can be problematic. That's because many Dachshunds retain their ancestors' hunting roots. Consequently, a family whose menagerie includes rabbits would do well to bypass adding a Dachshund to the household.

Trainability

Although the Dachshund is a very intelligent dog, he's not always the most eager student. These little canines have minds of their own. If you're expecting your short-legged hound to mindlessly obey your every command, you're in for a rude awakening. Patient teaching interspersed with lots of fun, games, and treats are important to helping the Dachshund reach his full potential.

However, the Dachshund is surprisingly versatile. These long-bodied dogs can be found performing in a variety of sports and activities, including:

Want to Know More?

More information about activities can be found in Chapter 11.

Agility

Yes, Dachshunds can compete in this exciting sport, which consists of an obstacle course with tunnels, hurdles, teeter-totters, A-frames, and other paraphernalia. The DCA holds agility trials every year at its National Specialty Show. Of course, the obstacles are sized to accommodate the breed's short stature.

Earth Tests

The Dachshund's heritage renders him perfect for these tests, which measure a dog's ability to hunt underground.

Field Trials

That same heritage makes the Dachshund a talented participant in field trials, which capitalize on a dog's ability to use his nose to track and quarry game above ground.

Obedience

The Dachshund's independence does not preclude his competing in either traditional obedience or the newer sport of rally obedience. Again, patient training and a willingness to enjoy the dog's comedic ability are critical to enjoying training for these events.

Tracking

Dogs with superior noses, such as Dachshunds, have the potential to excel in this event, which requires them to use a scented track to locate an article left by the person who laid the track.

CHAPTER 2

FINDING AND PREPPING FOR YOUR DACHSHUND PUPPY

Now that you've decided to welcome a Dachshund into your life, you should start on two important tasks: searching for the particular Dachshund who's right for you and making your home a safe place for that Dachshund to be. But first, you need to decide whether your new Dachsie should be a puppy or an adult.

WHY GETTING A PUPPY IS A GOOD IDEA

Face it: A Dachshund puppy is totally irresistible. Happily, you don't need to resist the temptation one of these bundles of perpetual cuteness embodies. That's because getting a Dachshund puppy instead of an adult has some real advantages:

First is that perpetual cuteness. There are few experiences more delightful than playing with your soft, warm, frolicsome little Dachshund puppy—except for maybe watching that puppy turn himself into a lapdog (on your lap, of course) when he tires out. And don't forget that puppies have that sweet, milky breath that you'll have the pleasure of smelling whenever your little canine charmer yawns or decides to bestow a puppy kiss.

Second is the lack of baggage. A well-bred

Dachshund puppy hasn't had the time or lived in an environment in which he could acquire any of the negative experiences that you might find if you decide to adopt an older dog. That same puppy also hasn't had time to develop bad habits that try the souls of dog owners, such as howling all day, wiggling into the open cabinet under your kitchen sink, or making off with one of your socks. In other words, a well-bred, well-raised puppy isn't a blank slate, but he's probably a clean slate.

With a Dachshund puppy whom you've purchased from a reputable breeder, you truly have the opportunity to start fresh and raise a dog right, right from the start. And that's true whether you plan to compete with that puppy in the show ring or simply raise him to be the best pet you could ever have. In fact, you'd definitely do well to buy a puppy from a breeder who's concluded that that puppy won't do well in the show ring because he doesn't adhere sufficiently to the breed standard (as described in the previous chapter). For example, a breeder might decide that a miniature Dachshund puppy won't qualify for dog shows because he's likely to grow bigger than the standard allows—but he can still be a terrific pet.

A well-bred Dachsie puppy is a unique individual with a special personality all his own.

Did you notice that phrase "reputable breeder"? That's because getting a great puppy requires finding a reputable breeder first. Here's how.

WHERE TO GET THE PUPPY OF YOUR DREAMS

To find a reputable breeder, you need to put in some research time, but the Dachshund Club of America (DCA) can be a great shortcut. Type the club URL (www.dachshund-dca. org/breederreferral.html) into your Web browser and you'll find a list of contacts for state Dachshund clubs. The contacts in your state can put you in touch with one or more breeders who expect to have or already do have puppies to place.

The DCA also has a state-by-state breeder directory that you can use to find a reputable breeder. Log onto www.dachshund-dca.org/ kennelads.html and you'll find oodles of advertisements from individual breeders, listed on a state-by-state basis. All of the breeders who advertise in this directory belong to the DCA, and they all offer contact information so that you can find out if a breeder who interests you has (or will soon have) puppies available.

You may have heard that attending a dog show and querying the breeders there about their dogs is a good way to find a Dachshund puppy. I don't agree. Breeders who exhibit their dogs at shows—both before and after their dogs enter the ring for judging—are often too distracted to spend much time with would-be puppy buyers. You might be able to collect a few breeders' business cards at a show, but don't count on having an extended conversation with them. Contact them a day or two later.

What to Ask a Breeder

When you first contact a breeder, tell her that you're thinking about buying a Dachshund puppy and ask her whether she has any puppies available now or in the near future. If the breeder can answer in the affirmative, she'll probably ask you a few questions about your dog-owning experience, your home, your lifestyle, and your family. Don't worry, though; you'll have a chance to be the interviewer! When you do, these are some questions you should ask:

Are the Parents of the Puppies More Than Two Years Old?

A good breeder will tell you that the puppies' parents are two years of age or older. That's because she knows that younger Dachshunds may not have the physical maturity needed to produce healthy Dachshund pups. A breeder who breeds dogs younger than two years of age may be less interested in producing healthy puppies than in making a profit.

How Many Litters Do You Breed Each Year?

The ideal answer is three litters or less. More than that may signal that the breeder's priority is healthy profits, not healthy puppies.

Do the Parents Have Final Health Clearances?

Because Dachshunds—like all other purebred dogs—have some inherited health challenges, conscientious breeders have their dogs evaluated for possible health problems before they breed them. If the evaluation determines that the dogs don't have such problems, the evaluating organization issues clearances certifying that the dog is healthy.

Clearances for Dachshunds should include one from the Orthopedic Foundation for Animals (OFA) that a dog's elbows are healthy and also from the Canine Eye Registry Foundation (CERF) certifying that the dog's eyes are problem-free.

Do You Show Your Dogs?

A conscientious breeder is working to improve the breed and does so in part by exhibiting dogs in shows where impartial judges determine how fully those dogs conform to the breed standard. Alternatively—or in

Finding a reputable breeder requires a little research and some patience.

addition—to showing dogs in conformation, the breeder may train dogs to perform in obedience, agility, or field trials. Still other breeders may not breed for either performance or show but for temperament. These efforts also indicate that they want to improve the breed.

How Long Have You Been a Breeder?

Ideally, your breeder has had plenty of experience raising Dachshund puppies. If the breeder responds that this is her first litter, ask about who is mentoring the breeder—that is, advising the breeder on how to breed Dachshunds. A response that includes the names of one or more experienced Dachshund breeders should at least partially offset a lack of experience.

How Do You Raise Your Puppies?

The ideal answer here is "in my house with my family." Home-raised puppies are likely to be better socialized than those raised in outdoor kennels. If the breeder says that the dogs are raised in outdoor kennels, ask how the puppies are socialized—for example, how often does each puppy get time inside the breeder's home interacting with family members and just experiencing the sights and sounds of a human household?

What Do You Charge for Puppies?

Be prepared for sticker shock here. A pet-quality Dachshund puppy from a good breeder was likely to cost between $900 and $1,500 in early 2010. A show-quality Dachshund may cost considerably more.

Home-raised puppies are likely to be better socialized than those raised in outdoor kennels.

What If a Puppy Turns Out to not Be Healthy?

If a post-purchase checkup with a veterinarian shows that a puppy has a serious medical problem, the breeder should allow you to return that puppy for a full refund, or if you prefer, a replacement pup. The purchase contract should include a provision for this.

Are the Parents on the Premises?

The ideal answer here would be that "the mother is" or "the dam is." If the breeder owns both parents, those parents may be a little too closely related to produce optimally healthy puppies.

What the Breeder Will Ask You

Don't be surprised if the breeder has some questions for you—and don't take offense at what she asks, even if her questions seem a tad personal. She just wants to make sure that one of her puppies will be the right one for you. Here are some of the questions she's likely to ask:

Why Do You Want a Dog?

Good answers to this question include wanting someone to nurture, wanting company, and wanting to give and get unconditional love.

A good breeder will want the puppy's new home to have people around for at least some of the workday.

Training Tidbit

Start looking now for a trainer or classes for your puppy. To start your search, log onto a website such as "Truly Dog Friendly" (www. trulydogfriendly.com), which has a national list of trainers who are committed to using positive, force-free training methods.

Not-so-good answers include looking for protection (a Dachshund is not suited to being a bodyguard), wanting to teach the kids responsibility (they shouldn't practice on a helpless Dachshund), and wanting a watchdog (Dachshunds can bark, but that doesn't mean that they'll bark at what you want them to).

Why Are You Interested in a Dachshund?

Right answer: "I like the way the way they (insert attribute from Chapter 1)." Wrong answer: "Because they look goofy" or "I dig Dachshund races."

When you visit the breeder, you should be able to meet the puppy's mother and see the litter.

Have You Ever Owned a Dog Before?

If your answer to this question is no, you don't need to worry. Your breeder is asking this question only so that she can determine whether to choose a calm puppy (which is better for a novice owner) rather than his more energetic littermate.

How Will You Exercise the Dog?

Bad answers: "Leave him alone in the backyard all day," "Let him out in the morning for all-day neighborhood carousing." Good answers: "Take him for long walks," "Teach him canine sports," "Play with him in an enclosed area."

Do You Have Children—and if so, How Old Are They?

The only right answer to this question is a truthful one. Generally, the breeder asks this question to guide her puppy selection—but if your children are under the age of six, she may hesitate to sell you a puppy at all. Dachshunds aren't always as patient with children as other breeds can be, and children under six often need closer supervision around dogs than parents realize, much less give.

Are You Allowed to Have a Dog in Your Home?

The breeder wants to know if you live in a rental apartment or home—and if so, whether you're allowed to have a pet. If you're a renter, bring along a copy of your lease or statement from your landlord saying that pets are permitted in your rental apartment or house.

How Long Will the Dog Be Alone Each Day?

Puppies are social animals and needy creatures, and they don't do well if they're left alone all day while the other household members are at school or work. They need to have someone around for at least part of the day. That's why a reputable breeder is likely to suggest that you consider looking for an adolescent, adult, or senior Dachshund if your house is empty all day long.

Who Will Be the Dog's Primary Caregiver?

The answer here should be "me" or "my adult partner." That's because a Dachshund puppy needs the care and supervision that only a responsible adult can give, although children can and should help out with puppy care. Even teenagers shouldn't be expected to take on primary dog duty; their lives are generally too full to perform such duty well.

Where Will the Dog Sleep at Night?

The breeder wants to know whether you understand that Dachshund puppies need lots of human company. The ideal answer is "in my room with me." Not so okay is "in the kitchen" or "in the basement." If you answer "on my bed," make sure to let the breeder know that you'll lift the dog on and off your bed and/or provide him a ramp or steps to get on and off by himself. Jumping on and off beds and furniture should be discouraged because of the strain such exercise can put on the Dachshund's long back.

How Do You Feel About Taking Your Dog for Training Classes?

The answer to this question should be a resounding "just fine, as long as the trainer uses positive methods." No matter what his age is, every dog lives more happily with people when he has at least a little training in basic

Trust your breeder to use her expertise to help make the right match between you and a puppy.

manners—but that training needs to be given in a gentle, dog-friendly manner with no harsh corrections or aversive practices.

Visit Your Prospective Puppy

If you and your breeder are satisfied with the answers to each other's questions, you can take the next step: making an appointment to meet your prospective puppy. During this visit, you should meet not only the puppy and his littermates but also his mother. As you interact with the puppies, look for the following:

Clear, Bright Eyes

Check for any discharge from or cloudiness in the puppy's eyes; the presence of either may signal an infection or other problem. Make sure, too, that the pup can follow a moving object with his eyes; if he can't, he may be blind.

Dry, Odorless Ears

Do the puppy's ears have a foul or yeasty odor? Either may signal the presence of an ear infection. Does he respond to the sound of clapping hands? If not, there's a strong likelihood that he is deaf.

Healthy Skin and Coat

Check to make sure that the puppy has no dirt or scabs on his skin or bald spots on his coat. That goes for the mother, too; there should be no bald spots, rashes, or scabs on her body.

Don't be surprised, though, if a Longhaired Dachshund mom lacks her usual gorgeous coiffure—nursing a litter is very depleting! Finally, make sure that neither mother nor puppies carry any little specks that hop around on the coat. Those are fleas, and their presence indicates that the dogs haven't had the best of care.

Normal Movement

Study the way each puppy walks. A puppy who seems to lack energy or who limps could have health problems that you might not want to tackle.

Sound Temperament

Like people, Dachshunds have their own special personalities: Some are more reserved than others; some are more active than others; some are more people oriented than others. Look for a puppy who's curious enough to approach you but calm enough to not start bouncing off the walls when you interact with him.

Once you've interacted with all of the available puppies, you and the breeder can talk about which one(s) you like best. Based on that conversation, you and the breeder may agree on which puppy is right for you, or the breeder may simply take your wishes into consideration in choosing your puppy for you. Either way is fine—just trust your breeder to use her expertise to at least help make the right match.

At this point, you'll probably be asked to sign a contract of your intention to buy the puppy, place a deposit equal to up to half the purchase price to reserve the puppy, and set a date for bringing him from the breeder's home to yours.

Documents and Guarantees

You should bring home papers along with your puppy when you pick up your new Dachshund from the breeder. Here's what those papers should include:

The Contract

When you pick up your puppy from the breeder, she should give you a copy of the purchase contract you signed when you placed your deposit. This contract should not only specify the purchase price of the puppy but should also include provisions relating to spaying and neutering requirements (if you and the breeder don't plan to show the dog), requirements to return the puppy if you can't keep him, and a health guarantee.

Registration Papers

If you want to show your puppy in conformation or have him compete in American Kennel Club (AKC) events such as agility, obedience, earthdog, field trials, or tracking, you need to register him with the AKC. If your breeder registered his mother with the AKC and the father is also registered, she should give you a signed bill of sale so that you can register your puppy. The bill of sale will list his date of birth, sex, breed, the parents' AKC-registered names, the AKC number for your puppy's litter, the date you purchased the puppy, and will include your breeder's signature.

The Pedigree

Another document your breeder should give you is a copy of your puppy's family tree—or in breeder speak, his pedigree. Depending on how many generations the pedigree includes,

A copy of your puppy's health records should be among the papers your breeder gives you.

you should be able to see the names of your new Dachshund's parents, grandparents, great-grandparents, and maybe even beyond.

Health Records
Still another important set of documents that you should receive from your breeder is a copy of your puppy's health records. The records should list his date of birth, dates of his visits to the veterinarian, dates his immunizations were given, and related information such as dewormings. Bring these records to your own vet at your puppy's first checkup, which should occur within a few days after you bring him home.

Health Clearances
The breeder should give you copies of all of the health clearances of both parents of your puppy.

Care Instructions
To help make your puppy's transition from the breeder's home to yours a smooth one, she should include written instructions on feeding and other basic care, plus a couple of days' supply of his regular dog food.

BEFORE YOUR PUPPY COMES HOME
Yes, you've picked your puppy, but now's not the time to sit back and relax. Take this time between picking your puppy and bringing him home to prepare for his arrival. Here are some ideas to help you do just that.

Puppy-Proof Your House and Yard
Just as you need to child-proof your home if you have babies and toddlers in residence, you also need to puppy-proof your home if a Dachshund is coming to live with you. Before he even crosses your threshold, study your

Puppy-proof your home to ensure that your puppy can't get access to items that could injure him, like electrical cords.

home's layout and remove as many hazards as possible from his reach.

Indoors
Start by conducting a sweep of the inside of your home. That means getting down on all fours and crawling around every room of your house so that you can get a puppy's-eye view of the mischief-triggering items those rooms contain. Among the items you should stash: shoes, socks, underwear, kids' toys, books, and magazines—all of which can be shredded or swallowed if they come into contact with your puppy's teeth.

Next, look for items that your puppy can get into, and block off his access to them. And don't think that because your Dachshund puppy has short legs that he can't get into fairly tall items. These little guys are surprisingly agile! That's why you need to put open wastebaskets up off the floor and either block off the kitchen garbage can with chairs or install a lid guard. Close your bathroom doors and for good measure install toilet lid locks. Put covers on your electrical outlets, and install door guards on your kitchen cabinets.

Third, pay special attention to dangling electrical cords. A curious Dachshund might find such objects way too interesting to resist chewing—with potentially disastrous results.

Finally, block off access to staircases until your Dachshund puppy has learned to navigate the stairs. Close any doors that lead to flights of stairs; if that's not possible, place baby gates at both ends of the staircase.

Outdoors

The outside of your house needs attention too. First, if you plan to exercise your Dachshund outdoors in your backyard without a leash, you need to invest in secure fencing—installed by either you or a fencing professional. Make sure, too, that the fencing doesn't contain any crevices or openings that your puppy can slip through. And check the perimeter often—not just for aboveground areas that your pup can use to escape but also for holes in the ground that your Dachshund may use to tunnel his way to freedom. Remember, Dachshunds were bred to work underground!

You might be tempted to install an electronic fence. However, most experts don't recommend these fences for two reasons. First, your dog may decide to venture across your property

A schedule helps you organize the many tasks that go into raising a young Dachshund and helps him make a smooth transition from his breeder's home to yours.

anyway but then refuse to come back so that he doesn't receive a second shock. The second reason is that other dogs, other animals, and people can enter your yard freely but your Dachshund can't escape from them unless he's willing to risk being shocked. That means that your dog is much more vulnerable to being attacked by an animal or stolen by a person than he otherwise would be.

Set Up A Schedule

Don't be surprised if you feel as though you're losing your mind when your puppy first comes home. He's curious about everything in his new world, and he's got the speed (despite those short legs) to get into trouble very quickly if you're not continually training an eagle eye on him. In addition, he's totally lacking in basic bathroom manners; he does his business wherever and whenever he wants. And just like any baby, he needs lots of opportunities to eat, drink, exercise, and sleep. How do you keep your sanity and still fill what appear to be his never-ending needs?

I've found that creating a schedule is a huge help. Writing down what you need to do with your Dachshund will help you organize the seemingly endless tasks that are part and parcel of raising a puppy. The schedule will give a road map for when to feed, potty, crate, and play with your pup. By following that schedule consistently, he'll learn what he needs to know—such as basic potty protocol—much faster than might otherwise be the case.

Build your schedule around the times your Dachshund puppy needs to go to the bathroom. A puppy under four months of age generally needs bathroom breaks first thing in the morning, after naps, after meals, after play sessions, and last thing at night before going to bed. Until he's around three months old, he may also need a middle-of-the-night trip to his bathroom. Use that knowledge to create a schedule similar to the one on page 43.

Use that knowledge to create a schedule similar to the one on page 43.

Be advised that a young Dachshund puppy may initially need many more potty breaks than this schedule calls for. Some of these little guys need hourly bathroom breaks, not to mention middle-of-the-night trips to the potty. This makes sense when you consider how tiny his bladder is (and thus how quickly it fills up). But take heart: This constant pottying won't go on forever. As his bladder grows and his ability to control his doggy downloads increases, he won't need to go out as often.

For detailed instructions on housetraining your Dachshund puppy, check out Chapter 4.

Purchase Supplies

Every Dachshund needs some special gear to feel truly at home—and you'll be one step ahead of the game if you shop for that gear now, before he crosses your threshold. Your shopping list for your puppy should include the following:

Bed

Just about any kind of bed is okay for a Dachshund—as long as that bed is his and on the ground. Sleeping in your bed is not a good idea. The chief reason: Hopping on and off your bed can injure your Dachshund's long back.

Clicker and Treats

You'll want to start teaching your puppy basic doggy manners as soon as possible once he settles in, and having a clicker (a small device

Want to Know More?

Chapter 4 provides detailed information on clicker training and how it works.

Sample Puppy Schedule

7:00 a.m	get up, take puppy to potty spot, put puppy in crate
7:30 a.m	feed puppy, offer water, take puppy to potty spot, play with puppy for 15 minutes, put puppy in crate for a nap
mid-morning	offer water, take puppy to potty spot, play with puppy for 15 minutes, put puppy in crate for a nap
noon	feed puppy, offer water, take puppy to potty spot, play with puppy for 15 to 30 minutes, put puppy in crate for a nap
mid-afternoon	offer water, take puppy to potty spot, play with puppy for 15 minutes, put puppy in crate for a nap
5:30 p.m.	feed puppy, offer water, take puppy to potty spot, play with puppy up to one hour and/or let him hang around with the family in the kitchen
7:00 p.m.	take puppy to potty spot, play with puppy for 15 minutes, put puppy in crate for a nap
Before bed	take puppy to potty spot, put puppy in crate
During the night	take puppy to potty spot if necessary

that makes a clicking sound when you press its button or metal strip) and some tasty treats makes that teaching a whole lot easier.

Collar

Your puppy needs a collar to hold his leash, his identification tag, and later on, his rabies and license tags. Resist the temptation to outfit your little darling in rhinestone or other blingy collars. For now, keep things simple with a soft nylon or thin leather collar that snaps or buckles.

Crate

A crate isn't cruel, and it's not a cage either. In fact, your Dachshund can learn to love a crate—and you can too while you're trying to housetrain him. Dachshund puppies grow quickly, though. To save money, buy a crate that's big enough to hold his adult size but that comes with a divider, which will allow you to adjust the size of the area inside the crate to which he has access. To keep him comfy, consider investing in a soft mattress or fleece crate pad to put atop the crate tray.

A wire crate is likely to come with the divider you need to adjust the size of your Dachshund's living area as he grows. Plastic crates are okay but much less easy to divide. Nylon crates, while much lighter in weight, are likely to fall prey to the ravages of a chew-happy Dachshund's teeth.

Dishes

Your puppy needs two dishes—one for food and the other for water. The best material for such dishes is stainless steel because it's dishwasher-safe and can't be damaged by your teething puppy's choppers. Plastic dishes can harbor bacteria, and ceramic dishes are breakable. Consider getting a third dish so that you can use one for the morning meal and one for the evening meal.

Food

You'll require a week's supply of dog food. Find out what your breeder has been feeding your puppy, and lay in a week's supply of the same. You may decide to change his diet later, but for now his tummy will be happier (and your floors will be cleaner) if you keep him on the same food that the breeder has been giving him.

Grooming Gear

For now, your Dachshund puppy needs a slicker brush, a mild shampoo formulated specifically for dogs, and doggy nail clippers. Later, depending on what sort of coat your adult Dachshund has, you may need to invest in additional grooming equipment. You'll also need a soft toothbrush and a tube of toothpaste made especially for dogs. (Toothpaste for people can upset a dog's stomach.)

Identification

Once you've decided what to name your puppy, buy an ID tag that contains his name as well as your address and phone number. In addition, plan to ask your vet to insert a microchip under his skin. If your dog gets lost, the microchip can help you recover him quickly because it has a number that's entered into a nationwide registry.

Leash

If you plan to take your dog out in public (and you should!), he needs a leash to keep him safely tied to you. Bypass the retractable leashes in your pet supply store; they can endanger human pedestrians, they encourage dogs to pull, and they're difficult for people to control. Instead, opt for a 6-foot (2-m) nylon or leather leash. Nylon costs less but can leave a painful abrasion on your hand if your dog pulls and the leash crosses your palm. Leather is gentler on human skin and lasts much longer than nylon does.

Pet Stain Cleaning Product

No matter how hard you work to housetrain your Dachshund, he will have accidents. When that happens, you must use a cleaning product that's especially designed to remove pet stains and odor. Look for a product that says "enzymatic cleaner" or otherwise indicates that it's been formulated specifically to eliminate the residue of puppy accidents.

Seat Belt

Just as people need seat belts to improve their odds of surviving a car crash, so does your dog. Canine seat belts utilize your car's seat belt system to give your

Invest in an identification tag that contains your Dachsie's name, address, and telephone number.

The crate is an essential tool to help with the housetraining process.

dog the same protection that you get whenever you buckle up. Try to get a seat belt that doesn't have a plastic clasp; such clasps can shatter if your car is hit hard from behind and your dog is sitting in the backseat.

Toys

Yes, your Dachshund puppy needs toys—but not very many and nothing fancy. Try giving him an empty plastic milk carton to bounce around your kitchen floor. If he loves to gum and cuddle up with soft things, he'll enjoy fleece toys. Nylon bones, like Nylabones, will keep his choppers off your furniture and shoes. Avoid rope toys (small pieces can get caught in your puppy's digestive tract), very small toys (the puppy could swallow one), and toys with squeakers (because the puppy can remove and swallow the squeaker).

BRINGING YOUR PUPPY HOME

At last the big day has arrived: You're bringing your new puppy home from the breeder.

And you're ready with all of the proper equipment, not to mention a puppy-proofed home and yard. You're probably excited and eager to bring home your new family member. But for just one minute, take a deep breath and relax.

Before you go rushing off to the breeder's to bring home your new puppy, put yourself in his place. You know that he's starting a wonderful new life with you, but he doesn't realize that—yet. For him, this day will mean that he's suddenly without his mother, littermates, and the human caregiver he's known for his entire (admittedly short) life. Consequently, he may not be thrilled with the day's proceedings. Instead, he may be confused, disoriented, or even frightened as he tries to process what's happening to him. Your job is to deal with him with compassion and empathy and use that compassion and empathy to help him through this transition. Eventually he'll realize that he has a great thing going in being part of your household.

The Car Ride Home

Start doing that job by bringing along the right equipment for the car ride home. That equipment should include:

Leash and Collar

Put a leash and collar on your puppy while he's in the car so that he can't run away if you stop for a bathroom break on the way home.

Car Restraint

Keep your puppy contained in the car by putting him in an inexpensive plastic crate for the ride home. Put him in the crate, put the crate in the backseat of your car, and secure it with a regular seat belt.

Blanket, Towels, or Sheet

Crate bottoms are rigid and hard. Soften your puppy's car crate by putting one or more of these items on the bottom for him to lie on.

Paper Towels

A roll of paper towels will come in mighty handy if your puppy gets carsick during the trip home. You can also use a paper towel to gently wipe his bottom if he has to potty on the way home. Save that soiled towel so that you can start housetraining him as soon as the two of you arrive home.

Plastic Bags

Use one to hold that soiled paper towel and another to hold any poop he offloads during the trip from the breeder's house to yours.

Treats

Take some treats with you on the trip to the breeder's. You'll use them for initial housetraining lessons when you get home.

Chew Toy

A toy to chew on will help distract your puppy from any stress he's feeling as he makes the trip from old home to new.

Upon Your Arrival

As soon as you get home, take your puppy to the outdoor area you've chosen for his potty. (See Chapter 4 for pointers on bathroom area selection.) Place a soiled paper towel on the ground, let your puppy sniff it—and then watch him squat and pee right on top of it. While he's anointing the towel, praise him enthusiastically but gently and give him a treat. And congratulate yourself for starting to housetrain your puppy before he even sets foot inside your home!

After your puppy has done his business and you enter your house or apartment, let him explore for a little while. Don't allow family members to fuss too much

Nylabone®

A chew toy will help distract your puppy from any stress he's feeling as he makes the trip from old home to new.

over him, and watch carefully for signs that he's about to perform a bathroom encore: suddenly stopping what he's doing, sniffing intensely, circling, and/or starting to squat. At the first sign of any such behavior, scoop him up and take him outside to the same place he pottied before. If he repeats his performance, praise and treat.

WHAT TO EXPECT IN THE BEGINNING

The most important thing to keep in mind during these next few days is that your new Dachshund puppy is trying to make sense of a world that for him has been turned upside down. Start implementing your schedule right away, and keep things as low-key as possible. Spend time with him, but give him time on his own too—like being in his crate to nap.

The first night he's in your home, and possibly for several nights thereafter, your puppy is likely to cry. Here again, empathy is the key to dealing with this situation successfully. Understand that your puppy is probably lonely. He's missing the warmth and comfort of snuggling with his littermates and may be frightened by his unfamiliar surroundings. To put an end to his nighttime yodeling and to jumpstart his bond with you, resist the temptation to isolate him in the kitchen or basement so that you can get a good night's sleep. Instead, put him into his crate and bring the crate and him into your bedroom. There he'll see and smell your presence, which will reassure him that he's not alone. If he continues to cry even after you bring him into your bedroom, go a step further: Bring him and his crate right up to your bed so that the door faces the bedside. Then dangle your fingers in front of the door so that he can sniff them. He

When your puppy first arrives in your home, start implementing your schedule right away, and keep things as low-key as possible.

will probably quiet down once he's assured that you're close by.

If your puppy goes to sleep but wakes up crying in the middle of the night, he probably needs to potty and is trying desperately not to do so in his crate. As you'll see in Chapter 4, this is behavior you want to encourage! That's why you should put on your shoes, bathrobe, and (if necessary) a coat and take him outside to his potty spot. Gently praise him if he goes, but then bring him back inside and put him back into his crate. Above all, don't stop to play or frolic unless you want him to get in the habit of demanding a play session at 2:00 a.m.!

CHAPTER 3

CARE OF YOUR DACHSHUND PUPPY

You're about to undertake one of life's greatest joys: sharing your life with your Dachshund puppy. But the fact that raising that puppy is a joy doesn't preclude another fact: that raising a puppy takes a lot of hard work. To help him grow up into the healthiest, happiest dog he can be, you must commit yourself to putting in the time and effort needed to raise him right. That commitment begins with taking good physical care of him 24/7. But while this job can be challenging and time consuming—at times you may feel that you've given your entire life over to this little creature—it can also be a magical time. That's because as you attend to your puppy's needs, you're also getting to know him and building a lasting bond between you.

This chapter shows you how to start building that bond by meeting your Dachshund puppy's physical needs.

FEEDING A PUPPY

Helping your cute little Dachshund puppy grow up to be a healthy, handsome (or gorgeous!) adult requires more than simply ripping open a bag of dry dog food and pouring it into his dish. No matter what his breed is, a puppy needs a healthy, nutritious diet with the right kinds of food in the right amounts to fuel his metamorphosis from cuddly little fur ball to sleek, streamlined good looks.

Feeding a puppy is as much an art as a science because there are no hard and fast you-must-feed-your-puppy-this-and-only-this rules to take into account. Instead, you need to consider his size, age, and past diet when deciding what's right for him. Here's how to take that knowledge and use it to make sure that your puppy's getting the nutrients he needs to not only survive but also thrive.

What to Feed a Puppy

For the first week or ten days after you bring your Dachshund puppy home from his breeder, plan to feed him the same food that the breeder was giving him. Because he has to get used to all kinds of new sights, sounds, and people in his move from his breeder's home to yours, it only makes sense to keep one part of his life consistent: his diet. And if the breeder has been feeding a high-quality puppy food, you might not need to make any changes at all, at least for the next several months. That said, if you have any doubts about what the breeder has been feeding your puppy, consult your veterinarian. If the vet agrees that a change of diet would be good for your puppy, go ahead and switch—but do so gradually, mixing the new food with the old over a week to ten days. Trying to make the switch any faster could upset your little dog's tummy.

How do you know that a puppy food is a high-quality product? One way to find out is to check the label on the package. The label should list a meat protein—most commonly beef or chicken—as the first ingredient. Moreover, that protein should be a true meat—not meat by-products, meat broth, bone meal, or other derivatives. Pay attention, too, to the protein content percentage listed on the label; for young puppies, the protein content should be at least 25 percent.

When your puppy reaches his four-month birthday, ask your veterinarian about whether to continue feeding him puppy food. Some vets advocate feeding puppy food to young dogs up until they are a year old or even longer. Others cite concerns that the higher protein content of puppy foods will cause an older puppy to grow

A puppy needs a healthy, nutritious diet with the right kinds of food in the right amounts to fuel his growth.

Training Tidbit

Wait for a quiet time of day to teach your puppy to accept being touched, examined, and groomed. The evening while you're watching television is ideal.

too quickly, which in turn could lead to bone and joint problems in the future.

To determine how much food to feed your puppy, start by asking the breeder how much food she's been feeding him and his littermates. As your puppy grows, though, check the label of your puppy's food for guidance. There, you'll find suggestions on how much to feed him each day; that said, try feeding a little less than what's suggested. Pet food manufacturers are sometimes overly generous in the portions they suggest feeding dogs—which stands to reason because they are in the business of making and selling pet food. Moreover, manufacturers' guidelines don't account for the fact that you'll be using treats to train your puppy, as explained in Chapter 4. Consequently, you should scale back your puppy's food portions so that he sports a sleek physique instead of looking like an overstuffed bratwurst. Conversely, if your puppy starts looking too thin, boost his food intake accordingly.

When to Feed a Puppy

Puppies require high-quality food to sustain their rapid growth, but they don't need to have food available round the clock. For that reason alone, experts discourage simply leaving a filled-up bowlful on the floor for your puppy to nibble on (or scarf!) whenever he chooses.

This practice, which is known as free-feeding, will keep your puppy's tummy full, but it's also likely to cause him to become overweight. Excess weight isn't good for any dog, but it's particularly dangerous for a Dachshund because the extra poundage puts a strain on his joints and long back.

Still not convinced that free-feeding is a bad idea? Consider this: If your dog's dish is full of food all the time, you won't be able to determine just how much food he's eating. Without such knowledge, you may take longer to notice when his appetite has fallen off—and appetite loss is a common sign of illness.

Finally, free-feeding makes housetraining much more difficult. As you'll see in Chapter 4, knowing when your puppy has eaten will help you determine when he needs a bathroom break. If you don't know when he's put something in his body, you won't be able to anticipate when he'll need to expel something else from that body. The result: unwelcome bathroom accidents.

That's why the wise Dachshund owner schedules her dog's meals at the same times every day. Up to the age of 16 weeks, puppies need three meals per day: breakfast, lunch, and dinner, along with fresh water at each meal. Each meal should contain one third of the day's total daily ration—do not give him a full day's worth of food at every meal!

When your puppy turns 16 weeks of age, you can cut back to two meals a day—one meal in the morning and one in the late afternoon or early evening—giving half the day's total ration at each meal.

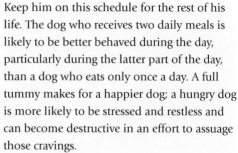

Keep him on this schedule for the rest of his life. The dog who receives two daily meals is likely to be better behaved during the day, particularly during the latter part of the day, than a dog who eats only once a day. A full tummy makes for a happier dog; a hungry dog is more likely to be stressed and restless and can become destructive in an effort to assuage those cravings.

Finally, make sure that your puppy's mealtime is a relaxing, stress-free time for him. He should be allowed to eat undisturbed. After his meal, take him outside to potty and give him at least an hour after his meal to digest his food before engaging in any strenuous activity.

GROOMING A PUPPY

You might think that because your puppy is probably just a soft (although undeniably cute) little butterball right now that grooming him isn't really necessary. But you'd be wrong. Grooming a dog from infancy is critical to maintaining his health and well-being for several reasons.

Why Grooming Is so Important

First, grooming your Dachshund puppy provides you with an opportunity to give him a health check. By regularly running your hands on his body and checking his fur as you brush, you can be on the alert for possible health problems that have symptoms such as unexpected lumps, hair loss, and skin rashes. Catching these

To determine how much food to feed your puppy, start by asking the breeder how much food she's been feeding him and his littermates.

The dog who receives two daily meals is likely to be better behaved during the day, particularly during the latter part of the day.

problems early greatly increases the likelihood that they'll be solved easily.

Second, grooming removes dead hair, and in the case of Longhaired Dachshunds, detangles that hair. Such removal not only reduces shedding but also stimulates the oil glands, which help keep the coat shiny.

Third, grooming your Dachshund not only helps you check up on his health but is also crucial to basic doggy maintenance. That's because grooming involves much more than brushing. Weekly ear cleanings help prevent ear infections; weekly pedicures ensure safe and comfortable walking; daily dental care helps prevent the onset of what can be life-threatening dental problems later in life.

Finally, grooming your young Dachshund gives the two of you a chance to spend some quality time together. By interspersing your brushing, ear cleaning, toothbrushing, and pedicures with treats, belly scratches, adoring looks, and cuddling, you'll build and strengthen your bond with your long-bodied baby.

Grooming Supplies

Grooming your Dachshund puppy doesn't require you to lay in a lot of fancy gear. Start with the following:

- a mild shampoo formulated especially for dogs
- a slicker brush
- a nail clipper or grinder
- a child's soft toothbrush or a toothbrush made for dogs
- toothpaste for dogs
- treats

Depending on whether your Dachshund is a Wirehaired, Longhaired, or Smooth, he may need additional grooming equipment when he matures. For now, though, the few items listed above are all you need.

Getting a Puppy Used to Grooming

The benefits of grooming may be very clear to you but may not be so obvious to your Dachshund puppy. That's why it's a good idea to sweeten his introduction to grooming with items he'll have no trouble enjoying: in a word, treats! By pairing grooming tasks with treats, you'll help your puppy associate those tasks with good things happening and reinforce cooperative behavior on his part.

When you want to examine your puppy's nails, touch one and then give him a tiny treat. When you peek inside his ears to make sure that he doesn't have an infection, give him another. Need to lift his lip slightly to look at his teeth or to brush them? Slip him another goodie immediately afterward. As you gently brush his puppy coat, let him take a treat from your hand. If you're consistent in these practices, your puppy will soon start looking for treats as soon as he sees his brush in your hand, and he won't mind submitting to other grooming rituals either.

Everyday Grooming Requirements

Later in life, your adult Dachshund may need more frequent grooming or even—if he's a Longhaired or Wirehaired Dachshund—the services of a professional groomer. But for now, there are a few tasks you should do every day. All of these introductory tasks have common elements: slow starts, short sessions, and liberal dispensation of treats. These elements will help your Dachshund accept and even enjoy being groomed, which will make the sessions something for you both to

look forward to in the months and years to come.

Brush the Coat

Use your slicker brush to gently brush your puppy's coat in the direction in which it grows. Initially, feed him a tiny treat every couple of strokes. Once he becomes accustomed to and enjoys being brushed, you can start dispensing fewer edible goodies.

Check His Ears

Unless your puppy already has an ear infection or makes a habit of rolling in dirt or mud, he shouldn't need serious ear cleaning at this point in his life. For now, just lift his ear flap gently, give him a treat, look for dirt inside the outer ear, and treat him again. Then lean a little closer, sniff his ear (really!), and give him another teeny tiny treat. You're sniffing to make sure that the ear has little or no odor; if you detect a truly foul smell or even a smell like bread baking in the oven, your puppy may have an ear infection. If that's the case, call your vet immediately. Ear infections can be very painful for a dog, and if left untreated, can result in permanent hearing loss.

Do His Nails

Persuading your puppy to accept a pedicure takes time, patience, and treats. Start by getting him used to having his feet touched with your hand, then with the clipper or grinder. Be sure to feed him a small treat each and every time you touch his foot with either your hand or the instrument. Only when he readily accepts

Want to Know More?

Chapter 6 explains how to perform essential grooming tasks.

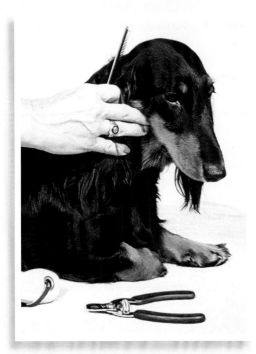

Later in life, your adult Dachshund may need more frequent grooming.

having his nails touched with the clipper or grinder should you attempt to clip his nails—and then only one nail per session and with a treat before and after each clipping. For more detailed information on how to persuade your pooch to accept a pedicure, check out Chapter 6.

Brush His Teeth

Here, too, you should have plenty of time, patience, and treats on hand. Start by wrapping your finger in some sterile gauze, gently lifting his upper lip from the side of his face, and rubbing his gum for a few seconds; follow with a treat. Repeat on the other side, then end the session. Once he accepts your gauze-covered finger readily, add a little doggy toothpaste to your finger and repeat as before. After he's comfortable with your toothpaste-covered finger, try using the toothbrush.

HEALTH

You can't keep your Dachshund puppy healthy all by yourself. Like every other dog owner, you need to partner with someone who's an expert at detecting and treating canine illnesses and who keeps up with the latest scientific research on how to keep puppies well. That someone, of course, is your veterinarian. This section deals with how to find the right veterinarian for you and your puppy, what your puppy's first visit to the vet will be like, and what conditions you need to watch for during the first year of your puppy's life.

Finding a Vet

If you didn't find a veterinarian before you bought your puppy, you need to do so now. That's because within a day or two of bringing him home, you need to take him to a vet for his first checkup. That initial checkup is an important event in and of itself, but it also, hopefully, will be the start of a fruitful partnership that you'll continue throughout your puppy's life.

If you've already had a dog and are happy with the vet you have, you needn't look any further. Otherwise, start by getting the names of a few veterinarians in your area. A good place to start is with the human guardians of dogs already in your neighborhood. You can also check online at websites such as Yahoo! or Switchboard.com, in a hard-copy phone book, or with local Dachshund or all-breed dog clubs. Another excellent starting point is an online search at the American Animal Hospital Association (AAHA) website (www.healthypet.com). The AAHA, which is a national organization that accredits U.S. and Canadian animal hospitals, has a searchable database on its website that will help you find a facility near you.

Once you've identified a couple of nearby

animal hospitals, pay a visit to each. During each visit, look for answers to the following questions. If the answers to all of the following questions satisfy you, congratulations—you've found a great vet. But if the answers don't satisfy you, don't settle. Instead, keep looking.

What Are the Office Hours?

A practice that's open only from 9 to 5 won't be very convenient for you if you're working similar hours. For most people, a facility that opens earlier in the morning, later in the evening, and on weekends might be a better choice.

What Forms of Payment Are Accepted?

Veterinary procedures can be expensive, and you can't always plan for them. If your Dachshund has a middle-of-the-night or weekend emergency that requires pricey intervention, such as ultrasound and surgery, you'll be glad that the practice you've chosen accepts credit cards. If you've purchased pet health insurance, make sure that the practice accepts the plan you've chosen.

What's the Hospital Like?

The hospital should be clean and odor-free, except for perhaps a whiff of antiseptic. The staff—vets, vet techs, and receptionists alike—should be courteous and client oriented.

Is the Hospital Close to Your Home?

The closer the hospital is to your home, the more likely you are to be conscientious about taking your puppy in for regular checkups, not to mention getting him to the vet if he's sick.

Does the Staff Keep Current?

The ever-changing field of veterinary medicine requires that practitioners and their staffs keep abreast of those changes. Look on the walls for certifications and diplomas, which show that vets and staffers are learning about new treatments and techniques and/or are developing specialties such as dentistry or emergency care. Make sure, too, that the facility itself is certified—check to see if there's an AAHA certificate or seal visible at the clinic. Generally you can find a seal right on the clinic's front door.

Are There Backup Systems?

Ask what procedures are in place if your Dachshund has an after-hours emergency. For example, does the practice have a veterinarian on call? If necessary, will the practice refer you to an emergency clinic (if the practice doesn't have such facilities itself)?

How Quickly Can the Vet See You?

A wait of more than two or three days for a nonemergency appointment may indicate that the practice is too busy or has too few veterinarians to meet your needs. The same may also be the case if you're consistently kept waiting in the lobby or an exam room for a long time before the vet can see you.

Is the Practice Computerized?

A computerized veterinary practice enables

Multi-Dog Tip

It's a good idea for any dog owner to keep written records of veterinary visits, but if you have more than one dog, it's crucial. Written records will help you keep track of who's gone to the veterinarian when, what occurred during those visits, and who gets what medication and diet.

you to be much more active in managing your Dachshund puppy's veterinary care. You can make appointments online, have access to his medical records, and receive notices by e-mail of when he's due for a checkup or procedure.

Do You Feel Good About the Practice?

The most important question you can ask about the practice is whether you feel good about it or at least comfortable. If you don't feel able to communicate with the veterinarian, ask any questions that come to mind, and understand the answers she gives you, helping your Dachshund receive the care that he needs will be much more challenging than would otherwise be the case.

The First Checkup

As soon as you bring your new Dachshund puppy home—or better yet, beforehand—make an appointment with the vet you've chosen for his first checkup. The appointment should be no later than two days after your puppy's homecoming.

This initial visit is important for several reasons. First, the visit gives you, your puppy, and your vet a chance to get acquainted. Second, the exam will allow your veterinarian to see what your puppy's like when he's healthy, which gives her a baseline against which to compare any readings she takes during future exams. Finally, the exam may uncover unknown or hidden health problems besetting your puppy, which your vet can begin treating right away. If the problem is serious, you may decide to return the puppy to the breeder; a provision for such a situation should be in the purchase contract's health guarantee.

Your breeder should have given you copies of the puppy's health records when you brought him home, which you should bring with you when you take him to the vet for his checkup. These records form the foundation of your puppy's medical file and will help the vet determine what shots and medications your dog will need during this initial visit. Along with the records, bring a sample of your puppy's stool so that your vet can check for the presence of parasites, such as worms.

In addition to examining your dog's health records and analyzing the stool sample, the vet will also probably:

- weigh your puppy
- measure his vital signs, including temperature, pulse, and respiration
- check his body for lumps, bumps, rashes, parasites, and signs of infection
- peer inside his ears for signs of parasites and infection
- look into his eyes for abnormalities
- check the genitals—in males, to see whether both testicles are fully descended; in females, to make sure that there's no discharge from the vagina
- inspect the teeth and gums for overall health and proper tooth formation

If the stool sample reveals the presence of worms, the vet will prescribe a deworming medication that will rid your puppy of these troublesome parasites. Eliminating worms is very important because they can deplete your puppy's energy and health—and he can also transmit these critters to you.

Vaccinations

Depending on his age, your puppy may also receive immunizations during this initial visit. These immunizations are important because they protect him from serious diseases. Although his mother transmitted her own immunity to such diseases in her milk when he was younger, that immunity won't be enough to protect him by the time he comes to live with you.

Generally puppies receive immunization against distemper, hepatitis, leptospirosis, parainfluenza, and parvovirus in a single combined shot commonly called a DHLPP. Puppies receive this protection in a series of several shots. The first shot is generally given at around six weeks of age, which means that your puppy should have received his first shot in the series while he was still with his breeder. Subsequent shots are given every three or four weeks until the puppy is around 16 to 20 weeks old. In addition, a puppy usually receives his first rabies shot at about 16 weeks of age. After this initial series of shots, you and your veterinarian can discuss how often your adult dog should receive immunizations.

Here are some of the diseases that immunizations can protect your puppy from:

The initial visit gives you, your puppy, and your vet a chance to get acquainted.

Bordetella (Kennel Cough)

This collection of respiratory viruses, often called kennel cough, frequently strikes dogs who spend time with lots of other dogs, such as at a dog park, a doggy day care facility, a boarding facility, or dog-centered events like dog shows and agility and obedience trials. Symptoms include a honking cough and discharge from the nose or eyes. Kennel cough doesn't usually require treatment; the condition resolves itself. Generally the condition isn't serious unless the dog is also lethargic, refusing to eat, or has a fever—which could indicate that he has a much more serious illness. Nevertheless, some doggy day care establishments, boarding kennels, and even dog training classes require proof of immunization against this condition before a dog is allowed to enter the premises. The immunization does not always provide full protection, but it can certainly limit the severity of its symptoms.

Coronavirus

This very contagious virus affects the dog's digestive tract, resulting in mild to serious diarrhea, vomiting, and depression. Coronavirus is particularly dangerous in young puppies because the diarrhea and vomiting it causes can deplete them very quickly. Although coronavirus isn't curable, it may resolve on its own over a two- to ten-day period.

Distemper

This deadly, highly contagious virus tends to strike young, unprotected dogs, as well as wild animals such as skunks, foxes, and raccoons. Symptoms include fever, appetite loss, and eye inflammation. Such symptoms may lessen or even disappear after a few days, only to reappear—along with other symptoms such as pneumonia and neurological complications. Treatment consists of containing the symptoms so that the dog's body has a decent chance of fighting off the disease.

Hepatitis
The symptoms of this highly contagious disease include a slight fever, congestion of the mucous membranes, depression, a significant decrease in white blood cells, and prolonged bleeding time. The condition is especially serious in young puppies. Treatment focuses on giving supportive care to maximize the dog's chances of recovery.

Leptospirosis
This multi-strain bacterial disease strikes mainly unprotected dogs who drink water that's been contaminated by an infected wild animal. Symptoms include lethargy, fever, shivering, vomiting, and dehydration. Dogs who enjoy outdoor activities, particularly swimming, might be especially vulnerable. Treatment consists of antibiotics, limiting exercise, and giving fluids. Immunization can protect from some strains for up to eight months.

Lyme Disease
Deer ticks transmit this condition to both dogs and people. A bite from an infected tick exposes the dog to the condition, but such exposure may not result in illness. Those dogs who do become ill may exhibit unexplained joint pain, fever, weight loss, lethargy, decreased appetite, and chronic ear and eye infections that do not respond to medication. They will also test positive for the presence of antibodies, indicating exposure. Complications can include kidney damage. The condition is treatable with antibiotics and can be prevented, at least to some extent, through the use of tick-controlling products.

Parainfluenza
Canine parainfluenza is sometimes mistaken for bordetella but is much more serious. Symptoms include not only a cough and nasal discharge but also fever, lethargy, labored breathing, and appetite loss. Complications can include pneumonia, which may be fatal. Treatment consists of giving an anti-pertussive medicine to control the cough; antibiotics may also be prescribed.

Parvovirus
This extremely dangerous virus attacks the lining of a dog's digestive system, which prevents the dog from absorbing nutrients in food. Symptoms include bloody, foul-smelling diarrhea, fever, lethargy, and appetite loss. Without treatment, most dogs die from dehydration. Unprotected dogs can contract the disease through contact with the stool of an infected dog. Treatment consists of

Kennel cough frequently strikes dogs who spend time with lots of other dogs, such as at a dog park or a doggy day care facility.

providing fluids and antibiotics, but it is not always successful.

Rabies

Rabies is a disease that is fatal once symptoms become evident. Symptoms among dogs include erratic behavior and uncharacteristic aggressiveness. Today dogs contract the condition much less often than wild animals such as raccoons, skunks, foxes, and bats do. However, because an infected animal's bite can transmit this extremely serious disease to an unprotected dog—who can in turn pass the condition to a person—immunization is vital. In fact, every state in the United States requires that dogs and other pets be vaccinated against rabies. Generally puppies get their first rabies shots when they turn 16 weeks of age and receive boosters at around their first birthdays. After the one-year booster, your dog will be immunized every one to three years, depending on local requirements.

Puppy-Specific Illnesses

The previous section talked about immunizations that protect puppies and young dogs from most of the really serious illnesses that can befall them. However, these same dogs are also susceptible to other illnesses that are not preventable through immunization—but which, fortunately, are generally much less serious. Among those illnesses are:

Demodex

This skin disease—which also is known as red mange, follicular mange, puppy mange, and demodectic mange—primarily strikes young dogs. The cause is one of two types

Want to Know More?

More information about worms and other parasites appears in Chapter 8.

of demodex mites that live on the skin of almost all adult dogs. However, some dogs' immune systems are too weak to keep the mite under control. The resulting proliferation of the mite causes crusty, red skin, hair loss, and perhaps a greasy or moist appearance to the skin. Most dogs who get demodex have mild cases with only a few lesions; such cases may resolve on their own as the dog matures and his immune system gains strength. However, the veterinarian may decide to accelerate the process with topical treatments such as a benzoyl peroxide gel.

In some cases of demodex, lesions appear all over the body. In addition, the skin may be inflamed and cracked and ooze a clear liquid. To help heal the skin and get the mites under control, a veterinarian may prescribe periodic dips in an antiparasitic drug called amitraz. The vet may also prescribe an oral antibiotic to heal the skin infections that may result from these cases. However, even widespread demodex usually resolves unless the dog's immune system is severely compromised.

Primary Acanthosis Nigricans

This genetic condition, which causes darkening and thickening of the skin and can lead to secondary infections, afflicts Dachshunds under one year of age. Although it's not curable, the condition can be controlled with injections of melatonin, administration of steroids, and frequent baths with shampoos designed to control seborrhea (a condition in which the skin becomes excessively oily due to heavy discharge from the sebaceous glands underneath the skin).

By spaying or neutering your Dachshund puppy, you may be decreasing the risks that he will develop some types of health problems.

Puppy Pyoderma

This skin infection, also known as puppy impetigo and juvenile pustular dermatitis, usually causes small pimples and/or crusted areas to appear on the skin. Generally the infection is limited to the chin, the abdomen, and the area under the front legs. Treatment may include an oral antibiotic to eliminate the bacteria that cause the infection and a topical antibacterial shampoo or spray. Such treatment is effective with most cases; however, stubborn cases may require further testing to determine whether an underlying condition is causing the problem.

Puppy Warts

This common puppy malady, which is caused by the canine papilloma virus, appears as small, cauliflower-like growths on the lips or inside the mouth. Usually they resolve on their own without treatment within a few weeks. However, if they become very large or interfere with the puppy's ability to eat, a veterinarian may decide to freeze the warts and then remove them.

Spaying and Neutering

The purchase contract for your Dachshund puppy probably specifies that you will spay or neuter your pup unless you plan to exhibit him in American Kennel Club (AKC) conformation events. Breeders include such provisions in contracts to ensure that dogs who don't conform to the breed standard enough to succeed in the show ring don't grow up to breed other dogs who also don't conform to the standard.

Advantages of Spaying and Neutering

There are good reasons to spay or neuter your puppy. If your puppy is a male, neutering eliminates the risk of testicular cancer and reduces the risk of prostate disorders. Neutering may also cut the risk that a male dog will mark your furniture or walls with his urine and that he'll roam beyond your property.

Spayed female dogs also experience beneficial changes. Females spayed before two and a half years of age are much less likely than unspayed females to develop mammary cancer, which is the most common cancer among female dogs. In addition, the removal of the uterus pretty much eliminates the likelihood that a female dog will develop pyometra (an infection of the uterine cavity). The spayed female dog also no longer goes into heat, which means that you won't have to worry about keeping intact male dogs away from her during her fertile period.

Early spaying and neutering may also be easier than if those procedures occur later in a dog's life. The surgery is easier for vets because there's much less fat in the abdominal cavity than may be the case for older animals. In addition, younger animals are believed to recover more quickly and suffer less pain than might be the case with older postoperative patients.

Risks of Spaying and Neutering

Spaying and neutering do carry some risks. As is the case with any surgical procedure, the use of anesthesia can lead to occasionally fatal complications, although this already minimal risk is further reduced if the veterinarian runs blood tests on your dog beforehand.

Recent research also indicates that while spaying and neutering decrease the risk of some canine cancers, the procedures may increase the risk that a dog will develop others. One study has shown that dogs neutered before one year of age have a bigger chance of developing osteosarcoma, or bone cancer. Another study showed that spayed

female dogs could be at a higher risk of developing hemangiosarcoma, a blood cancer.

Spaying and neutering before six months of age have also been implicated in the development of cruciate ligament ruptures, a painful injury that often requires surgery and weeks of recuperation time. Other problems that are more likely to appear after early spaying or neutering include hypothyroidism, and in female dogs, urinary incontinence. Usually such incontinence is easily treated with a short course of estrogen replacement. Hypothyroidism, which is a shortage of thyroid hormone, is also easily treated by giving the dog artificial hormones for the rest of his life.

The Verdict?

If you don't plan to breed or show your puppy, how should you apply this information? The answer to that question isn't an easy one. That's because if you spay or neuter your Dachshund puppy, you'll probably reduce the risks that he'll develop certain health problems, but you may also increase the risks that he'll have to deal with others—especially if he's spayed or neutered before six months of age. In the end, you and your vet need to discuss this question and determine together when your dog should be neutered or spayed.

CHAPTER 4

TRAINING YOUR DACHSHUND PUPPY

Training your Dachshund puppy is a crucial aspect of taking care of him, but don't think that you've done the job just by signing up for a group class with a professional trainer. A training pro can teach you a lot—but in the end, you're the one who will teach your puppy how to be a model doggy citizen. It's worth taking the time to do the job the right way.

Doing the job the right way does not mean that you have to act like a drill sergeant who's running a boot camp for your Dachshund puppy. As you'll see in this chapter, acting tough or like a boss is exactly the opposite of the approach you should take. Instead, I suggest that you consider yourself to be your dog's partner in his effort to become a well-mannered pet. In this chapter, I'll show you how to take advantage of your Dachshund's natural instincts and impulses and use them to direct and guide his behavior.

INTRODUCTION TO TRAINING

Some people don't train their dogs—perhaps because they don't think that they can do the job or perhaps because they don't think that they'll have the time. Others might believe that training a dog is unnatural and manipulative. Those in the latter category may have a point if they're referring to old-fashioned training methods that involve coercion, aversives, physical manipulation, and at times even (by today's definitions) mistreatment of the dog.

Why Training Is Necessary

Using modern positive methods to train your Dachshund puppy is an entirely different story. Instead of forcing your dog to do something, you gently show him what you want him to do—and then reward him when he does so. This method is a win-win proposition because by doing something you want, your Dachshund gets something he wants.

More importantly, though, training saves dogs' lives. Studies have shown that problem behaviors are the most common reason that people relinquish their dogs to animal shelters—and that many such dogs are surrendered after spending less than 90 days with their families. Moreover, many shelter dogs are adolescents—older puppies who lost their homes because their families couldn't or wouldn't cope with their totally normal but nevertheless out-of-control, untrained behavior. Inevitably, some of these surrendered dogs are euthanized because they're not adopted into new homes and the shelter must make room for new, potentially more adoptable dogs.

In short, if you want your Dachshund puppy to live happily ever after with you, start training him now. The earlier you start to school him in the ways of life with humans in general and your household in particular—not to mention how to behave properly at home and away from it—the better off you'll both be.

The Importance of Positive Training

But as mentioned earlier, not all training methods are created equal. Old-fashioned methods—examples include jerking on a leash and a choke collar to teach a dog to walk politely or pushing his tush to force him to sit or lie down—don't work well with any dog, but they're especially counterproductive when training the independent, sometimes feisty Dachshund. Many Dachshunds simply won't work with people who attempt to force train them; others might react aggressively by snapping, growling, snarling, or even biting. But even if your Dachshund simply complies

and appears to have no negative reaction to such training, attempting to force him into submission could cause irreparable harm to your relationship with him. Assuming that you've acquired your Dachshund for companionship, why would you do anything that would diminish that companionship?

Fortunately, there's a better way to train: positive training. The basic premise of this method is that you concentrate on showing the dog what you want him to do rather than coercing him into obedience or correcting him for mistakes. In other words, you reward your dog when he responds appropriately—usually with a treat but also with praise, affection, and/or a short play session—and if possible, ignore him when he responds inappropriately or incorrectly.

A dog who's trained with positive methods behaves differently from a dog who's trained the old-fashioned way. The dog who's been rewarded for doing the right thing will work hard to continue receiving such rewards. If he's received a treat for sitting when asked, he'll sit again in hopes of scoring another treat. If he's received some playtime for bringing you a tennis ball, he'll keep bringing that ball to you. You won't have a merely obedient dog—you'll also have a happy dog who's eager to work with you and engage in new activities with you. In short, by training with positive methods you'll be bringing out your Dachshund's true nature—clever, sociable, and always thinking.

The Clicker or Marker Word

To the newbie owner or trainer, positive training may seem like a slow way to teach a dog. One would understandably wonder whether there's a way to cut the time it takes to teach a new behavior or cue (we're not using the word "command" in this book!) without doing any corrections. Such a shortcut or tool would enable a dog to recognize immediately that he's done something right and that he's about to be rewarded for doing so.

There is indeed such a shortcut: It's called a marker. The marker can either be verbal, such as a happy exclamation of "Yes!," or it can be physical, as in the use of a clicker. These days, trainers and owners alike are finding that the clicker can greatly accelerate the speed at which a dog learns basic good manners or anything else.

The clicker is a small plastic box that's about 2 inches (5 cm) long and 1 inch (2.5 cm) wide that contains either a little button or small metal strip on top. By pressing the button or strip, the user produces a clicking noise. Consistent use of the clicker, followed immediately by a treat, will soon help the dog realize that he's just performed a behavior that will be rewarded.

Before you start using a clicker to train, however, you need to show your dog that the sound of the clicker means that goodies will follow. For that reason, your first clicker session with your puppy should be a simple click-and-treat session. Starting with the clicker behind your back (because the sound will be softer), click the clicker and immediately give your puppy a treat. Repeat this procedure until he starts looking for a treat as soon as he hears the click. If your puppy is like most Dachshunds, that won't take very long! In essence, you're "charging" the clicker before you use it, just as you would charge up a cell phone or other electronic device.

Some people do find it cumbersome to juggle a puppy, a clicker, and treats all at the same time. Not to worry. If you'd rather ditch the clicker, just use a marker word—like "Yes!"—to mark the desired behavior instead.

Rewards

Rewards are a crucial component of positive reinforcement training, and for most dogs the best rewards are soft, tasty treats. For training, you should make a concerted effort to find goodies that are especially flavorful so that you can offer your Dachshund a strong incentive to learn. Experts call such treats "high-value treats" because the flavor causes your Dachshund to value them so highly that he'll do just about anything to earn them.

Make sure that the treats you use can be broken into small pieces. That way, your Dachshund puppy won't pork out during the training process. Tiny pieces of hotdog (cold or microwaved to a crisp), canned chicken (drained), cheddar cheese, or meat roll treats all provide the flavorful, aromatic incentive your puppy needs to do his best to learn basic good manners.

Positive training focuses on rewarding a dog—with treats, for example—for performing a desired behavior.

When and Where to Train

Another way to make your training more effective is to hold your training sessions at a time when your dog is more likely to appreciate those treats; in other words, when he's hungry. For just about any dog, that would be right before mealtime. The dog's empty tummy will make him more eager to work for those tasty rewards.

Keep in mind that any beginning student—whether human or canine—learns more quickly when he's in an environment with few if any distractions. That's why it's a good idea to start teaching any new behavior at a quiet time and in a familiar place, such as in your home when no one else is around. Later, when your Dachshund performs that behavior proficiently in that quiet environment, add distractions such as other people milling around or being outdoors. Of course, if you're training outdoors, make

Training Tidbit

Start training in an environment with few distractions—for example, inside your house when all is quiet. (If other family members are home, close the door to the room you're in and ask that you not be disturbed.) Once your puppy has mastered a behavior in that environment, you can start building in distractions a little bit at a time: opening the door to the rest of the house, training with other family members coming back and forth, training in your fenced backyard.

sure that he's on the leash unless you're in a securely fenced area.

HOW TO FIND A TRAINER

Finding a dog trainer isn't very difficult—but finding a trainer who's truly committed to using positive training methods can be a little more challenging. Not to worry, though; several organizations offer online databases to help you begin your search. Those organizations include:

Truly Dog Friendly (www.trulydogfriendly. com/blog/?page_id=4): This coalition of dog trainers and behavior consultants eschews electronic collars and other coercive equipment in dog training. The Truly Dog Friendly website includes a link to a searchable database of trainers who are committed to using gentle, pain-free methods to train dogs.

Association of Pet Dog Trainers (www.apdt. com): This 6,000-member-plus organization, better known by its APDT initials, educates and encourages trainers in the use of positive training methods. Like Truly Dog Friendly, the APDT site has a searchable database of trainers.

International Association of Animal Behavior Consultants (www.iaabc.org/Divsn/ dog.php): This organization's dog division includes among its members not only dog trainers who teach group classes but also behavior professionals who work one on one with dogs and their families to solve problem behaviors. The organization's website doesn't specifically mention positive training methods, but the member-written books listed on its website are all based on these principles.

Once you've identified a few trainers who live near you, start contacting them to see whether their philosophies and services mesh with what you and your Dachshund need.

Here's what to ask any trainer you're considering:

Seeing a trainer in action can give you a good idea as to whether you and your dog will be comfortable working with her.

What Is Your Training Philosophy?

Most trainers today will answer that question by saying "positive" or "dog-friendly" or something similar—but don't blindly accept a canned answer. Instead, pursue the issue a little further. Ask a trainer how she would address specific behaviors, such as jumping. Some trainers will use their knees or the leash to correct the dog's jumping; others will try to teach the dog to find a different way to get the attention he's seeking via jumping. A truly positive trainer opts for the second approach.

What Equipment Do You Use?

The answer to this question will provide additional insight into a trainer's methods and philosophy. A trainer who uses choke chains, prong collars, electronic devices, or anything else that causes discomfort to the animal is not truly positive. Pain isn't necessary to train a dog.

What Is Your Background and Experience?

A trainer's answer to this question will tell you a lot about her philosophy. If she says that she uses devices to administer "corrections"—e.g., choke chains, electronic collars, prong collars, or anything else that causes discomfort—the trainer is not truly positive. You don't need pain to train!

May I Observe a Class?

Firsthand observation is a valuable tool for deciding whether to take a particular class. You'll get a better idea of whether you and your dog will be comfortable with a trainer by watching her work with other dogs. Firsthand observation will also help determine the ratio of dogs to instructors; ideally that ratio should be no more than six dogs for every instructor or assistant instructor. Note too how the trainer explains and demonstrates new exercises, answers in-class questions, and deals with disruptive canine students. And after the class, don't hesitate to ask some of the human students what they think of the class.

Do You Have References?

A trainer should be happy to give you references to former students. If your prospective trainer does so, call or e-mail the people she's listed. Ask the people to whom she's directed you what they learned and whether they'd recommend her class or services. If the trainer refuses to give you any references, steer clear and bypass her class.

Do You Offer Both Private and Group Classes?

A trainer who offers both group classes and private instruction may be more experienced and creative than a trainer who offers only group instruction. However, trainers who work exclusively in one-on-one consultations are generally good at individualizing their approaches to solving canine problem behaviors, so don't automatically reject such a trainer for not also conducting group classes.

SOCIALIZATION

Your most important reason for acquiring a Dachshund puppy probably was to add a new and very special friend to your life, and you want to be the same for him. But if you and your family are your dog's sole companions and if he never goes anywhere except to the vet's, you may be jeopardizing his emotional health and well-being. That's because no matter how great a life you provide for him, he'll still be missing something that's crucial to his becoming a happy, well-adjusted dog. That missing element is a social life.

Not to worry: Being your Dachshund's social director isn't very hard. You don't need to overprogram him into a complex set of activities to which you must drive him all over creation. You only need to take the time to systematically expose him to people, pets, sights, sounds, and places beyond what's familiar to him in your home. This process—which should continue throughout your dog's life but is especially important to a puppy's mental and emotional development—is what experts call socialization.

What Is Socialization?

Socialization is the process in which you systematically expose your Dachshund to unfamiliar people, sounds, sights, surfaces, and experiences in a manner that helps him feel positive about those experiences. The well-socialized Dachshund doesn't get fazed at surprises and faces new experiences with confidence. He's happy to welcome a visitor to his home, take a walk in a public area, or ride in the car to visit a friend. He's a confident, well-mannered individual who's a pleasure to live with and a pleasure to meet.

The unsocialized Dachshund, by contrast, can be a challenge to live with. He could even become dangerous, both to his human family and to those he encounters for the first time. Because he hasn't been systematically exposed to new experiences, people, and places, he's likely to react much more fearfully to a novel situation or encounter than his well-socialized counterpart will. Some fearful Dachshunds show their feelings by hiding behind their people, under some furniture, or in a corner. Others, however, deal with their apprehension by growling, snarling, or biting—not because they're aggressive but because they're scared. To ramp down your Dachshund's fear factor, it's crucial to enrich his life with lots of positive social experiences, starting right now.

How to Socialize

If you're lucky, your puppy's breeder has already begun to socialize him. Simply taking him out in her backyard to walk on some grass, mulch, concrete, or other noncarpeted surface can be exciting to a puppy. Even walking on a floor after being accustomed to carpet can be new and novel. So can learning to walk up and down stairs (dogs are not born knowing how to navigate stairways!), as can taking a car ride to the vet's for his first round of shots. Most exciting of all may be the opportunities the breeder gives the puppy to meet lots of people, learn to enjoy having people hold and pet him, and experience everyday life in a human household.

But you need to continue the socialization process your breeder has started. Introduce him to lots of people of different ages and ethnicities and make sure that those experiences are fun and positive. Take him for car rides—and not just to the vet's but to lots of other places as well.

However, socialization is not a one-size-fits-all process. Your puppy is unique and needs a socialization process tailored to his personality. Some Dachshunds are more outgoing than others; they'll approach a new person or dog or object with heads up, happy panting, and loosely wagging tail. Others may be a little more hesitant and may exhibit downward tucked tails and ears held down and back and otherwise exhibit a more uncertain demeanor. If your Dachshund seems to fit the latter description, don't push him beyond his comfort zone. Be patient, take your time, and let him adjust to a novel situation at his own pace.

Although they realize the importance of socialization, some veterinarians hesitate to endorse the process at such a young age. They worry that meeting other dogs could expose

Multi-Dog Tip

The other dogs in the house can create some challenging distractions to your Dachshund puppy-in-training. For that reason, keep those dogs away from your puppy during the initial stages of training a new behavior. As he masters new behaviors in this dog-free environment, you can start practicing when your other dogs are nearby. Not only will you offer your puppy a new challenge, but you may also find that your other dogs benefit from getting a refresher course in their behavior basics!

puppies to serious contagious diseases such as rabies and distemper. Immunizations protect puppies from these and other diseases, but those immunizations aren't complete until puppies reach 16 to 20 weeks of age, when the window for optimal socialization is closing.

The vets have some reason for concern. Until he's finished his shots, a puppy's risk of contracting serious contagious diseases is heightened. However, keeping a puppy away from all other dogs can make socialization difficult—and failure to socialize imperils a dog's mental and emotional health.

Fortunately, the socialization/immunization issue need not be an either/or proposition. You can socialize your puppy without putting him at excessive risk. Here's how:

Bring the World to Him

If you don't want to take your puppy outside, just bring that outdoor world inside to him. Ask

Even just feeling a variety of surfaces under his feet will help socialize your new puppy.

put him on your lap. By giving him a lap's-eye view of the world, he'll be both safe and socialized, and you'll get in some extra cuddle time!

Treat Him Right

Your Dachshund-turned-lapdog can still be socialized to new people and novel environments if you exercise a bit of ingenuity. Simply take him to a public place where there's a park bench. (I especially like one outside the local supermarket.) When people pass by, ask them to feed your new pup treats. Most people will be happy to oblige—and doing so may well be the high point of their day!

people with well-behaved, fully immunized dogs to come over and play with him—and bring him to their homes too. Keep those playdates to one-on-one encounters, though, until you have a better idea of how your puppy plays with other dogs.

Seek Out Dog-Free Zones

Your Dachshund puppy is safe any place where dogs don't congregate. In other words, you can take him anywhere except dog parks, pet stores, and other pet-friendly public locations. Don't take him to those spots until his puppy shots are complete.

Make Him a Lapdog

If you're uncertain as to whether a place is safe for your little Dachsie, just scoop him up and

CRATE TRAINING

Crates are indispensable to Dachshunds and their people. When used properly, the crate helps your puppy learn his bathroom manners much faster than would otherwise be the case. The crate also gives you a place to put your puppy when you can't watch him and gives him a place of his own to retreat to when he needs to nap or otherwise have a little alone time.

But not all puppies immediately appreciate the advantages of being crated. If your puppy fits that description, you need to crate train him before you start crate-dependent lessons such as housetraining. Once your puppy can stay calmly in his crate for 30 minutes, he's sufficiently crate trained to begin the housetraining process.

What Is Crate Training?

Crate training is the process of gently introducing your puppy to the crate before you start using it for other training. If you're lucky, his breeder may have already completed or at least started this process—but it's more likely that you'll need to take on the job. The process need not take long, but when you're done your puppy will know that his crate is his very own safe, special place. In fact, one of the Dachshunds to whom this book is dedicated regularly chose to chill out in her crate throughout her 12-year life span. If you do it right, your Dachshund puppy could learn to view and use his crate the same way.

How to Crate Train

Teaching your Dachshund puppy to love using his crate isn't difficult, but it does require a little bit of time and patience. Here's what to do:

Let Him Sniff the Perimeter

Throw some treats around the perimeter of the crate to encourage your puppy to sniff the crate's exterior.

Encourage Inside Exploration

Take a small treat and throw it inside the crate, preferably toward the back. If your puppy goes into the crate to get the treat, praise him. If he hesitates, move the treat close to the front of the crate so that he need not enter the enclosure right away. After he takes treats comfortably at the door, place the treat farther and farther back in the crate until he's completely inside. Each time he takes the treat, praise him lavishly.

Close the Door

Close the door—but only for a moment. Once your puppy consistently enters the crate without hesitation, use a treat to encourage him to enter; then, when he's inside, shut the door for no more than five seconds. During those five seconds, speak to him softly and encouragingly. Then open the door and give him another treat when he steps out. Repeat this sequence, gradually increasing the amount of time the door is closed until your puppy remains comfortably in the crate for about five minutes.

Leave

At your puppy's next meal, put his food in a small bowl and place the bowl inside the crate. Then toss a treat inside the crate to encourage him to enter. When he does, shut the door and leave the room for a minute or so; then check to see how he's doing *without his seeing you*. If he's eating happily, leave again and return a few minutes later. Once he's finished his meal, let him out of his crate, praise him, and give him a small treat. After he's taken his meal in the crate a couple of times, start enclosing him in the crate without a meal. Gradually extend the time he's in the crate until he stays comfortably for about 30 minutes.

HOUSETRAINING

Unfortunately, Dachshunds have a reputation for being more challenging to housetrain than other breeds. The reasons for the apparent inability of these long-bodied little dogs to immediately grasp the intricacies of proper bathroom behavior are not clear. One possible reason might be that the Dachshund puppy's bladder is so small that he needs more frequent bathroom breaks than his people think to provide for him. Another might be that because the Dachshund puppy *is* quite small, his people overlook his errant puddles and piles.

Your Dachshund, though, can give the lie to this reputation if you work with him consistently to perfect his bathroom behavior. For the record, each of the three Dachshunds to whom this book is dedicated learned proper potty protocol quickly and maintained their bathroom manners throughout their long lives.

What Is Housetraining?

Housetraining is the process of teaching your puppy to eliminate only at the times and in the places you want him to. The concept may sound simple, but the actual process hasn't always been so.

That's because not so many years ago, most people didn't really know how to housetrain. We didn't know much about our dogs' basic bathroom instincts, much less how to capitalize on those instincts. The result was that people would unintentionally set up their puppies to make mistakes. Then they'd berate the puppies for such mistakes—even though the puppies had no idea what their people were angry about, much less that they themselves had goofed.

Fortunately, today we know better. We now understand that dogs like to have special places, or dens, of their own and that they'll do just about anything to avoid pooping or peeing in those dens. That's why crates are so important in housetraining. By confining your puppy to his crate when you can't watch him—and by carefully supervising him when he's not in the crate—you will help him develop the control that's necessary for him to have reliable bathroom manners.

When you housetrain your Dachshund puppy in this way, you can say goodbye to rolled-up newspapers, rubbing his nose in his mistakes, and other old-fashioned methods that have never really worked. Instead, you and your puppy will be working together to help him become a housetraining ace.

How to Housetrain

Housetraining isn't a complicated process, but it does require time, patience, and consistency. Follow these steps and your Dachshund housetraining student will be a housetraining graduate sooner than you think.

Establish the Bathroom

Ideally, you will have chosen where your puppy will do his business before you bring

Want to Know More?

More information about the advantages of bathroom schedules and a sample schedule appear in Chapter 2.

him home from his breeder. The best place for your pup's bathroom is outside in your backyard and close enough to your house that he won't have to go too far to eliminate. If you don't have a backyard, take your puppy to the median strip between the sidewalk and street, have him do his business there—and be sure to clean up whenever and wherever he poops.

Throw in the Towel

The very next time your puppy pees, gently blot his sanitary area with a paper towel and put that paper towel in a plastic bag. You'll use this soiled paper towel, also known as a scent cloth, to show him where his bathroom is.

Show Him Where to Eliminate

Once you've created the scent cloth, take your puppy out to his designated bathroom the next time he needs to eliminate. Bring the scent cloth and a very small treat with you. Once you reach the potty place, place the scent cloth on top of it. The scent from the puppy's urine will draw him to the towel, and in all likelihood he will pee right on top of it. Praise him and give him the treat. Bring him here for all subsequent bathroom breaks.

Create a Schedule

Young puppies generally need to eliminate first thing in the morning, after naps, before and after meals, after play sessions, and last thing at night. A puppy may also need a middle-of-the-night break until he's at least three months old. That means that he'll need a potty break at least every couple of hours or so during the day. To help you organize all of these bathroom breaks, write out a schedule and adhere to it as closely as possible. That way, you'll condition your puppy to eliminate only at those times and to hold his fire in between potty breaks.

Supervise Closely

Whenever your puppy is not in his crate, you need to watch him carefully to make sure that he doesn't get into any mischief and to prevent accidents. Any time that you can't supervise him, he should be in his crate. This step is crucial: You want to do as much as you can to prevent him from having an accident.

Watch for Pre-Potty Signals

Your puppy will learn proper potty protocol faster if you can keep him from having accidents. If you see your little darling suddenly halt in his tracks, sniff the ground closely, or begin pacing either back and forth or in circles, he's probably getting ready to perform a doggy offload. Pick him up and get him to his potty place as fast as you can—and if he performs there, praise and treat.

Expect Accidents

No matter how hard you try or how diligent you are, your puppy will have at least a couple of accidents until he figures out the whole housetraining thing. When that happens, don't scold or berate him, and certainly don't whack him with a rolled-up newspaper or rub his face in the offending puddle or pile. Instead, take him to his crate and clean up the accident without comment. Make sure, too, that you use a cleaner that's formulated specifically to deal with pet stains and odor. Failure to do so could easily prompt your puppy to return

to the scene of his accident and repeat his performance.

Troubleshoot the Accident

If your Dachshund puppy does commit a potty foul, the fault generally lies with you, not him. Did you fail to watch him closely? Did you make him wait too long between potty breaks? Did you fail to heed a signal that he needed to go? Did you fail to thoroughly clean up the scene of an earlier accident? An answer of "yes" to any of those questions could illuminate the reason behind your puppy's doo-doo boo-boo.

Crate training is the process of gently introducing your puppy to the crate before you start using it for other training.

By confining your puppy to his crate when you can't watch him, you will help him develop the control that's necessary for him to have reliable bathroom manners.

Be Patient

Puppies don't become housetraining graduates overnight. They need time to figure out where and when they can potty, as well as develop enough physical control to refrain from eliminating until their scheduled bathroom breaks. In fact, most puppies—Dachshunds included—don't really master their bathroom basics until they're about six months old; some take even longer. If your Dachshund reaches that half-year mark and hasn't had an accident for a month or so, you can consider him to be a housetraining graduate and pat yourself on the back for a job well done.

BASIC GOOD MANNERS CUES

Not so very long ago, we thought that dog training was all about us being alpha leaders and our dogs being our willing, obedient students. (And if they didn't obey, we would correct them or discipline them, sometimes in rather bizarre ways.) Now we understand that just like humans, dogs need a reason to learn

Puppy Kindergarten

One very good way to socialize your puppy is to take him to a puppy kindergarten class or puppy play group. Such classes or groups are usually conducted by a dog trainer, and depending on the size of the class or group, some assistants. Think of a small-scale version of Animal Planet's annual *Puppy Bowl* telecast, and you'll have a good idea of what a puppy play group is like. A puppy-K class may also include some basic behavioral instruction. Either way, you'll be awash in puppy cuteness!

A well-run puppy-K or play group gives your juvenile Dachshund a safe, supervised way to meet other puppies and people. It also gives you a chance to learn from an expert about general puppy behavior and how to raise your particular puppy. With a puppy-K class, you'll also get a head start from an expert on teaching your puppy basic behaviors that can help you and him live happily together.

The process for finding a good puppy kindergarten class or play group is similar to that of finding a good trainer and/or obedience class for older puppies and adults. Log onto websites such as Truly Dog Friendly (www.trulydogfriendly.com) and the Association of Pet Dog Trainers (www.apdt.com), and search their databases for trainers who offer group classes. Check with those trainers to see if they also conduct puppy-K classes and/or play groups. Once you've narrowed your search to a few candidates, visit each of their facilities. Then, in addition to finding out basics such as when the classes are held and what they cost, get the following questions answered:

What's your impression of the facility? Here you're looking for a place that's clean, well lit, and has enough room for puppies to run and play but not so much room that the puppies will be too busy exploring the room to bother with one another.

What's the trainer-to-puppy ratio? The more puppies are playing, the more trainers or assistant trainers should be present to supervise the action. The maximum ratio should be one trainer or assistant to five or six puppies; a lower ratio is better.

How are the puppies screened? Not every puppy should participate in a puppy-K class or play group. Large puppies, particularly those over six months of age, don't belong in a puppy kindergarten class unless it's limited to big pups only. Size compatibility is important; at this stage, big puppies shouldn't be playing with small puppies.

What vaccinations are required? The trainer should require that every puppy be immunized as is appropriate to his age and should ask for records of such vaccinations before puppies are allowed to play together.

and perform. For humans, the incentive to do a job or task is a monetary paycheck; for dogs, the incentive most often takes the form of a treat but can also be something else like a toy or a play session.

That's why you won't see the words "command" or "obedience" in this section. Instead, I talk about "cues": verbal prompts that signal to our dogs that we want them to perform specific behaviors.

This section isn't about teaching Dachshunds "obedience." (The highly independent Dachshund would probably object strenuously to such a term if he could!) Instead, it deals with good manners. A well-mannered dog of any breed, including a Dachshund, is a joy to be around. A person can take a well-mannered dog anywhere, anyplace, anytime and be confident that the right cue is all that's needed to help him behave appropriately.

Here, then, are some basic cues that every well-mannered puppy knows.

Name and Attention

If your dog doesn't pay attention to you, you'll have a tough time training him. That's why I recommend that you teach your Dachshund puppy his name before you try to teach him anything else. A puppy's name is the best way to get his attention. That's because the name is a one-word cue that tells him to look at you right away and wait for additional instructions.

Because you'll use your puppy's name so often, make sure that you choose one not only that you will enjoy using but also that he'll enjoy responding to. For that reason, keep the name short (no more than two syllables) and simple, and resist the temptation to make the name an object of humor. Translation: Don't name your Dachshund "Bratwurst" just for laughs.

How to Teach It

To teach your puppy his name, have treats in one hand (or within very easy reach) and your clicker in the other. Then:

1. Wait until your puppy is looking at you. As soon as he does, say his name, click the clicker (or say "Yes!" if you don't use a clicker), and give him a treat.
2. Do this several times until he clearly associates his name with the click and treat.
3. Now wait until your puppy is looking away from you. Then say his name. If he turns back to look at you, click and treat. If he doesn't, don't repeat his name; instead, make a noise to get his attention (a kissing noise is good), then click and treat.

Many puppies find it easier to lie down than to sit.

In addition to many other times, young puppies generally need to eliminate after play sessions.

Sit

The *sit* is one of the easiest cues you can teach your juvenile Dachshund. Think about it: Your puppy already knows how to sit, so all you need to do is help him understand that the word "sit" means that he should plunk his bottom downward. Teaching this cue will help both you and your puppy feel successful right away and will allow you to feel more confident about teaching him other cues later.

How to Teach It

You need a clicker and treats to teach this cue. Put the clicker on one hand a treat in the other. Then proceed as follows:

1. Hold a treat in front of your puppy's nose. Make sure he sees it, but don't let him eat it.
2. Slowly move the treat upward, then back over his head.
3. Your puppy will follow the treat with his eyes—and as he does, he'll sit. As soon as his bottom hits the ground, click the clicker (or use a verbal marker) and give him that treat.
4. Repeat this sequence until you're sure that he will sit for the treat.
5. Now add the verbal cue. In a cheerful tone of voice, say "Sit" as you move the treat over his head and his bottom heads downward. When his tush hits the ground, click and treat.
6. Repeat the previous step until he consistently sits when he hears the cue.
7. Now you're ready for the last step: asking him to sit without using the treat to lure him into position. Start by putting your arms behind your back so that your puppy can't see the treat. Ask him to sit. If he does,

click and treat. If he doesn't, use the treat to guide him into the sit as you did in steps 2 and 3, then click and treat—and keep practicing!

You may need more than one session to teach your puppy this cue. If so, don't worry. Just keep each session short—no more than ten minutes—and make sure that you end on a positive note.

Down

Your puppy may learn to lie down on cue faster than he learned to sit, simply because many pups find it easier to recline than to park their tushes on the ground. Still, your puppy should know how to sit on cue before you teach him the *down*.

How to Teach It

When he sits, proceed as follows:

Your puppy already knows how to sit, so all you have to do is help him associate the act of sitting with the word "sit."

1. Hold a treat in front of his face at eye level. Make sure that he sees it.
2. Tell him "Down," being sure to draw out the cue so that you're really saying "Dowwwwn," and keep your voice cheerful.
3. At the same time you use the cue word, begin moving the treat slowly downward toward your puppy's paws. When the treat is near ground level, move it outward several inches (cm). The effect should be that you move the treat in an L-shaped path.
4. As your puppy follows your hand with his eyes, he should lie down. When he does, click and treat.

Come (Recall)

The *come* cue, also known as the *recall*, is truly one of the most important cues you can teach your Dachshund puppy. If you and he are in a situation where he needs to return to you immediately—for example, if he slips out of his collar—a truly reliable *recall* can save his life.

How to Teach It

There are two ways to teach this cue—by yourself and/or with a human partner. Start by working just with your puppy as follows:

1. Leash him and have him sit a few feet (m) away from you.
2. Say his name and the word "come" in an enthusiastic, excited tone of voice.
3. As your puppy comes toward you, squat down and open your arms.
4. When he reaches you, praise lavishly and click and treat.
5. Repeat this sequence. Gradually increase the distance between you each time.

After he's mastered the *recall* with the leash on, remove the leash. Be sure, though, that you practice off-leash *recalls* in enclosed settings, such as in a fenced yard or inside your home. And keep practicing periodically for the rest of your dog's life; he can never be too good at the *recall*.

To teach the *recall* with a partner, proceed as follows:

1. Leash your dog. Have your partner hold the leash.
2. Move several feet (m) away from your partner and your dog.
3. Say your dog's name and the word "come" in a high, happy voice. At the same time, your partner should drop the leash so that your dog can go to you.
4. When he reaches you, praise lavishly, click and treat, and pick up the leash.
5. Repeat the previous four steps, with you holding the leash and your partner calling your dog. Keep calling your dog back and forth for five to ten minutes.

Not every puppy figures out the *recall* immediately. For such puppies, try one or more of the following fixes.

1. Puppies love to chase their people, and you can use that desire to your advantage. Have your dog sit, then run away from him—but tell him to come as you do so. When he catches up to you, praise and click and treat. Repeat until he consistently runs to you. Then switch back to having him sit and you squatting a few feet (m) away from him.
2. Make sure that you're using high-value treats—that is, treats that your puppy truly adores.
3. Don't rush the process. If your puppy's having trouble responding in a high-distraction environment, go back to practicing in a quieter environment.
4. Be very careful to reward him every time he comes to you. Never ask him to come if you're going to end his playtime, scold him, take something away from him, or do anything that he'd find unpleasant. In such

Nothing makes a walk more pleasurable than being accompanied by a Dachshund who knows how to behave himself while he's on the leash.

instances, go to him instead. That way, he won't associate coming when called with a negative consequence.

Walk Nicely on Leash

A Dachshund who behaves himself while on leash is a pleasure to walk with. Unfortunately, learning proper leash behavior can be problematic for many dogs, including Dachshunds. That's understandable— with so much to investigate around him, staying close to you may not seem all that stimulating. Your strategy here is to show him otherwise; in other words, that better things happen when he stays with you than when he tries to run ahead or otherwise leave your side.

How to Teach It

1. Leash your Dachshund and place the leash loop around your wrist.
2. With your looped hand, grasp the leash just below the loop.
3. Place your dog next to you on the side opposite your looped hand. The leash should fall diagonally across the front of your body.
4. Say to your dog "Let's go!" in a happy but firm tone of voice.
5. Walk fairly briskly. (Take advantage of your dog's short little legs!) By setting a brisk pace, your short-legged Dachshund will have to hotfoot it to keep up with you. As you walk, talk to your dog so that you keep his attention.
6. To keep him close to you, click and treat with your unleashed hand every couple of steps initially. As he improves his walking-on-leash skills, you can walk for longer distances before clicking and treating.
7. If your Dachshund makes like a sled dog and bolts in front of you, stop immediately. By stopping consistently when he pulls, he'll eventually learn that pulling gets him nowhere. Resume your walk when he heads back toward you and the leash slackens.
8. When you stop at a corner, place your unleashed hand a few inches (cm) in front of your Dachshund's face so that he also stops. Click and treat.

PREVENTING PROBLEM BEHAVIORS

Alas, not even Dachshunds are perfect. As wonderful as they are, even they can develop problem behaviors. Chapter 10 discusses these problems and how to solve them if they occur. However, the best way to solve problem

Trouble With the Walk Nicely *Cue?*

If mastering this exercise really seems to be beyond your puppy's ability, try the following remedies:

1. When he bolts, turn around and go in the opposite direction. But do so *very* carefully. Do not snap the leash or jerk his head in any way. Just turn around in one smooth motion, and be sure to click and treat him when he catches up and begins walking politely next to you.
2. Let him work off some steam with some exercise before you start teaching this behavior. A puppy who's sizzling with energy may find polite walking nearly impossible to perform no matter now enticing the goodies are.
3. If your puppy pulls continually, invest in a front-clip harness. This handy device is much more effective at arresting the antics of a would-be Iditarod dog than a choke collar, prong collar, or even a head halter—and they're much kinder to the dog too.

Keep in mind that walking nicely on leash isn't the same thing as formal heeling. The latter requires that the dog's head be parallel with his handler's left knee and that the dog stop and sit next to her left knee whenever she stops. The formal *heel* is beautiful to watch, but such precision isn't needed for a dog to walk politely while on leash.

Struggling With the Down Cue?

For some puppies, learning the *down* cue is a bit of a struggle. If your Dachshund is among the strugglers, just experiment a bit. For example, if your puppy likes to lie down on one hip, try moving the treat down toward his paws and then outward on the side that's opposite the hip on which he likes to lie down. If he won't lie down at all, move the treat more slowly and perhaps use a different treat (one that's tastier or he otherwise really wants). Above all, be persistent and patient.

behaviors is to prevent their occurring in the first place. By teaching your Dachshund puppy or adult dog the cues in this section, you'll do a lot to head off undesirable behaviors such as guarding food or toys and picking up forbidden objects.

Trade

A puppy who picks up something that he's not supposed to needs to give up that something willingly. Teaching him to surrender a forbidden object is a whole lot easier if you offer him something that's even more desirable than the object he already has.

How to Teach It

Here's how to do that:

1. Give your puppy a chew toy that you know he likes but isn't totally crazy about. Let him engage with that toy for a minute or two.
2. Bend down or sit on the floor next to him and hold his favorite treat in front of his nose.
3. Say "Trade" and use the treat to lure his nose away from the toy. When his nose is well clear of the toy, give him the treat and pick up the toy.
4. Give the toy back to him right away.
5. Keep practicing this exercise until he consistently drops the toy as soon as you say "Trade."

Practice periodically, but make sure that your Dachshund associates the *trade* cue with getting something better than what he already has. That way, if he happens to get hold of a forbidden object that you can't give back to him, he'll nevertheless relinquish that object readily.

Off/Take It

The *off* cue teaches your puppy to not pick up a forbidden object at all. If your puppy is about to pick up something he shouldn't and hears you tell him "Off" (or "Leave it"), he should stop immediately and leave the object where it is. By contrast, the *take it* cue gives your puppy the go-ahead to pick up an object.

How to Teach It

Teach him both cues this way:

1. Sit on the floor with your puppy in front of you.
2. Have a tasty treat in the palm of your hand and show him your palm, but don't let him take the treat.
3. As your puppy goes for the treat, shut your hand in a fist so that the treat's not accessible and say "Off." Each subsequent time he noses your hand, repeat the cue.
4. Then after about four or five times, open your fist so that the treat is visible and tell him to "Take it."
5. Practice these two cues regularly, even after your puppy has mastered them.

PART II

ADULTHOOD

CHAPTER 5

FINDING YOUR DACHSHUND ADULT

There's no question that Dachshund puppies epitomize cuteness. They're soft, they're cuddly, and they have incredibly big eyes with which to look upon you beseechingly. Who could possibly resist bringing such adorableness into a family?

Well—maybe you.

Maybe you don't want to deal with middle-of-the-night puppy potty breaks, cleaning up puppy accidents, and dealing with everyday puppy mischief. And even if those puppy challenges were okay with you, paying $1,000 or even more for a purebred Dachshund puppy from a reputable breeder might not be. If those "maybe's" resonate with you, a better choice might be an adult Dachshund: a dog who's a year or more old.

WHY ADOPTING AN ADULT IS A GOOD IDEA

Raising a puppy is much more than basking in his cuddliness and cuteness. At times, this enterprise is a huge hassle. Puppy raising can be incredibly rewarding, but it's not for everyone.

For example, a household in which all of the family members are gone all day is probably a household that's unsuited to raising a puppy of any breed, Dachshund or otherwise.

That's because puppy raising—especially housetraining—requires a lot of human time and attention. The juvenile Dachshund housetrainee needs trips to the potty at least every couple of hours, and in the first week or two, may need to make pit stops even more often. Such a schedule is pretty much impossible in a household where all of the family members are at school or work for the entire day. And even if you can find someone to take care of your puppy when you're not around, you'll still need to put a lot of time into raising him when you are around. Who wants to have to do that on top of a full-time job, home maintenance, running errands, and all the other activities that are necessary to 21st-century living? Trying to crowd puppy raising into your already stuffed-to-the-gills daily schedule is likely to result in both you and your puppy feeling shortchanged.

But if you don't want to deal with the perpetual challenge of caring for a puppy, are the joys of living with a Dachshund off-limits to you and your family? Not necessarily. Instead, you can open your heart and home to an adult Dachshund.

Still need some convincing? Here are some more pluses to offering a home to a grown-up Dachshund:

By the Numbers

Dachshunds are considered to be adults at one year of age.

He May Already Have Good Bathroom Manners

Many adult Dachshunds have mastered their bathroom basics. That said, even if your particular Dachshund has missed out on Housetraining 101 as a puppy, he can catch up quickly. That's because an adult Dachshund has the physical control needed to hold his poop and pee between pit stops and he can wait a lot longer between trips than his younger counterpart can.

He May Already Know the Ropes

Most adult Dachshunds have already lived in human households and are likely to have acquired some basic good manners training. They may understand not only some basic cues such as the *sit*, the *down*, and coming when called; chances are that they also know that they're not supposed to chew on shoes or attempt to board the living room sofa.

He'll Cost Less Than a Puppy

As mentioned earlier, a Dachshund puppy from a reputable breeder can cost $900 or even more. By contrast, a Dachshund from an animal shelter or rescue group generally costs far less than half that amount. For example, in early 2010, Central Texas Dachshund Rescue charged $250 to adopt a dog of any age. Such fees are generally designed simply to offset the shelter or rescue group's expenses in caring for the dog.

You May Save One or More Lives

Most adult Dachshunds in shelters or rescue groups are homeless—and in many cases, they've lost their homes due to circumstances beyond their control. In some cases, changes in an owner's circumstances—divorce, home foreclosure, moving to a home that doesn't allow pets—may cause her to relinquish her dog. Other Dachshunds lose their homes because they have behavioral challenges that their owners couldn't or didn't want to try to solve—but that doesn't mean that you can't succeed where others have failed. Finally, some Dachshunds lose their homes because they've been neglected or even abused. But no matter why an adult Dachshund loses his home, your willingness to take him in gives him a second chance at having a happy life. You also will not only spare him the euthanasia that could occur if he were not adopted but will make room at a shelter or rescue group for another dog in need of a home.

ADOPTION OPTIONS

Fortunately, you have several choices if you're looking to add an adult Dachshund to your life. Here are the most common:

Breeders

Sometimes a reputable breeder will sell an adult Dachshund. For example, if a breeder shows a dog only to find that the dog doesn't like being in the show ring, she might conclude that he would be better off simply being a family pet. Or maybe a puppy whom a breeder thought would be a good dog show prospect has grown up to be not so stellar; he could be oversized, undersized, or otherwise not conform enough to the breed standard to do well. However, a dog who doesn't do well in the show ring could still do great as a pet.

If you want to buy an adult Dachshund from a reputable breeder, log onto the Dachshund Club of America's (DCA) regional clubs' page at www.dachshund-dca.org/clubs/html and peruse the list of regional and state clubs you'll find there. Click on the link(s) for your state or region. You may also find one or more listings for breed referral coordinators who often can tell you whether any breeders in your area are trying to find homes for their adult Dachshunds.

Be advised, however, that you are likely to pay much more for an adult Dachshund obtained through a breeder than would be the case if you adopted one from a shelter or rescue group.

Animal Shelters

If you thought that animal shelters offer only mixed-breed dogs for adoption, you'd be wrong. The Humane Society of the United States (HSUS) reports that up to 30 percent of the dogs in shelters are purebred dogs. And because the Dachshund is one of the most popular breeds in the United States, the odds are fairly good that your local shelter might at least occasionally have a Dachshund available for adoption.

A quick way to find out whether your local shelter or rescue group has Dachshunds or Dachshund mixes available to adopt is to check out the listings on Petfinder. Just log onto www.petfinder.com and follow the prompts on the lefthand side of the page to search the site's nationwide database of Dachshunds available from rescue groups and animal shelters.

Most of the adult Dachshunds who are up for adoption are homeless.

Rescue Groups

A lot of regional, state, and local Dachshund clubs have committees that concentrate on finding new homes for Dachshunds who have lost the domiciles they had. Committee members—who are almost always volunteers—bring the homeless Dachsies to temporary (also known as foster) homes, care for the dogs, evaluate potential adopters, match adopters and dogs, and raise the money needed to finance these activities. Many committee members take on several of these jobs. You can find these committees by logging onto the DCA's rescue page at www.dachshund-dca.org/rescue.html. By contacting the individuals listed on this page, you'll be able to determine whether their groups have any adoptable Dachshunds available.

You can also find a local rescue group by contacting a local Dachshund club directly.

Training Tidbit

Many adult Dachshunds received some training during puppyhood, but your particular Dachshund may not be among them. And even if he did get some early schooling, the stress of having been relinquished from one home and having to get used to a new one may cause him to at least temporarily forget what he's learned. But don't worry. Just turn to Chapters 4 and 10 and do some of the training exercises described there. He'll remember what he's forgotten or learn quickly if being taught these behaviors for the first time.

To find such a club, access the DCA's local club list at www.dachshund-dca.org/clubs.html. From there, scroll down the list to find a club located near you, and click on the link to that club's website. Most of the local club websites either list the person who heads the club rescue committee or direct visitors to the rescue committee's own website. In addition, Petfinder's database includes listing for Dachshunds available from rescue groups.

Still another way to find a Dachshund from a rescue group is to go to an adoption fair that the rescue group may be holding. At such events, the group's foster care providers bring adoptable Dachshunds to introduce to potential adopters and encourage those adopters to submit applications. Your local Dachshund rescue group probably has information on upcoming adoption events on its website.

HOW TO FIND AN ADULT DACHSHUND FROM A SHELTER OR RESCUE GROUP

Because adult Dachshunds are only rarely available from breeders—and because those Dachshunds are likely to cost far more than the adoption fees a shelter or rescue group charges—you're much more likely to find an adult Dachshund from the latter venues. This section shows you how to find a Dachshund from a shelter or rescue group. That said, many of the points discussed can also apply to selecting an adult Dachshund from a breeder. For more on selecting a dog from a reputable breeder, check out Chapter 2.

Once you've identified one or more groups that have adult Dachshunds available for adoption and found an adoption prospect, it's time to visit the shelter or rescue group foster home and meet those Dachshund candidates in person, so to speak. When Dachshunds are

An adopted adult Dachshund can bring great joy and fulfillment into your family's life.

involved, such meetings aren't simple. That's because it's all too easy to fall in love with any and all Dachshunds that you encounter, but falling in love with those Dachshunds doesn't make any, much less all, of those objects of your affection right for you.

The truth of the matter is that when it comes to Dachshund adoption, love is not enough. You need to cast an objective eye on each dog you meet, ask the right questions of the shelter or rescue group volunteer, and answer the questions that those volunteers put to you.

Do you need more specific suggestions on how to find the right adult Dachshund? Here are some tips:

Don't Go It Alone

Finding and choosing an adult Dachshund can be challenging. That lovable but rambunctious young adult may not do as well in your home as the quieter, somewhat older Dachshund who always seems to be overlooked. That's where having someone along can help. If you live alone, bring a friend or family member to help you make the right choice; if the dog will be a family pet, everyone in the household should come along. Another option—particularly if this Dachshund will be your first-ever dog—is to hire a dog trainer to help you choose.

Look at Every Dachshund

If you're at an adoption event or otherwise are seeing multiple Dachshunds in a single setting, don't zero in on one dog right away. Instead, give all of the dogs a once-over first. Identify which dog is the most sociable and interested in the world around him, and/or who's most interested in interacting with you. The dogs who meet both criteria merit an additional, more extended look. If you're meeting only one dog right now, you can still apply those criteria; just spend a little time with him to see whether he's interested in spending a little time with you.

Get Some Info

Many shelters and rescue groups perform a formal assessment of a dog's behavior before putting him up for adoption. Ask the shelter staff or rescue group volunteer for details

Finding and choosing an adult Dachshund can be challenging, so having someone come with you can help.

on the assessment of the dog who interests you. Pay special attention to whether he likes children, likes other animals, and/or has any problems such as being possessive with toys or food. If the assessment form indicates that any of these areas is a problem, think twice about adopting this dog—particularly if you have children or other pets.

Look at Your Favorite Dog(s)

Ask the shelter personnel or rescue volunteer whether you can take each dog, one at a time, to a quiet place to get better acquainted. There, look to see how interested he is in interacting with you—with or without toys—and whether he plays nicely without biting. See too (with the shelter volunteer or shelter's permission) whether he's interested in any food you offer; a dog who takes treats readily will be much easier to train than one who doesn't.

Make Up Your Mind

Now that you've become acquainted with the individual dogs who caught your eye, it's time to decide. If the dog(s) you've looked at doesn't seem right for you, don't be afraid to say "not this one" and keep looking. However, if you think that you have found your canine soul mate, go ahead and take the plunge.

Answer Questions

At some point in the process, the shelter or rescue group volunteer will have you fill out an adoption application. The application gives you a chance to describe your experience and history with dogs and to supply references that attest to your suitability as a dog owner. Answer all of the questions fully and truthfully.

Bring Housing Info

Expect the shelter or rescue group to ask for a

Multi-Dog Tip

Make sure that the dog you already have is okay with adding an adult Dachshund to the pack. Both shelters and rescue groups generally allow prospective adopters to bring the pets they already have to their shelters or foster homes to meet the new dog before an adoption is finalized. In fact, some groups require such meetings.

copy of your lease or your landlord's contact information if you rent your home; they want to avoid having you be evicted because you've broken the no-pets clause of a lease, or your being forced to give up the dog to stay in your home.

Pony Up

When you formally apply to adopt the dog, you'll probably be asked to at least place a deposit on the adoption fee, with the balance to be paid when you actually bring the dog home. You may also be asked to pay a deposit on spaying or neutering the dog if that hasn't occurred already.

Sign the Contract

The shelters or rescue groups will almost certainly require you to sign a contract in which you'll agree to care for your new Dachshund properly and to return the dog to the shelter or rescue group if you can't keep him. The contract may also require you to spay or neuter the dog within a certain time period if the procedure hasn't already taken place.

Prepare for Company

Many shelters and rescue groups won't finalize adoptions until a volunteer actually shows up on your doorstep to ensure that your home is suitable for the dog. Don't take this personally—both you and the shelter or rescue group want to make sure that the dog will get the best possible home.

Bring Your New Dachshund Home

Once the adoption is approved, you can pay the rest of the adoption fee and bring your new Dachshund home. You'll probably also be given some other items such as care instructions, contact information for veterinarians and dog trainers, and your dog's health records. Bring those records to your veterinarian when you take your new dog for his first checkup—which you do within a day or two of his arrival in your home.

Want to Know More?

Read Chapter 2 for pointers on preparing for your Dachshund's arrival.

CHAPTER 6

DACHSHUND GROOMING NEEDS

The Dachshund's striking, streamlined appearance doesn't happen all by itself. He benefits not only from great genes but also from good health and good grooming. Just as human beings need to bathe their bodies, style their hair (or get a buzz cut), and tend to their nails—among other tasks—to look and be their best, so too do Dachshunds. The difference, of course, is that while humans can do those tasks for themselves, Dachshunds need humans to perform those tasks for them. That said, the services of specialists can be a big help to both species.

This chapter explains how to handle most, if not all, of your Dachshund's grooming tasks yourself. It also discusses how to find a grooming pro if the job proves too time consuming for you to do, if you just need a break, or if some grooming chores are too complicated to handle on your own.

BRUSHING

Your adult Dachshund needs regular brushing—and not just to look good. Regular brushing also prevents tangling of the coat (if your Dachshund has long hair), removes surface dirt from all three Dachshund coats, allows air to circulate through the coat to the skin, and stimulates the shine-producing oil glands in the skin. Regular brushing can also help limit shedding, whether the hair is the little needle-like hairs from a smooth coat, the long tresses of the longhaired coat, or the coarse hair of the wirehaired coat. Removal of the shed hair prevents the coat from matting, which can result in painful skin sores if not dealt with.

Brushing also gives you an opportunity to check your Dachshund for skin irregularities. As you move your hands over his body, you can be alert for lumps and bumps and can visually inspect him for fleas, cuts, and rashes.

Finally, regular brushing of your Dachshund can be a pleasurable activity for you both. Many Dachshunds enjoy being brushed. If you do the job right, you may find that your Dachshund comes running to you whenever he sees you holding his brush.

The right way to brush your Dachshund depends on what kind of coat he has.

How to Do It: Smooth Dachshunds

If your Dachshund is a Smooth Dachshund, you'd be wrong in thinking he doesn't need a regular brushing. The fact of the matter is that he does—just not as much. Here's how to do the job:

1. Gather your gear: a hound brush (a glove with little nubs on it) and a soft bristle brush.
2. Stroke your dog with the hound brush all over his body in the direction the hair grows. Be careful not to exert too much pressure. You want him to feel as though he's being petted or being given a very gentle massage.
3. Stroke your dog again, this time with a soft bristle brush, in the direction the hair grows. That's it!

How to Do It: Wirehaired Dachshunds

The Wirehaired Dachshund requires a little more maintenance. While much of his coat is short, it still sheds and needs attention.

Brushing removes the shed hair, which can get caught within the living hair of the coat and form mats. Here's what to do:

1. Gather your gear: in this case, a pin brush and a slicker brush.
2. With the pin brush, brush your dog's hair all over his body against the direction in which it grows. This will lift the shed hair out from underneath the hair of the coat.
3. Use the pin brush to brush his hair in the direction it grows to smooth the coat down.
4. Finish by brushing the dog's hair in the direction it grows with the slicker brush.

Wirehaired Dachshunds also need additional grooming that, at least the first few times, is best left to a grooming professional. Twice a year, their coats need to be stripped to remove any hairs that aren't removed with regular brushing. The groomer will use a special stripping knife to do the job. If you

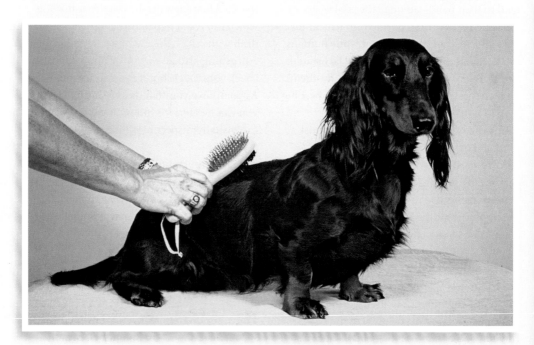

Regular brushing prevents tangling of the coat if you have a Longhaired Dachshund.

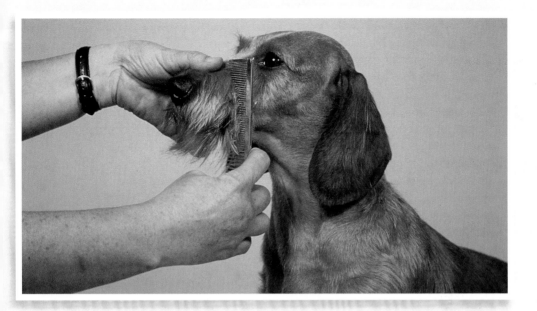

Wirehaired Dachshunds need additional grooming that is often best left to a grooming professional.

want to do this yourself, ask the groomer to show you how to do so. At the same time, ask the groomer to show you how to trim your Wirehaired Dachshund's long, soft eyebrows and mustache.

How to Do It: Longhaired Dachshunds

Not surprisingly, Longhaired Dachshunds require the most time and effort when brushing. Those glorious tresses don't get gorgeous all by themselves! Here's what to do:

1. Gather your gear. You'll need a slicker brush, a medium-toothed comb, a soft-bristle brush, and a dematting claw.
2. Get into position. Unless you're using a grooming table, have your dog lie down on his side and either kneel or sit next to him, facing his tummy.
3. Start brushing. With your slicker brush, start brushing the hair at the base of your dog's tail. Brush gently, from the skin outward, in the direction the hair grows. Brush a little bit at a time, using one hand to hold aside the hair that's immediately ahead of the section that you're brushing.
4. Start the next row. When you reach the dog's shoulder, go back to the base of the tail and gently brush the next row up to the shoulder. Repeat, row by row, until you've completely brushed your dog's side.
5. Lift the front leg. Gently lift your dog's front leg so that you can see the hair in the armpit. Brush this hair gently and carefully. If you encounter any tangles, use the dematting claw to gently untangle them. Continue brushing the hair on his tummy from the skin outward in the direction the hair grows. Be careful when brushing the tummy area, which is very sensitive.

6. Lift the rear leg. Gently lift the dog's rear leg so that you expose his sanitary area, and carefully brush the hair there and on the inside of the leg—again, from the skin outward, in the direction the hair grows.

7. Brush the hair on the legs, rear, and tail. Use the brush to gently tend to the feathers on your dog's legs; then move to the tail and hair on the rear (sometimes known as the dog's pants) on the side that you've been brushing.

8. Do the chest. Have your dog change from a reclining to a sitting position. Brush the hair on his chest outward from the skin in the direction it grows.

9. Reposition your dog. Have him lie down on his other side, and repeat the first seven steps.

If your Dachshund doesn't like to be combed or brushed, introduce him to it a little bit at a time.

Training Tidbit

Some Dachshunds love being groomed, but others are ambivalent about such rituals. Still others like some aspects of grooming but despise others. If your Dachshund is less than enthusiastic or out and out hates being groomed, pairing grooming with tasty treats might help him change his mind.

10. Run the comb over his entire body.

What should you do if your Dachshund doesn't like being brushed? Introduce him to the pleasures of brushing a little bit at a time, and use treats to help him associate brushing with something positive. Feed him a treat, brush for a minute, give another treat, and then end the session. Continue brushing and treating him in very short sessions—even if it takes you a couple of days to do so—until he's completely brushed. The idea here is for your dog to connect being brushed with getting treats. Once he does, he's likely to look forward to being brushed rather than run away at the sight of one.

BATHING

Every dog needs periodic bathing, and your Dachshund is no exception. Even if he doesn't ever roll in yucky stuff, regular baths—perhaps monthly—will help keep his coat and skin in optimum condition.

Where to bathe your Dachshund depends on what's most convenient for you. An obvious venue is your bathtub, if your house has one and if you're willing to buy a handheld shower attachment. Another option is a self-service dog wash, which can be found at doggy day cares and some pet supply stores.

How to Do It

These how-to's can help get the job done better and more easily:

1. Brush beforehand. This is especially important for Longhaired Dachshunds. Brushing your dog thoroughly before the bath ensures that all tangles and mats are gone before he gets wet. Failure to brush before the bath may cause the wet hair to clump together into doggy dreadlocks. Such clumps are very difficult to untangle after they dry—and may require that your Longhaired Dachshund get a coat shave that makes him look more like a Smooth Dachshund.

2. Block the ears. Place a cotton ball in each ear to keep water from getting inside. Water in either or both ears can cause discomfort to your dog.

3. Dilute the shampoo. Experts recommend diluting your dog's shampoo to help it lather and rinse more easily—generally three or four units of water per single unit of shampoo is a good ratio.

4. Put him in the tub. Your Dachshund may think he's agile enough to get into the tub on his own—but to be on the safe side, lift him carefully into the tub. A bathmat on the bottom will keep his feet steady.

5. Keep him steady. If your Dachshund is one of those dogs who don't immediately appreciate the pleasures of being bathed, keep a steady hand on him to forestall any attempts to exit the tub.

6. Water him down. With a handheld shower attachment, pour warm (never hot) water over your Dachshund. Start at the top of his head and neck, then proceed to wet the length of his backbone. After that, water his sides, chest, legs, and tail. Make sure that the water goes all the way down to his skin.

7. Lather up—but not too much. Once your Dachshund is completely wet, apply enough diluted shampoo to work up a lather all over his body—but not such a heavy lather that you see billowy clouds of bubbles in either the tub or on your dog. (If you do, use less shampoo next time.)

8. Rinse, rinse, rinse. Once you've finished soaping your dog, use the handheld shower attachment to rinse him off. Apply the water in the same way as when you started the bath: front to back and top to bottom. To ensure removal of all the shampoo, keep rinsing for five minutes or until the rinse water runs clear—whichever comes last. A less-than-thorough rinse will leave your dog's skin dry, flaky, and itchy.

9. Wrap him up. After you've thoroughly

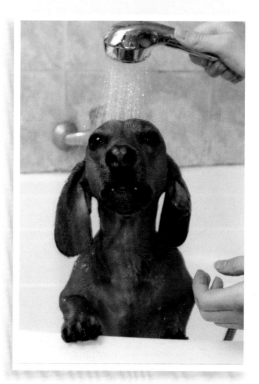

Once you've finished soaping your dog, use the handheld shower attachment to rinse him off.

rinsed your Dachshund, wrap him in an extra-large bath towel or bath sheet and remove the cotton from his ears. Gently blot the excess water from his coat and skin. Do not rub—rubbing could cause the coat to mat or tangle. After you've blotted the excess water, let your dog indulge in a post-bath breakneck run. When he's done with his post-bathing zoomies, towel him some more or use a blow dryer if he tolerates it (if he's a Longhaired Dachshund.)

10. Blow dry with care (for Longhaired Dachshunds). Don't expect your Longhaired Dachshund to tolerate a sudden introduction to a blow dryer. Many dogs freak out at the loud noises and moving air of these appliances, and some find the dryers themselves very menacing if the dryer is pointed at them. Instead, introduce the dryer gradually—preferably well before his first bath. Start by letting your dog sniff the dryer, and give him a treat while he does. Then turn on the dryer while it's still lying on the floor and encourage him to come over and inspect it. If he does, give him a treat. Repeat this sequence several times until he's clearly comfortable around the dryer while it runs. At that point, try picking up the dryer and actually drying his coat. With the dryer on a low-heat or a cool setting, start

from his rear end because that's the part of his body that's farthest away from his head and ears. Gently brush the hair as it dries. After his rear end is dry (or nearly so), give him a treat. Continue drying and treating, section by section, until your dog is reasonably dry.

11. Brush him out. Most Dachshunds need a post-bath, post-drying brush-out. Just use your usual brush the way you did before his bath. When you're done, your Dachshund will look as strikingly handsome (or beautiful) as you know he can be.

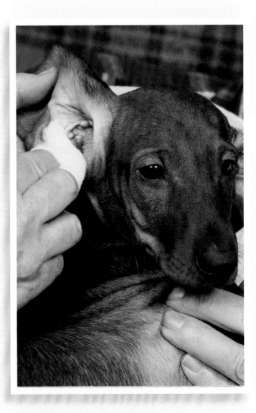

Use a cotton ball to clean your Dachshund's ears, never a cotton swab, which could damage the ears.

EAR CARE

Your Dachshund's ears make it possible for him to hear not only everything that you do but also a whole lot of other things that you can't hear. But those same ears can make him mighty uncomfortable. That's because a Dachshund's ears may be prone to infections more than may be the case with many other breeds. The chief reason for that vulnerability is that the floppy, downward-hanging Dachshund ear flap makes the ears more likely to trap moisture, particularly during a bath or a swim. That long-standing moisture can become a breeding ground for infections, and ear infections are more than just a nuisance. They can be very painful to your Dachshund and can, if not treated, lead to hearing loss.

For those reasons, weekly ear care should be part of your Dachshund's grooming routine.

How to Do It

1. Obtain a sprayable ear cleaner from your veterinarian, or make your own ear cleaning solution. Pour one part white vinegar to one part rubbing alcohol into a spray bottle. (Check with your vet to be sure that this is safe for your particular dog.)

2. Lift your Dachshund's ear flap and spray a little bit of the cleaner directly into his ear canal. While you do, inspect the ear and the inside of the ear flap to be sure that there's no (or very little) visible dirt or debris. Take a sniff too and make sure that there's no yeasty or foul odor.

3. Rub the solution in. To do this, fold over the ear flap back toward the face. Then gently massage the flap for a minute or so. After you're done, your dog is likely to shake his head. That's okay.

4. To blot up excess moisture and further clean the ear, use a cotton ball. Then

---

Multi-Dog Tip

If you have more than one dog, the prospect of grooming them all on the same day might seem a tad overwhelming. To keep that I-don't-have-the-time-to-do-all-these-dogs feeling from prompting you to skip doggy grooming altogether, try grooming just one of your dogs per day. For example, if you have three dogs, schedule Dog #1's weekly grooming for Monday, Dog #2's day for Wednesday, and Dog #3's day for Friday.

However, consider bagging the one-at-a-time maxim if you take your dogs to a professional groomer. Instead, try bringing them all to the groomer on the same day, and see if you can score a multiple-dog discount.

---

inspect the cotton ball—it should have little or no debris on it, and the debris should not have any sort of odor other than the smell of your cleaning solution. If that's not the case or your dog's ear is very red or he's showing signs of discomfort such as frequent head shaking or rubbing his ear on the ground, have your vet check him out.

5. Give him a trim. The long hair at the entrance to your Longhaired Dachshund's ear canals can further trap debris and moisture, which in turn can result in ear problems. To reduce that hazard, use some small scissors to trim the hair. And if you take him to a groomer, ear trims should be among the services he's given there.

EYE CARE

Your Dachshund's eyes also need regular attention and care, but vigilance and common sense are all you need to complete this task.

How to Do It

More specifically, you should:

1. Inspect regularly. Look at your Dachshund's eyes for squinting, cloudy discharge, or redness. Pay special attention if he's been pawing at his eye. If you see any of these conditions, put in a call to your veterinarian.
2. Each morning—and whenever else it's necessary—dampen a cloth or cotton ball with cool water to gently wipe your dog's face and eye area. This daily cleansing will remove those crusty "sleepies" we all get after a nap or good night's sleep.

NAIL TRIMMING AND FOOT GROOMING

Many women (and men too) love the look of high, stiletto-heeled shoes. They make a woman's legs look like they go on forever and add an undeniable note of elegance to many outfits. However, stilettos also throw a woman's hips and legs out of alignment and cause her balance to be precarious at best.

What do these thoughts on footwear have to do with your Dachshund? Simple. If you don't trim his toenails regularly, he'll have the same balance problems that stiletto-sporting high-heeled women have—but because his legs are

Each morning (and whenever else it's necessary), dampen a cotton ball with cool water to gently wipe your dog's face and eye area.

so short, there's no way those toenails will ever make his legs look longer!

That's why regular nail trims need to be part of your Dachshund's grooming routine. Keep his nails at his toes short enough be off the ground when he's standing still, and keep the dewclaws (the nails that are found higher up on the leg near the ankle) short enough to keep them from curving back into the skin of the leg.

How to Do It

Here's how to care for the nails and feet:

1. Take a relaxed approach. Pick a quiet time of day—maybe after dinner while you're watching television in the evening—and have your Dachshund with you. Pet him for a few minutes until he lies down, and keep doing so for another minute after that.

2. Once your dog is clearly relaxed, pick up one of his paws with your hand. Gently press on a toe to extend the nail outward.

3. Look for the quick. The quick is the blood vessel inside the nail that runs all the way down to the tip. Even a small nick to the quick can trigger a lot of bleeding. For that reason, it's important to know where the quick is to avoid accidental nicks. In light-colored nails, the quick is the pink area inside the nail. In dark nails, the quick can't be seen—which means that trims need to be very conservative.

4. Trim just a bit. Pick up your dog's nail clippers and place them around the very tip of the extended nail. Squeeze the clippers very quickly to trim off the nail tip. Continue trimming a little at a time until you see a black dot in the center of the trimmed nail. The black dot signals the start of the quick.

5. Don't panic. If you trim too much nail, hit the quick, and bleeding ensues, don't

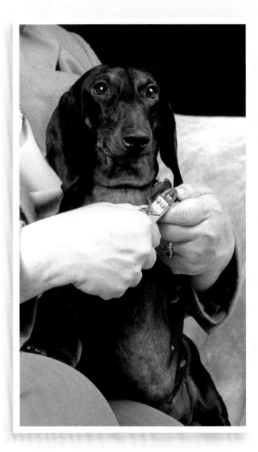

When clipping your dog's nails, trim off just a bit at a time to keep from cutting into the quick.

panic. Simply apply some styptic powder (available in pharmacies) to the nail tip. If you don't have any styptic powder, you can still stanch the bleeding by placing the paw in a small bowl of ordinary baking flour.

6. Trim the pawpad hair. If you have a Longhaired Dachshund, use a pair of baby scissors or small grooming shears to carefully trim the hair that grows from the paws. The completed trim should show the fur following the shape of the paw. Then turn the paw over and clip the hair between the pads as short as possible.

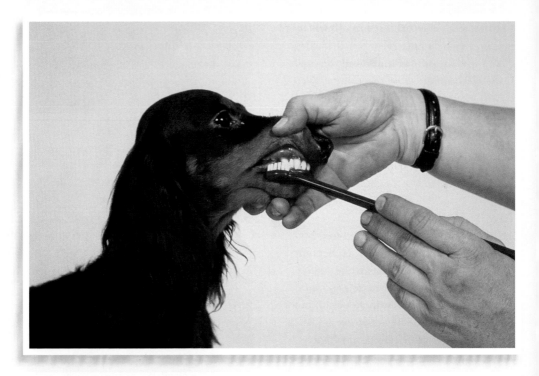

A great way to invest in your Dachshund's health is to brush his teeth.

If your Dachshund hates having his nails trimmed, a little bribery and a lot of patience can help get the job done, albeit at a much slower pace than with a dog who tolerates his pedicures. Here's how to deal with a pedicure-hating Dachsie:

1. Start slowly. Wait until your dog is relaxed, have a clicker and some treats on hand, and pick up one of your dog's paws. If he tolerates your picking up his paw, click your clicker (or say "Yes!" if you don't use a clicker) and give him a treat.

2. Focus on the toe. Once your Dachshund is comfortable having his foot picked up, press gently on one of his toes to extend the nail. Click and treat if he tolerates this action. Repeat over the course of several sessions until he's clearly relaxed when you perform this action.

3. Show him the clippers. If he sniffs at or otherwise investigates them, click and treat.

4. Touch a nail. Once your dog is comfortable having the clippers around—he either pays no attention to them at all or simply gives them a little sniff before ignoring them—pick up the clippers and touch one nail. If your dog tolerates the touch, click and treat. Repeat this sequence until he is totally comfortable with having his nail touched by the clippers.

5. Perform the first trim. Trim just one of your dog's nails, then click and treat. Then end the session for the day.

6. Once your dog tolerates getting one nail trimmed per day, start adding a second nail to the daily regimen and again use the clicker and treats to aid the process.

7. Introduced slowly, even a clipper-phobic dog

may learn to tolerate a session with the hated instrument. However, some experts believe that guillotine clippers, which are the most common type of nail clipper, put too much pressure on the nail and don't cut the nail efficiently. They recommend using scissor clippers or a nail grinder instead. Because scissor clippers are stronger and sharper than guillotine clippers, they put less pressure on the nail. A grinder is a rechargeable device originally intended for precision drilling, sanding, shaping, and detailing of wood and other building materials. Today, however, companies are manufacturing nail grinders especially for dogs.

8. If your Dachshund truly won't tolerate your doing his nails, have a grooming pro do the job. The pro may allow you to bring your dog without an appointment and clip his nails on the spot—and the cost may be only about $1.00 per nail.

DENTAL CARE

A great way to invest in your Dachshund's health for pennies a day is to brush his teeth. By paying attention each day to his teeth and gums, you take a giant step toward preventing dental disease—which, according to the American Veterinary Dental Society (AVDS), befalls more than 80 percent of all dogs by age three. Symptoms of this condition include bad breath, inflamed gums, and tartar on the teeth. Without treatment, dental disease can cause the tooth to separate from the gum, and the infections from the gum can spread to other organs in the body. Frequent brushings remove the food particles, saliva, minerals, and bacteria that form a coating of bacteria-breeding, infection-causing plaque on the teeth.

How to Do It

Brushing your dog's teeth need not be difficult. Here's what experts suggest that you do:

1. Equip yourself. You'll need some sterile gauze, a child's toothbrush or doggy toothbrush with bristles soft enough to clean the teeth and gums without irritating them, toothpaste made especially for dogs, and some treats. Avoid using toothpastes for people, which can upset your Dachshund's stomach.

2. Start slowly—you don't have to wield the toothbrush immediately! Instead, get your Dachshund accustomed to having his teeth touched. Wrap some gauze around your finger, lift his lip, and gently rub his gums for a few seconds. If he tolerates the gum rub, give him a treat. Next, add toothpaste to your gauze-wrapped finger and rub as before. If he's okay with the toothpaste, give him another treat.

3. Add the brush. When your dog tolerates the finger and toothpaste consistently, try using a toothbrush and toothpaste. Gently lift your dog's lip on one side of his mouth and brush the teeth for a few seconds. Give him a treat. Repeat on the other side and treat afterward.

4. Build tolerance. Over time, gradually extend your brushing sessions to one or two minutes on each side of the mouth. As he becomes more tolerant, you can phase out the treats.

5. Be consistent. Make a point of brushing your dog's teeth at the same time each day.

Want to Know More?

For more on what happens at a vet visit, see Chapter 8.

A professional groomer can take the stress out of grooming your Dachsie and make both of your lives a lot easier.

Dogs love structure, and knowing what to expect when will help your dog feel more confident.

6. Get regular checkups. Your veterinarian should inspect your dog's teeth once a year, and if necessary, schedule a professional tooth cleaning. These routine procedures are similar to those for humans except that doggy dental cleaning occurs while the dog is under anesthesia. That said, if you brush your Dachshund's teeth regularly, he won't need professional cleanings very often.

HOW TO FIND A PROFESSIONAL GROOMER

Although it's certainly possible to groom your Dachshund by yourself at home, it's not always easy. Longhaired Dachshunds are certainly more challenging to groom than Smooth Dachshunds are, and grooming of Wirehaired Dachshunds may be well beyond the abilities of their people. Moreover, any Dachshund—no matter what kind of coat he has—may feel more than a tad uneasy about having his nails trimmed or his ears cleaned by his uncoordinated owner. And finally, some people don't have the time it takes (as much as a couple of hours) to give their Dachshunds the full spa treatment.

That's where a professional groomer can help. Knowing that you can drop your dog off at a groomer and feel confident that he'll be brushed, bathed, pedicured, trimmed, and cleaned leaves you time to just enjoy your long-bodied, short-legged best friend. However, not all groomers are created equal. Here's how to find a grooming pro for your very special Dachshund:

Decide Where to Go

Many groomers have traditional brick-and-mortar enterprises, while others have installed grooming equipment in a truck and meet their canine clients at their homes. Figure out which would be more convenient for you.

Consult Experts

Your vet or doggy day care provider may be able to recommend a groomer to you; in fact, many of these facilities actually have grooming pros on their staffs. Trainers and pet sitters also may be able to point you in the right direction.

Ask Around

Most people love to share the names of their own hairdressers, and they're probably equally happy to share the names of those who coif their dogs. If you're in a training class, a dog park, or even just out on the street, don't be afraid to query a person whose dog looks drop-dead gorgeous. Pay particular attention to any Dachshunds you see; if you observe one who looks exceptionally well groomed, ask the owner who grooms him. (And if the owner says that she's the groomer, ask for pointers!)

Check Out Some Groomers

Once you've gotten some groomers' names, pick up the phone and chat with each briefly. A few minutes on the phone can serve up lots of info about prices, cancellation policies, and the groomer's experience with dogs in general as well as Dachshunds in particular. If you like the answers you're given, consider taking the next step.

Visit the Shop

If you like what you've heard from a groomer so far, ask if you can pay her a visit. When you get there, look around carefully. The shop should be reasonably clean; a little hair on the floor is to be expected, but huge piles of hair are not. Odors should not overwhelm. The fragrance of dog shampoo is fine; the stinkiness of doggy accidents isn't. Look too at how the groomer and her staff interact with the dogs they're tending. Are the dogs relaxed? Do the groomer and staff try to put the dogs at ease? Are dogs constantly attended when they're on the grooming table? A negative answer to any of those questions should prompt you to keep looking.

Give It a Try

If you like what you saw at the shop, book an appointment for your Dachshund. When you and your dog arrive, pay attention to how the staff interacts with him and what they do to make him comfortable. At pickup time later in the day, check to make sure that everything you've asked to have done has been accomplished. If you and your Dachshund are both happy, terrific! Pat yourself on the back for having found another partner in your dog's care.

CHAPTER 7

DACHSHUND NUTRITIONAL NEEDS

When you were a child, did you get tired of your mom telling you to eat your peas or your dad commanding you to down your lima beans so that you'd grow up to be strong and healthy? You probably couldn't even visualize yourself as an adult, much less a strong and healthy one. Consequently, the adage "you are what you eat" probably didn't make much sense to you then—but of course, it didn't have to. The adage did make sense to your parents, who did their best to put more nutritious food into your body, even if that meant you couldn't always have the junk food you craved.

The same is true with the Dachshund. He doesn't understand the importance of having a balanced diet—but you do (or will, after you finish this chapter). A balanced diet and good nutrition will help a Dachshund be the healthiest, handsomest dog he can be. The Dachshund who gets highly nutritious fare will probably have a healthier body and a healthier mind than one whose diet consists of cheap eats.

This chapter details not only what a Dachshund needs to eat to get healthy and stay that way but also when and how he needs to do so.

WHY IS GOOD NUTRITION ESSENTIAL?

Dachshunds need good nutrition for the same reasons any other living being does: to become and remain healthy and strong and to be able to fight off ailments that might otherwise befall him. Equally important, good nutrition can keep a Dachshund lively, alert, and more willing to learn, not to mention enabling him to remain the picture of robust good health. In short, a healthy diet will help your Dachshund be the dog you wanted him to be when you welcomed him into your family.

A good way to think of nutrition is as a building, with individual nutrients composing the materials that make up that structure. Just as high-quality materials make a building's structure sounder, high-quality nutrients make for a healthier Dachsie. Here are descriptions of different nutrients and the roles they play in a Dachshund's diet.

Carbohydrates

Carbohydrates start with a combination of carbon dioxide and water. Plants such as corn, wheat, rice, and soybeans use sunlight to transform these substances into energy.

Many commercial dog foods contain high

The Dachshund who gets highly nutritious fare will probably have a healthier body and a healthier mind than one who doesn't.

percentages (often anywhere from 30 to 60 percent) of carbohydrates because the plants from which the carbs are derived are usually cheaper food sources than other nutritional sources, such as meat. Moreover, the starches in carbohydrates give dry dog food texture and structure.

But while carbohydrates are a cheap source of nutrition and energy, experts no longer agree on whether they're necessary for dogs. Traditionally, experts have contended that carbs are crucial to dietary health for dogs. In recent years, however, owners and experts have realized that some dogs find the grains from which most carbs come—especially wheat and corn—difficult to digest. Moreover, dogs in the wild generally don't eat any grain at all, which means that they take in miniscule levels

of carbohydrates. These observations have prompted some experts to believe that dogs don't really need carbohydrates.

Consequently, some—but not all—breeders and veterinarians now suggest withholding grain from dogs' food regimens. The result for many such dogs is far less consumption of carbohydrates—and for some, improved health and quality of life. To determine whether your Dachshund needs carbohydrates and in what amounts, consult your vet.

Fats

Fats are compounds that result when glycerol (a carbon-oxygen-hydrogen compound) combines with fatty acids. Healthy fats come from meats such as chicken and lamb and in oils such as sunflower oil, fish oil, and safflower oil.

Fats play a hugely important role in maintaining your Dachshund's health (yes, really!). They help maintain the health of his skin, brain, eyes, hair, and other tissues, as well as keep his body temperature stable and promote healthy digestion. They also, believe it or not, are very important sources of energy because they contain more calories than either proteins or carbohydrates.

Although you certainly want to keep your Dachshund on the lean side—more information about that topic appears later in this chapter—fats still need to be a significant component of his diet.

Proteins

Proteins are complex groups of very large molecules that contain carbon, hydrogen, nitrogen, and (usually) sulfur and that are linked by chains of amino acids. They not only are the building blocks of many organs, muscles, bones, blood, tissues, nails, and the immune system; they also enable the body to convert food into energy.

Proteins are available in many foods, but the best sources are meats, poultry, fish, eggs, and dairy products. Dogs of any breed who don't get sufficient protein may have poor coats, less-than-optimum muscle development, weakened immune systems, and low red blood cell counts. Puppies whose diets don't have enough protein may have growth problems.

Proteins are available in many foods, but the best sources of protein are meats, poultry, fish, eggs, and dairy products.

By the Numbers

An overweight Dachshund should lose only one or two percent of his total body weight per week. In other words, a 35-pound (16-kg) Dachshund should lose no more than 11 ounces (0.5 kg) a week or about 2.75 pounds (1.5 kg) every four weeks.

Vitamins and Minerals

Most foods contain very small quantities of vitamins and minerals, but those small quantities do some mighty big jobs: enabling the body to properly process proteins, carbohydrates and fats; helping maintain the body's immune system; helping maintain the quality of the dog's coat; and preventing many health problems. Owners who want to give their dogs vitamins and minerals can find them in commercial supplements and also in some dog foods.

Water

A Dachshund could go for a couple of weeks without much food, but he couldn't last for more than a couple of days without water.

Your Dachshund needs water for the same reasons that you do. Water helps regulate body temperature and serves as the foundation of the body's transportation systems: the circulatory system, which moves nutrients within the body, and the urinary system, which transports waste products outside the body.

That said, not all water is created equal. Obviously, clean water is better than water that's allowed to become scummy and filled with food particles. Tap water is way better than water your dog might lap from a puddle. And some veterinarians and dog enthusiasts believe that bottled or distilled water is better for a dog than water from the tap.

Cool, clean water should be available for your Dachshund at all times unless otherwise directed by your vet.

WHAT TO FEED

The ways that the previously mentioned ingredients are combined together—or in the case of carbs, sometimes omitted—are what make for such a wide variety of dog foods from which to choose. Here, to help you determine which combo is right for you and your Dachshund, is a brief description of the most common types of dog food, including both the advantages and disadvantages of each.

Commercial Food

Technically, commercial dog food is any food product that you can buy for your dog from a retail outlet, whether online or at your local shopping center. The pet food industry offers an incredibly wide range of dog food options, including:

Dry Foods

Also known as kibble, dry

Dry food consists of baked bite-sized pellets usually made from grain, meat or meat by-products, and other ingredients.

food is generally the least expensive type of commercial food, especially if you buy larger bags rather than smaller ones. This food consists of bite-sized baked pellets usually made from grain, meat or meat by-products, and other ingredients.

A big advantage to dry food is its incredible convenience: You can just pour some into your dog's dish and serve it. Another advantage to kibble is that its rough texture makes it an edible toothbrush by scraping plaque and tartar off the teeth. Still another kibble upside is that it stays fresh longer than any other type of food once it's opened.

But kibble also carries some disadvantages. Some dogs find an all-kibble-all-the-time regimen boring and may become finicky eaters as a result. Another problem is that kibble often contains a relatively high percentage of grains, which some dogs might have trouble digesting or be allergic to. Also, some of the cheaper dry foods contain poor-quality protein, which is one of the reasons those companies can keep the cost down.

Canned Foods

Dog food that's sold in cans has much more moisture than kibble does and is far tastier to most dogs than kibble is. Canned fare is also easier to digest. Offsetting those two advantages, however, is the fact that canned food doesn't stay fresh nearly as long as kibble does and must be refrigerated after being opened. And the high moisture content means that canned food is less economical than kibble is because you have to feed more to satisfy your Dachsie's appetite.

People who feed noncommercial foods have total control over what their dogs eat.

Semi-Moist Foods

This type of food, also called soft/moist food, usually comes in boxes that contain single-serving pouches or bags. They contain more water than dry food but less water than canned. These foods make good training treats (broken up, of course) and are very convenient for traveling. However, they often contain more salt, sugar, and preservatives than either canned or dry foods do to maintain freshness while keeping the food soft. For these reasons, experts don't recommend a steady diet of semi-moist foods.

Noncommercial Food

The pet food recalls of recent years have heightened owner concerns about commercial pet food quality. These concerns have prompted an increasing number of dog owners to bypass commercial fare and prepare their dogs' meals themselves. In addition, owners whose dogs are allergic to ingredients found in most commercial foods may also choose to fix their dogs' meals in their own kitchens. Each group of do-it-yourselfers enjoys two big advantages: They have total control over what their dogs eat, and they can prepare food that they know pleases their pooches' unique palates.

However, prepping your dog's food yourself also has a downside. Home preparation can be both inconvenient and time consuming, particularly if you're traveling with your dog and need to feed him while you're on the road. Another possible pitfall has been the challenge of fixing a meal that not only pleases your Dachshund but also fulfills his nutritional requirements.

Despite the hassles involved in preparing food oneself, many Dachshund owners find that the pluses supersede the minuses. Moreover, those minuses are diminishing because pet food manufacturers are creating products that augment rather than replace home preparation.

Proponents of raw diets believe that raw food promotes better overall health.

Home-Cooked Diet

This diet is self-explanatory: food for your dog that you cook at home. A typical home-cooked meal for your dog would be a stew that includes meat, fresh fruits and vegetables, and (perhaps) a grain such as rice.

To make sure that the diet is really as good as it tastes, consult your veterinarian—or alternatively, other expert sources. One such source is *The Healthy Dog Cookbook* by Jonna Anne (TFH); another is the recipe created by veterinarian and syndicated columnist Michael Fox at www.twobitdog.com/DrFox/Dr-Fox-Homemade-Dog-Food.

Pet food manufacturers are capitalizing on owners' interest in home preparation by creating dog food products to which owners can add fruits, vegetables, or cooked meats to create a complete meal.

Raw Diet

This diet also is exactly what it sounds like: a regimen that consists entirely of uncooked food. Proponents of this diet believe that uncooked food is better for dogs than cooked food because the raw product is closer to what dogs eat in the wild. They also believe that raw food promotes better overall health, cleaner teeth, and smaller stools. In addition,

they contend that because there is little to no processing to raw food, dogs who go raw may have fewer allergies and other adverse reactions.

Moreover, what was once a big drawback to feeding raw—difficulty and inconvenience of buying and preparation—is now no longer the case. Until recently, raw food devotees needed to visit their butcher to procure raw meats and bones, grind up the meat themselves, add fresh vegetables and fruits, and keep the product fresh for a few days—at which point the whole cycle would begin again. Even for a small dog like a Dachshund, that would make for a whole lot of food prep. Now, however, more and more companies are manufacturing raw food products that blend raw meat with vegetables and fruit, and they sell them in frozen patties or chubs (tubes).

However, many veterinarians contend that raw foods aren't safe to feed. They may have a point—raw meat frequently contains a whole host of harmful bacteria such as *Salmonella* and *E. coli*, not to mention parasites as well (such as the *Trichinella* worm in pork, which can cause trichinosis, although freezing pork at 5°F [-15°C] can kill the worm.). Raw diet devotees counter that a dog's digestive tract is much shorter than that of a person, which means that dogs are less likely

Want to Know More?

Chapter 8 of this book discusses food allergies in greater detail, including how to detect them and how to choose foods that don't trigger allergic reactions in your Dachshund.

to be affected by such bacteria than humans are. If you're interested in this type of diet, check with your vet for more information.

If you decide to feed raw foods to your dog, wash your hands thoroughly with soap and hot water after handling, and clean any utensils and food preparation surfaces thoroughly if they're touched by raw meat.

Special Diets

Some Dachshunds can't or shouldn't eat regular commercial dog food or even certain home-prepared foods. One reason is to combat food allergies; many dogs are allergic to one or more common dog food ingredients such as wheat, corn, beef, and/or chicken. Other conditions that may necessitate special diets are excess weight, higher-than-normal energy requirements (such as female dogs who are pregnant or nursing puppies), cancer, and old age.

If you think that your Dachshund has a condition that could benefit from a special diet, consult your veterinarian.

Treats and Bones

If you want a well-behaved Dachshund, count on using plenty of treats to encourage such behavior. Treats come in a wide variety of products, some of which are better for your Dachshund than others. Those products include:

Cookies and Biscuits

Your Dachshund will probably like them, but they may not like him. That's because they're often very high in calories, which could put too much weight on your Dachshund, straining his already vulnerable back and joints. And because they're hard, you'll have a tougher time breaking them off into the smaller-sized pieces that make for optimum treats. In addition, some cookies and biscuits may also have dyes; these should be avoided.

Soft Treats

Dachshunds and other dogs generally like these treats even more than cookies and biscuits because they have more flavor. Moreover, because they break apart easily, they're ideal for training. With soft treats, you can give your dog more food rewards without causing him to put on weight.

Plastic Treats

Some Dachshunds are enthusiastic chewers, which makes them likely to enjoy chew toys such as Nylabones, which are made from plastic or nylon but are extremely durable.

Animal-Derived Treats

Pet food manufacturers have been incredibly creative in sourcing chew treats for dogs.

Some Dachshunds are enthusiastic chewers, which makes them likely to enjoy a variety of chew toys.

Choosing the Right Food for Your Dachshund

As you try to figure out which foods and treats are best for your Dachshund, the sheer number of available options may seem overwhelming. To make sense of them all, you need to know what to look for. Here's how to gain that knowledge.

Read product reviews. *The Whole Dog Journal*, a monthly newsletter that doesn't accept advertising, publishes product reviews of dry and canned dog foods every year. These reviews can save you a lot of time evaluating possible foods for your dog. To learn more, log onto the newsletter's website at www.whole-dog-journal.com.

Study ingredient lists. To learn more about a dog food you're considering, check the ingredients listed on the label. If one or more meats are listed first, that means that the product contains more meat than any other ingredient. That's a sign of good quality; lower-quality food tends to list grains or grain by-products first.

Study the meat. Not all meats listed on a dog food ingredient label are created equal. "Meat by-products," for example, may mean that your Dachshund is eating a chicken beak or other equally unsavory part of the animal. A label that simply lists a meat—chicken, beef, duck, ostrich, or other food product derived from livestock or fowl—indicates a dog food that's a much better choice.

Check for additives and preservatives. Make sure that the ingredient list doesn't include butylated hydroxyanisole (BHA) and/or butylated hydroxytoluene (BHT), two preservatives that have been used to prevent fats in food from spoiling. Studies have shown that high levels of either BHA or BHT can cause serious problems in animals.

See whether your dog likes the food. Once you start using the food, watch to see whether it agrees with your Dachshund. Signs that a food isn't a good fit include bulky, soft, and/or extremely smelly stools, flaky skin, flatulence, and weight gain. And if your Dachshund turns his nose up at the food you've chosen, respect his preference and find something else if you can.

Those sources include pig ears, pig snouts, deer antlers, cow hooves, and bull penises. No matter where the chew treats come from, though, the results are good for dogs and people—they provide chewing pleasure for dogs, but carpets and couches are left untouched by their teeth.

Straight-From-the-Kitchen Treats
Your own kitchen probably contains edibles that are good for your Dachshund and that he would enjoy. Examples include low-calorie treats such as sliced apples, carrots, or frozen green beans and high-value treats such as canned chicken (drained), cheddar cheese, or pieces of hot dog. Chapter 9 explains why high-value treats play such an important role in training your Dachshund.

Meaty Bones
Experts agree that owners shouldn't give their dogs cooked bones to chew. The reason:

Cooked bones can splinter and puncture the digestive tract. However, some experts say that it's okay to give an adult Dachsie raw, meaty bones to chew. If you choose to offer this special treat, do so in an area where the floor can be cleaned easily or where you can cover a carpet with a shower curtain or tarp. Watch your dog carefully while he eats such a bone, and remove the bone as soon as he chews it down to a size where he could swallow it and choke.

The same supervision should apply if you give any type of treat that's meant to be chewed over at least a few minutes, such as hooves, pig ears, and other animal-derived treats. The reason's the same: You need to monitor your dog's chewing progress and make sure that he doesn't choke on the treat.

WHEN TO FEED

When your Dachshund becomes an adult, you can put him on a regular feeding schedule. That said, one Dachsie's feeding schedule may differ from another's. To learn more about how to determine when is the best time to feed your particular dog, read on.

How Often

You may have heard that an adult dog needs to eat only once a day—and that's generally true. But what a dog needs—*needs* in this case meaning simply what he can scrape by on, what he requires as an absolute minimum—and what's best for him may be two different things. The Dachshund who gets his daily meal in the evening may find himself feeling hungry all day, which isn't a pleasant sensation. Doing the once-a-day meal in the morning is no better; your Dachshund is more likely to wake up in the middle of the night feeling hungry, and that hunger could in turn prompt him to wake you up to tell you he needs some chow.

A twice-daily food regimen is good for your Dachshund because it keeps his tummy fuller for a longer period.

That's why a twice-daily food regimen is much better for your Dachshund. Feeding him twice a day, once in the morning and once in the evening, keeps his tummy fuller for a longer period both day and night. Two meals a day are also easier on your Dachshund's digestive system than would be the case if that system needed to process a whole day's worth of food at once.

The twice-daily meal plan is also great for the Dachshund who spends a lot of time alone during the day. The dog who gets a morning meal is more likely to feel sleepy after that meal, which means that he may be more interested in doing some snoozing than in going on a destructive tear in your home. The same principle will probably be true at night as well—an evening meal will help him (and you) get a good night's sleep.

But while feeding your Dachshund twice a day is better than doing so just once a day, making food available to him 24/7 is not. This practice, known as free feeding, isn't advisable for several reasons. For one thing, it's tougher to determine whether a free feeder is having appetite changes than a dog who's on a regular feeding schedule. Because appetite changes, particularly appetite loss, are often a sign of illness, the Dachshund whose owner sees such changes sooner stands a better chance of recovering quickly from an illness than one whose owner took longer to realize that the dog's food intake had altered.

If your Dachshund is one of several dogs in your household and you leave one food bowl out for all

of your dogs to eat from, you'll have an even bigger challenge. Not only will you have more difficulty realizing that one of your dogs has had a change in appetite, but you'll also have a tougher time figuring out which dog in your pack is having that problem.

Housetraining is also a lot tougher for the free feeder than for the dog who's fed on a schedule. What goes in must come out—so if you don't know exactly when your dog ate, you're going to have a tougher time anticipating when he's going to need a potty break. The possible result: a lot more accidents and a longer road to housetraining graduation than is generally the case for a dog whose mealtimes—and by extension, need for potty breaks—are more predictable.

Need another reason to bypass free feeding? Try this one: Leaving food out all day for your Dachshund can be an open invitation for other creatures—namely cockroaches and mice—to share that food with him. Those creatures not only are a nuisance but are also unsanitary and may carry disease.

What Times

Plan to feed your adult Dachshund once in the morning and once in the evening at whatever time is convenient for you. Some owners feed their dogs before they have their own breakfasts and dinners; others prefer to eat first, then feed their dogs. Either way is fine. (No, you will not be telling your dog that he's the boss if you feed him before you feed yourself. In fact, if his tummy is full from eating his breakfast, he may be less inclined to try to score some of yours!) No matter what time you feed your dog, however, it's

Wash your Dachshund's dishes as often as you wash your own for the sake of cleanliness.

important to make sure that his mealtime is happy and stress-free. Here's how to do just that:

Divine His Dining Preferences

Some Dachshunds prefer to eat in solitude and quiet, while others would rather eat in the kitchen surrounded by other members of the household who are going about their business. Still others like having just one person around. Study your Dachshund to see which conditions (if any) he prefers—and once you have a sense of what those preferences are, cater to him a little. Doing so doesn't mean that you're spoiling him; rather, you're helping his body absorb his food more fully, and you're preventing after-meal digestive stresses such as belching and flatulence.

Let Him Eat Undisturbed

Any Dachshund, no matter when he eats and what his preferences are, has the right to enjoy his meal without being interrupted. Such interruptions are, at the least, stressful to the dog; at worst, they can provoke growls, snapping, and even bites. Therefore, keep your toddler from waddling over to the dog's dining corner while the dog is eating; older children and adults should also leave your dog alone at mealtime.

Let Him Linger

Unless your Dachshund is a fussy eater, don't be too quick to pick up his dish after mealtime. By giving him 15 minutes or so to eat his meal, you'll reduce the likelihood that he'll scarf it down too quickly, which in turn will decrease the odds that he'll get a post-dining tummy upset.

Wash Those Dishes

For the sake of cleanliness, wash your Dachshund's dishes as often as you wash your own. That means washing the food dish by hand or by machine after every meal and

Training Tidbit

Mealtimes can be wonderful training opportunities. Once your dog knows how to sit and stay (see Chapter 9 to learn how to teach this behavior), have him sit and stay for each meal. Hold his food dish off the floor and give him the *sit-stay* cue. When he's sitting, place the food dish on the floor. Wait a few seconds, then tell him "Okay." By having to wait politely for his meal, you teach him self-control—and you avoid getting mowed down as he races to grab his grub!

washing the water dish (and changing the water) at least once a day. Many Dachshund owners keep two sets of dishes, one for each meal, so that they can put one set of dishes in the dishwasher and have a second set ready for the next meal.

OBESITY

Without a doubt, Dachshunds are terrific. However, when considering individual Dachshunds, it's most definitely possible to have too much of a good thing. In other words, a fat Dachshund is not a healthy Dachshund. Even a little plumpness isn't pleasing.

If your Dachshund is packing on too many pounds (kg), he's far from alone. According to Pfizer Animal Health, a company that manufactures pharmaceutical products for animals, veterinarians consider 47 percent of their patients to be overweight. Pfizer also counts the Dachshund among those breeds that are more prone than others to gaining weight.

The main cause of excess weight and obesity

is the same for Dachshunds as it is for other breeds and even for people: eating too much and exercising too little. More specifically, if a Dachshund is overweight, the number of calories he takes in when he eats exceeds the number of calories he expends when he exercises. The difference between what he takes in and what he uses are excess calories, which his body stores in the form of fat.

However, other factors can also play a part in creating weight problems in Dachshunds and other dogs. Being spayed or neutered can be a factor because either procedure may slow down a dog's metabolism and result in weight gain if the dog's food intake isn't adjusted accordingly. Another factor can be hormonal disorders such as hypothyroidism, a condition in which the thyroid gland produces insufficient thyroid hormone. Finally, age alone can cause a pooch

If your Dachshund is looking a bit portly, feeding him smaller amounts and making sure that he gets enough exercise may be enough to help him slim down.

to pork out. Just as many people develop a "middle-aged spread," so can Dachshunds by the time they're five or six years of age.

But no matter what the cause, excess weight jeopardizes a Dachshund's health. An overweight dog is at greater risk than his thinner counterpart for developing a variety of serious illnesses, including arthritis, heart disease, breathing problems, heatstroke, and skin problems. Overweight dogs also increase their risk of developing spinal problems—conditions that the Dachshund is already predisposed to. In addition, excess weight can compromise the dog's immune system and heighten the risks associated with surgery and anesthesia.

Excess weight also can shorten a dog's life span. A study by Nestle Purina showed that dogs whose food intake was restricted over their lifetimes—and thus maintained ideal weights—lived 15 percent longer than dogs who were allowed to eat as much as they wanted.

So how do you know whether your Dachshund weighs more than he should? Sometimes it's hard to tell—especially if the dog is a Longhaired Dachshund, whose luxuriant coat might conceal a spare tire or two. But if a dog's looks don't tell, his ribs will. Run your hands firmly along the sides of his body; if you can't feel his ribs easily or determine where one rib ends and the other begins, he probably weighs more than he should. Another way to assess your dog's physique is to give him a bath or take him for a swim. With his wet fur matted against his body, you'll find it easier to see whether he is in the shape he should be.

If a rib check or a dunking doesn't yield clear-cut results, check out Nestle Purina's Body Condition System at www.purina.com/dogs/health/bodycondition.aspx. There you'll find nine ratings that can help you determine whether your Dachshund is too thin, too heavy, or just right. If you're still uncertain, try taking Pfizer's online Body Assessment Rating for Canines (BARC) at www.stopcanineobesity.com/barc.aspx. If the verdict is "too heavy," you need to take steps to help your Dachshund achieve a sleek physique. Here's how:

Have Him Checked Over

Your veterinarian may discover that a medical problem, such as hypothyroidism, is causing your Dachshund to pork out. By uncovering any such condition and correcting it with medication, your dog's weight problem could be solved very easily. And even if no medical cause for your dog's weight gain is found, your vet can still help you put together a diet and exercise plan that will enable him to take off those extra pounds (kg) and keep them off.

Nix Free Feeding

If you've been leaving a dish of food out all day for your Dachshund and filling it up as he empties it, now's the time to end that practice. Many Dachshunds don't know when to stop eating. If you keep filling up his food bowl, he'll keep filling his tummy and banking the excess food as fat.

Limit Intake

With your vet's help, gradually reduce the amount of food you give your Dachshund. Cut enough food to help him lose weight but not so much that he's constantly hungry and begging for food.

Feed More Often

Notice that the suggestion here is not to feed more food but to take that reduced amount of food and divide it into more than one or two meals per day. Frequent small meals will help your Dachshund's tummy stay full longer so that he doesn't feel as hungry between meals.

Multi-Dog Tip

If you have several dogs in your home in addition to your Dachshund, it's important to be careful when you feed them to prevent food fights. If you feed them at the same time, feed each dog in a different location of your house. If you feed them in the same location, feed one dog at a time.

Add Fiber

To help fill your Dachshund's tummy without adding many calories, try adding some fiber-filled fruits or vegetables to his daily fare. Apples, carrots, frozen brussels sprouts, frozen green beans, and canned pumpkin are all good options. Be ready, though, to have to take your dog out for a bathroom break more often. That's because fruits and veggies act as natural laxatives for dogs, just like they do for people..

Adjust for Treats

If you're teaching your Dachshund new behaviors and using treats to do so, reduce his mealtime portions to compensate for the extra calories he's consuming while he's learning.

Get Moving

Exercise not only mellows out a Dachshund but can also speed up weight loss. By pairing decreased calorie intake with increased calorie utilization, your dog will lose weight faster than he will with just smaller meals alone.

Go Gradually

Your dog is more likely to keep off weight that he's lost slowly than weight that he's lost quickly.

CHAPTER 8

DACHSHUND HEALTH AND WELLNESS

Watching a healthy Dachshund go about his business is pure joy. His unusual looks, big-dog disposition, and uninhibited appetite for life bring chuckles to all who see him. Chances are, though, that that Dachshund's good health didn't just happen. It's more likely that his owner has worked hard to keep him healthy and been proactive in dealing with any possible illnesses that might have befallen him. This chapter explains how you can do the same with your Dachshund.

THE ANNUAL VET EXAM

Just as people need regular checkups, so also do Dachshunds. Your dog needs an annual checkup, or wellness exam, every year until he reaches his eighth or ninth birthday. At that point, he may well be the canine equivalent of a senior citizen—even though he has a life expectancy of 12 to 14 years—and needs a wellness exam twice a year instead of just once.

The wellness exam serves as an inventory designed to confirm that your Dachshund is in good health. A wellness exam generally includes the following tests and measurements:

• The vet or clinic staffer will place your dog on either a floor scale or table scale to see how much he weighs.
• The vet or clinic staffer will measure and record your Dachshund's respiration, pulse, and temperature.
• The vet will look at your Dachshund's eyes and inside his ears for signs of ear or eye problems such as redness, discharge or odor.
• The vet will check for lumps, bumps, or tender areas by running her hands over his body. She also will probably check his weight by seeing if she can feel his ribs easily and will look at his skin for anything out of the ordinary such as flakiness or a rash.
• To check for signs of dental disease, the vet will look at your dog's gums for redness or puffiness and at his teeth for plaque or tartar.

Be prepared for the vet to also ask you for samples of your Dachshund's stool or urine; by analyzing both, she can check for parasites, urinary tract infections, and nutritional problems. And if your dog is due for an immunization, she'll probably give him one during this visit.

Sometimes a wellness exam will reveal health problems that had previously escaped detection. More often, though, this type of exam gives your vet a snapshot of what your

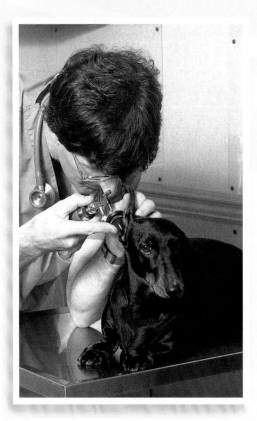

The wellness exam is a checkup to make sure that your Dachshund is doing as well as he appears to be.

dog is like when he's well and a basis of comparison for results in future exams.

PARASITES

A variety of parasites would love to take up residence inside or outside your Dachshund's body. (The choice of canine real estate depends on the type of parasite.) And while they're very small, they can all cause your Dachshund a lot of discomfort as well as endanger his (and possibly your) health. Here are the parasites most likely to besiege your dog and recommendations on how to get rid of them.

Internal Parasites

Parasites that do their dirty work inside your canine companion include:

Heartworms

This parasite is spread by mosquitos. When a mosquito that's carrying heartworm larvae bites a dog, the mosquito transmits the larvae into the dog's body. There the larvae mature over several months into adult worms that reproduce and take up residence in the dog's heart, lungs, and circulatory system. The first sign of a heartworm problem is usually a persistent cough; later the dog may become lethargic and breathe abnormally.

Heartworm is treatable, but the treatment can be debilitating. The veterinarian may prescribe an arsenic drug compound—which will require that the dog be hospitalized—or will inject another compound called melarsomine dihydrochloride. Either way, though, treatment can result in complications. For example, the dead heartworms may obstruct the blood vessels. Such obstructions may cause the dog to develop a fever, a worsened cough, and blood in the liquid he coughs up. For this reason, dogs being treated for heartworm aren't allowed to exercise.

Heartworm is much easier to prevent than to treat. Chewable preventives include tablets of ivermectin and milbemycin oxime; topical treatments consist of selamectin and moxidectin. Usually heartworm preventives are given once a month. However, your dog should be tested for heartworm before preventive treatment begins because using a heartworm preventive in heartworm-positive dogs can cause severe negative reactions.

Hookworms

The bloodsucking adult hookworm lives and mates inside the intestine of its canine host, and the resulting eggs are expelled in the dog's stool. The eggs hatch in the soil and develop into larvae. Then they infect another dog, either by entering any part of a dog's skin that touches the ground or by being present in soil that the dog licks when he cleans himself.

Hookworm infection is especially common in puppies and can be fatal if not treated. Signs of infection include pallor, physical weakness, iron deficiency, and possibly diarrhea. Hookworms can also infect people.

Getting rid of the hookworms requires two treatments of a dewormer such as mebendazole, albendazole, or pyrantel pamoate. Severely infected dogs may need blood transfusions and/or an iron supplement.

Heartworm preventives are also effective in preventing hookworms.

Roundworms

These parasites are very common in puppies, but a dog of any age can acquire them. Ingesting feces from an infected animal (for example, a rodent) that contain roundworm eggs or stepping on soil that contains roundworm eggs and then licking a paw and swallowing them causes those eggs to enter the body and arrive at the dog's intestinal tract. There the eggs hatch into larvae, and the larvae migrate to other parts of the body and reproduce. The eggs are expelled through the dog's stool.

Symptoms include coughing, diarrhea, vomiting, and a swollen belly. Analysis of a stool sample confirms the diagnosis. Treatment consists of one of a variety of dewormers the vet may prescribe. The worms can be prevented if a dog takes heartworm prevention products that also contain medication that kills roundworms.

Tapeworms

If your Dachshund has tapeworms, he also has

Heartworms are spread by mosquitoes, which transmit the larvae into the dog's body.

fleas. That's because the tapeworm's sole mode of transport to a dog is through a flea that he swallows. From there, the tapeworm travels to the dog's intestine, latches onto the intestine wall, and sheds segments of its body. The dog expels those segments through his rectum when he poops. Each segment resembles a grain of rice and can be seen not only in the dog's poop but also around his anus and even on his bed. Tapeworms are treated with either injectable or oral dewormers; an effective flea control program prevents them.

Whipworms

A dirt-eating Dachshund stands a good chance of getting whipworms. That's because whipworms reside in soil and will take up residence in your Dachsie's intestines if he eats infested soil, and the eggs they lay will leave his body through his stool. (Contact with infected stool can also result in whipworms.) In mild cases, symptoms often don't show up,

but severe cases cause bloody diarrhea that can be fatal if left untreated. Unexplained weight loss is another symptom. Treatment is with a dewormer that is prescribed by a vet.

External Parasites

Some parasites live on your Dachshund's skin. These include:

Fleas

For such tiny creatures, fleas can cause a lot of misery. A single bite can make some dogs itchy almost beyond endurance, but itching isn't the only problem they cause. To relieve the itch, your Dachshund may scratch bitten areas so hard that they bleed and cause hair loss. Moreover, fleas ingest your dog's blood—so without treatment, he may develop anemia. A Dachshund who's scratching himself constantly needs to be checked for fleas. Inspect his tummy and groin for black spots, then mix those spots with water. If the spots

Check your dog for fleas and ticks after he's been playing outside.

turn red, you'll know that your dog has blood-filled flea poop, which can only come from fleas. Another way to check for fleas is to run a flea comb through his coat. If fleas are present, you'll see them crawling around the teeth of the comb when you examine it.

Luckily for you and your Dachshund, pharmaceutical companies have developed lots of flea-eradicating products. Some work by stopping flea eggs from hatching; others focus on killing adult fleas that bite a treated Dachshund. Better still, some anti-flea products are multitaskers that also prevent internal parasites from infecting your dog. For any of these products, though, you need a prescription from your veterinarian.

Sarcoptic Mange

Another itch-inducing parasite is the mite that causes sarcoptic mange, also known as scabies. The mites tunnel under the skin, often near the ears, elbows, belly, or armpit. In addition to constant scratching, inflammation and hair loss may occur at the affected areas. If the vet suspects sarcoptic mange, she'll perform a skin scraping to see if mites are present.

To treat sarcoptic mange, the vet is likely to prescribe a flea and/or heartworm preventive treatment. These remedies are often very effective in ridding a dog of this very uncomfortable condition.

Ringworm

Ringworm isn't a type of worm; rather, it's a fungus that affects not only dogs but also cats and people. An infected animal or contaminated item transmits the infection. The most common sign of a ringworm infection is a small, round, hairless lesion; the lesion may also have scaly skin in the center. Generally, the lesion is seen on the head, but it can also appear on the legs and tail.

By the Numbers

Your dog should have his first adult wellness exam by the time he celebrates his first birthday.

To diagnose ringworm, the vet will collect scales from the lesion and perform a culture. If the culture is positive, she'll prescribe a topical or oral antifungal product. Meanwhile, the lesion itself should be treated by clipping the hair at the lesion site as short as possible. Any grooming equipment should be sterilized immediately after it's used.

Ticks

These insects can transmit serious diseases such as Lyme disease, Rocky Mountain spotted fever, and ehrlichiosis. Symptoms of these illnesses in dogs include weight loss, lethargy, decreased appetite, unexplained lameness, and ear or eye infections that don't respond to medication. Antibiotics are used to treat these conditions.

Ticks can also be prevented by keeping your dog out of the high grasses or low shrubs where they like to congregate and (if your veterinarian approves) by using topical tick treatments. Another effective preventive is to check your dog regularly for ticks. They're easy to spot: ladybug-sized dark bugs that cling to the dog's skin. If you see one, remove it promptly and properly. Here's what to do:

1. Don a pair of rubber gloves and pick up a pair of tweezers.
2. Grab the tick's body with the tweezers. Pull the tick straight off the dog without jerking or twisting.
3. Check to see that you've removed the entire tick; sometimes the head remains behind.

4. If the removed tick is headless, remove the head from the dog by using a needle dipped in alcohol. Put the removed tick in a bowl of alcohol to kill it, and clean the area from where you removed the tick with soap, water, and alcohol.

BREED-SPECIFIC HEALTH ISSUES

Like any breed, Dachshunds have some breed-specific health problems, although reputable breeders are working to at least greatly reduce occurrences of those problems by not breeding affected dogs. Unfortunately, not-so-reputable breeders fail to test their breeding stock for such conditions. The results of such failures can be tragic not only for the resulting puppies but also for the people who buy those puppies.

For these reasons, you should watch your

Dogs infected by a tick-borne illness may experience symptoms such as weight loss, decreased appetite, and lethargy.

adult Dachshund for signs of the genetic problems described in this section, especially if you adopted him from a shelter or rescue group and don't know about his parentage. You should be equally vigilant if you bought your dog from a breeder who didn't give you copies of his parents' health clearances. And no matter where you got your Dachshund, consult your vet immediately as soon as he shows signs of a problem. Early treatment can greatly increase the chances that his condition can be controlled, if not resolved—but early treatment requires early detection.

There's no single disease that befalls only Dachshunds, but a number of illnesses are of particular concern to those who care about the breed. These conditions include:

Alopecia
Several forms of alopecia, or hair loss, are known to afflict Dachshunds.

Color Dilution/Mutant Alopecia
Color dilution/mutant alopecia afflicts Dachshunds with diluted black or fawn coat colors. Hair of these colors begins to thin when the dog is about six months of age. There's no cure for this condition, but veterinarians generally caution against excessive grooming or harsh shampooing of affected dogs, and you should take steps to protect the skin against any bacterial infections that might result from this condition.

Estrogen–Responsive Dermatosis
Still another form of hair loss is estrogen-responsive dermatosis, which can occur in spayed female Dachshunds. Symptoms of this condition are hair loss that starts at the flanks and moves frontward on the body. The hair color may also fade. The standard treatment is estrogen replacement therapy.

Want to Know More?

For more information on acanthosis nigricans, see Chapter 3.

Pattern Baldness

Finally, Dachshunds are among the breeds that are susceptible to pattern baldness, also known as pinnal alopecia. Between six and nine months of age, the hair begins to thin at the temples, underneath the neck, on the chest and abdomen, and the backs of the legs on female dogs; males lose hair on their ears. The hair loss may continue until the affected areas are completely bald, and the skin thickens. There is no treatment for this condition, but the dog doesn't usually experience any discomfort.

Primary Acanthosis Nigricans

One type of hair loss is primary acanthosis nigricans, which can afflict Dachshunds less than one year of age (as explained in Chapter 3).

Elbow Dysplasia

When the bones and cartilage of the elbow fail to fit together properly, elbow dysplasia results. A Dachshund with this condition will exhibit lameness in one or both of his front legs. To confirm the diagnosis, a vet will use an X-ray. Treatment depends on the nature of the improper bone-cartilage fit. For some dogs, regular low-impact exercise can help; for others, surgery is needed.

Eye Diseases

Dachshunds are susceptible to a number of eye diseases. These include:

Cataracts

In this condition, the lens of the eye becomes cloudy, which can partially or completely block light from reaching the retina. In Dachshunds, a hereditary form of cataracts may form before the dog reaches his second birthday. Cataracts can also develop in conjunction with PRA. (See below.) A veterinarian may choose to treat the condition with medicated eye drops, or she may suggest surgery to remove them.

Progressive Retinal Atrophy (PRA)

This genetic disorder causes cells in the retina at the back of the eye to degenerate and die, resulting in night blindness. There is no cure for PRA.

Intervertebral Disc Disease (IDD)

Intervertebral disc disease (IDD) is a spinal condition that can result in paralysis of a

Progressive retinal atrophy causes cells in the retina at the back of the eye to degenerate and die.

dog may hold his head strangely, experience sudden excruciating pain, and exhibit varying degrees of paralysis in all four legs. If the rupture or displacement occurs farther down the spine, the dog is more likely to experience back pain and weakened, wobbly rear legs. Rear leg paralysis may also occur.

A dog who exhibits any of the above symptoms needs immediate veterinary attention. The vet may perform a myelogram (an X-ray of the spine after a dye has been inserted into the spinal fluid) or may order either a CT scan or magnetic resonance imaging (MRI).

Treatment depends on how severe the problem is. A dog with a mild case of the disease may respond to a month of crate rest and administration of a corticosteroid such as prednisone. More severe cases, such as when a dog needs help to get up from a reclining position, require surgery and several weeks of postoperative crate rest.

Patellar Luxation

The unusual anatomies of toy dogs and short-legged, long-bodied dogs like Dachshunds place unusual strain on their kneecaps. Such strain can sometimes cause the kneecap to pop out of place; when that happens, the dog suffers from patellar luxation. An affected dog may stop suddenly while running and cry out in pain, extending the affected leg behind him. A dog who exhibits this symptom needs immediate veterinary attention. If the condition is severe, surgery may be needed to put the kneecap back into its proper place.

GENERIC HEALTH ISSUES

Many other health problems that Dachshunds face are not necessarily the result of genetic bad luck. Here are some of the most common nongenetic health problems besetting

The Dachshund's long back makes him especially vulnerable to intervertebral disc disease (IDD), which is one reason why he shouldn't be allowed to jump or sit up.

dog's rear legs or all four legs, depending on the location on the spine where the condition occurs. IDD is caused by the leakage or displacement of one or more of the fluid-filled discs that are located between the bones of the vertebrae to cushion them from each other. The Dachshund's long back makes him especially vulnerable to this problem.

Symptoms vary according to where on the spine the condition occurs. If the rupture or displacement occurs in the neck, the affected

Dachshunds and how you can help your dog deal with them.

Allergies

Many dogs have allergies, and Dachshunds are no exception. A dog whose ear infections never seem to clear up—or recur almost as soon as they do—may have an allergy problem. So too may the dog who frequently licks or chews his feet, rubs his face, or scratches his armpits. Other signs of allergies include frequent biting or scratching of the tail and thighs and development of a rash or even a bacterial infection in the bitten areas.

A veterinarian usually takes a two-pronged approach to treating allergies. First, she acts to relieve the immediate discomfort caused by the allergic reaction. Effective remedies may include antihistamines, ear washes for ear infections, and short-term corticosteroids or topical treatments for skin reactions.

The second step involves determining the root cause of the allergy. However, doing so can be easier said than done because canine allergies can result from one or more of a long list of possible triggers. Common offenders include flea bites, dust mites, house dust, mold, pollen, and food.

A year-round allergic reaction—especially if accompanied by vomiting and diarrhea—may lead your vet to suspect that a food allergy is plaguing your dog. She will probably suggest putting your dog on a food elimination trial (also known as an elimination diet). These trials can be very effective at finding a food allergen, but they're challenging. The dog is placed on a strict diet that consists of one protein and one starch that he has never eaten before. No other foods—including table scraps—treats, supplements, or ingestible drugs are allowed. For the trial to work, owners and their families must be vigilant in making sure that the dog eats only those foods permitted in the trial.

A food-allergic Dachshund who's on an elimination trial will probably experience significantly milder symptoms (and maybe even none at all) from eight weeks to four months after the trial starts. At that point, a second phase begins: adding foods from the previous diet one at a time to see if an allergic reaction returns. However, many owners decide not to perform this phase of the trial; instead, they either keep the dog on the same foods as are in the food trial or gradually switch him to other foods that he's never had up till this point.

If a food trial doesn't improve your dog's symptoms, your vet may refer you to a veterinary dermatologist. This specialist can perform a blood test or skin test to pinpoint your dog's allergic triggers. Depending on the results, the dermatologist may formulate a program of allergy shots. These shots involve injecting gradually increasing (but always minute) amounts into the dog's skin of the allergens identified in the test. The objective is to desensitize him to the allergic trigger(s). Allergy shots can be very effective but can take as long as a year to work.

Another common allergic trigger is fleas; many dogs are allergic to the saliva that fleas leave on the skin when they bite. Treatment requires ridding the dog of the fleas.

Cancer

As a breed, Dachshunds are no more likely to get cancer than other breeds and are less likely to fall victim to this condition than some. However, like all breeds, the chances of a Dachshund developing cancer increase as he ages. In fact, according to the Animal Cancer Center at Colorado State University, 50 percent of all dogs develop cancer if they live ten years or longer.

Many dog deaths from cancer reflect the fact that modern veterinary medicine helps our

Some dogs are allergic to certain foods and must be put on an elimination diet to determine the ingredient that's causing the allergy.

dogs live longer than they did a generation ago or before. That said, you can do a lot to help your dog win a battle against cancer by knowing what the symptoms of canine cancer are. They include:

- Abnormal swellings that appear suddenly, persist, or continue to grow. In all likelihood, the lump is harmless or at least noncancerous, but you can't know for sure that that's the case until your vet assesses the lump.
- Sores that don't heal. In a healthy dog's body, a cut or sore heals within one or two weeks. A sore that doesn't heal within that period indicates that all may not be well within his body, and one reason could be the onset of cancer. If you observe a slow-healing or nonhealing lesion on your Dachshund, contact your vet.

- Unexplained weight loss. If your dog is losing weight for no apparent reason, he needs to see his vet as soon as possible.
- Appetite loss. Most dogs, including Dachshunds, love to eat. Consequently, if your Dachshund suddenly shows no interest in food, something's probably wrong. Call your vet.
- Bleeding or discharge from any body opening. Blood or the leakage of any other fluid from the nostrils, mouth, ears, anus, or urethra (other than urine from the latter) isn't normal and merits an immediate call to your veterinarian.
- Offensive odor. Like all dogs, a Dachshund loves to roll in smelly stuff or otherwise do something that makes him stink.

Other conditions can cause him to smell bad too, such as a yeasty odor from an ear infection or bad breath due to dental disease. However, an offensive odor with no apparent cause may indicate that something serious is amiss with your Dachshund. Call your vet as soon as possible.

- Difficulty in eating or swallowing. Painful teeth and gums can cause your Dachshund to have trouble eating or swallowing, but so can a tumor that's blocking the esophagus. Put in a call to your vet.
- Hesitation to exercise or loss of stamina. Dachshunds aren't necessarily the most active dogs in the canine kingdom, but healthy ones are almost always up for a brisk walk. If your dog's normal short-legged trot becomes a slow shuffle for no apparent reason, he needs a vet's attention.
- Persistent lameness or stiffness. If your dog is middle aged or older, don't assume that his stiff gait is a result of aging. Have

Hesitation to exercise or loss of stamina is one of the signs of cancer.

your veterinarian check to see if a tumor is causing the problem.

- Difficulty in breathing, urinating, or defecating. A dog who can't poop may be suffering from a blockage caused by a tumor, as can a dog who has difficulty peeing or a dog who has trouble breathing. Any sudden problems your dog experiences in performing these vital functions merit your vet's attention.

Diabetes

Diabetes, also known as diabetes mellitus, is the disease that results when a Dachshund's pancreas doesn't produce enough insulin (a hormone needed to help the body process sugar in the blood), or the body can't use the insulin the pancreas does produce. Because many Dachshunds are overweight, they may be more prone to acquiring this condition than other dogs are. Age also increases the risk of developing diabetes.

The main symptoms of diabetes include increased thirst and urination, weight loss despite an increased appetite, and cloudiness of the eye. However, because these symptoms also appear with other conditions, lab tests are needed to confirm the diagnosis. Among the tests that a veterinarian may order if diabetes is suspected are assessments to measure glucose (a type of sugar) in the urine and blood, an analysis of the urine, and a complete blood count.

Diabetes is a chronic condition that cannot be cured but can be managed. The primary treatment is twice-daily injections of insulin to replenish what the dog's body can't produce or process on its own. Your veterinarian can show you how to perform the injections yourself.

During the initial stages of treatment, the amount of insulin injected will probably need to be adjusted several times to achieve maximum effectiveness. Your vet will perform blood tests to measure the amount of glucose in the blood to determine whether your Dachshund is receiving the right amount of insulin. In addition to insulin injections, your veterinarian may also order dietary changes.

Ear Infections

Ear infections have many causes. They can result from infestations of yeast, bacteria, or mites; a foreign body in the ear; or allergies to food or elements in the environment. For that reason, effective treatment of ear infections may take a two-pronged approach: getting rid of the immediate infection and trying to determine and treat the underlying cause.

Symptoms of ear infections include a dark, goopy discharge from one or both ears, a yeasty or unpleasant odor from the ears, persistent head shaking, and persistent scratching or rubbing one or both ears. Any of these symptoms should prompt a call to your vet for an appointment to have the ears examined. A physical exam is usually all that's needed to confirm the immediate diagnosis of infection. However, the vet may also examine any ear discharge under a microscope in an effort to pinpoint an underlying cause of the infection.

Often a vet will suggest using a topical over-the-counter product or a prescription cream or ointment to treat a mild or first-time ear infection. In addition, she may prescribe an oral antibiotic to kill infection-causing bacteria. If ear mites are causing the infection, the vet may prescribe ivermectin, an anti-parasite treatment; to prevent recurrence, she'll suggest using a preventive anti-parasite product.

If the ear infections keep coming back, there's probably an underlying condition that's causing the problem. A vet can discuss with you whether your dog should be tested for food and/or environmental allergies, which often trigger ear

Because of their long hanging ears, Dachshunds are more prone to ear infections than some other breeds are.

infections that never seem to go away or seem to occur one after the other.

Epilepsy

Epilepsy is fairly common among many dog breeds, including Dachshunds, but in all too many cases the cause of the condition can't be determined precisely. Such epilepsy is known as idiopathic epilepsy, and many experts speculate that this condition may be genetic in origin.

In idiopathic epilepsy, the first seizure usually occurs during the first third of the dog's life—generally between six months and four years of age. Unless he's already lying down, a seizure usually starts when the dog falls on his side. His head and neck arch, his mouth opens wide, and the limbs extend fully, after which they begin to move in a jerky manner. The dog may urinate or defecate and may also froth at the mouth. Most last about two minutes, although some can continue for longer. After the seizure is over, the dog may sleep for about 20 minutes. When he awakens, he may walk aimlessly and be extremely hungry or thirsty.

If your Dachshund has a seizure, the best immediate course of action may be inaction. Simply leave him alone unless he's near a flight of stairs and in danger of falling; in such instances, just move him to a safer place.

If your Dachshund has more than one seizure, take him to your veterinarian. The vet will perform an extensive examination and will order lab tests to determine whether the seizure has an obvious cause, such as a brain tumor. If no such cause is found, the usual course of action is to prescribe phenobarbital or potassium bromide for the dog to control the seizures.

Eye Problems

A dog's eye problems may be rooted in any one of several causes. Among the more common are:

Conjunctivitis

Also known as "pink eye," conjunctivitis is an inflammation of the tissue that coats the inner aspect of the eyelids and a portion of the outer surface of the eyeball. The ailment can result from allergies, bacterial or viral infections, foreign bodies in the eye, irritation from shampoos and dips, and a number of eye diseases. Symptoms include redness in the white parts of the eye and/or the eyelids, squinting, and pawing at the affected eye. There may also be a discharge, although the nature of the discharge often depends on the underlying cause of the conjunctivitis.

Treatment starts with a topical antibiotic and/or a corticosteroid to reduce eye irritation and knock out the infection. The vet will also try to determine whether the condition has

an underlying cause; if she finds one, she'll prescribe additional treatment.

Corneal Ulcer

Also known as ulcerative keratitis, this condition is a break or scrape on the outer layer of the cornea. Causes include trauma, eyelid abnormalities, and tear duct problems. Symptoms include a red, painful-looking eye, watering of the eye, a mucus or pus-like discharge from the eye, and squinting. A veterinarian can diagnose a corneal ulcer by performing a complete examination of the eye and cornea, including the placement of a diagnostic dye in the eye. Superficial ulcers generally heal in a few days with the help of topical medications and treatment of the underlying cause. Deeper ulcers and/or those that don't heal may need surgical treatment.

Glaucoma

This condition results when fluid can't drain from the eye into the circulatory system. The blocked fluid accumulates and takes up space in the eye, causing intraocular pressure to increase. As the pressure increases, the optic nerve becomes irreversibly damaged. Ultimately, the dog loses sight in the eye.

Symptoms of glaucoma include a reddened eye, sensitivity to light, dilated pupils, loss of vision, eyelid spasms, eye enlargement,

> ## Multi-Dog Tip
>
> If you have more than one dog, ask your local animal clinic if it offers a multiple-dog discount for bringing all dogs in for their wellness exams at the same time.

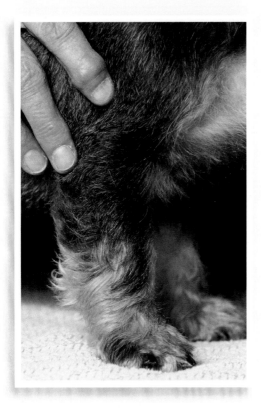

Any unexplained lumps or bumps warrant a trip to the vet.

however, the vet may suggest removing the eye completely so that the dog doesn't suffer any infection or pain from the disease.

Keratoconjunctivitis Sicca (KCS)

This condition, also known as KCS or "dry eye," occurs when the eye produces insufficient tears. Symptoms include a red eye, a thick mucus discharge, and squinting. Causes can include allergies, side effects from medications, and age.

To diagnose KCS, a veterinarian will give the dog a test that measures the amount of tears he can produce in one minute. If the test shows that tear production levels are lower than normal, the vet will prescribe twice-daily administration of cyclosporine cream or liquid. She may also prescribe antibiotics, artificial tears, lubricants, or topical corticosteroids.

ALTERNATIVE THERAPIES

In addition to the marvels that 21st-century conventional veterinary medicine has devised, there are many other therapies that can enhance your Dachshund's health and well-being. Those therapies include:

Acupuncture

Acupuncture is an ancient Chinese medical practice that is designed to provide beneficial influences to the body's energy flow. Traditional Chinese medicine is based in part upon the principle that the body's energy flows along unseen pathways called meridians, which in turn are believed to influence other parts of the body. Normally the energy flows smoothly along the meridians—but if that energy is disrupted, the body becomes sick. Acupuncture aims to restore the smooth flow of the energy by stimulating specific points on the meridians that influence the part of the body that needs help to heal.

discoloration or cloudiness of the cornea, and rubbing or pawing of the eye area.

To diagnose glaucoma, the veterinarian or veterinary ophthalmologist measures the amount of pressure within the eye. If secondary glaucoma is suspected, blood and urine tests may be performed to determine the underlying cause; X-rays or ultrasound may be used to locate a suspected tumor.

The treatment for glaucoma depends on how far the disease has progressed. If sight remains in the affected eye, the vet may recommend surgery to either bypass the blockage or diminish fluid production. Carbonic anhydrase inhibitors, beta blockers, and miotics can help reduce pressure within the eye. If vision is completely lost,

Acupuncture is commonly used to treat muscle injuries and arthritis. However, the practice may also be helpful in treating other conditions, such as allergies, skin problems, and digestive problems.

Acupressure is related to acupuncture. However, instead of using needles to treat one or more physical conditions, the practitioner uses her fingers. The fingers are placed where the acupuncture needles would go.

More information about veterinary acupuncture is available by logging onto the International Veterinary Acupuncture Society (IVAS) website at www.ivas.org or the American Academy of Veterinary Acupuncture (AAVA) at www.aava.org. You can also find qualified practitioners by logging onto these sites.

Chiropractic

Chiropractic is a treatment system that centers on the belief that certain conditions, such as incontinence and arthritis, result from a lack of normal nerve function. To restore normal nerve function, the chiropractor manipulates and adjusts the spine's position by using specific techniques and equipment.

Veterinary chiropractors may be veterinarians who have received postgraduate training in chiropractic, while others are doctors of chiropractic who have chosen to focus on animals. Either route, however, requires postgraduate training in veterinary chiropractic from one of only five facilities in the world. Three of those facilities are located in the United States. In addition, the prospective practitioner must pass an examination given by the American Veterinary Chiropractic Association (AVCA). More information on veterinary chiropractic and a listing of practitioners are available from www.animalchiropractic.org.

Hands-On Therapies

More often than you might think, a knowledgeable touch can heal a Dachshund who's suffering from aches, pains, stress, or mobility issues. Here are descriptions of the more common therapies that require a laying on of hands.

Conventional Physical Therapy

This type of therapy, also known as rehabilitation or rehab, involves the use of directed exercise such as working on a treadmill, exercising underwater, or having a trained therapist work an injured limb. Other forms of physical therapy include heat therapy, which helps relax the muscles and loosen the joints, and cold packs, which decrease swelling. While this therapy has long been popular for humans, it's only more recently emerged as a treatment option for animals. The University of Tennessee, which offers a certificate program in canine rehabilitation, maintains a listing of qualified practitioners; you can access that listing by logging on to its website at www.canineequinerehab.com/practitioners.asp.

Massage

This practice, which is probably the most common form of hands-on therapy that people can give to their dogs (not to mention to each other!), requires a person to rub and knead her dog's muscle tissue with her hands. When performed properly, massage can loosen muscle fibers that have become tense or sore during exercise, and it increases the circulation of blood to those muscles. And it's not an exotic technique—simply petting your Dachshund can also be a form of massage. Just stroke your dog's head, neck, and body in long, slow motions.

As beneficial as massage can be, it's not applicable in every instance. Conditions such

Training Tidbit

Teach your Dachshund to accept a veterinarian's examination by pretending to give such exams yourself. Periodically run your hands over his body, and give him treats for good behavior. Do the same when you pick up his feet, look into his eyes and ears, or exert very gentle pressure on his sides. The Dachshund who can accept these procedures calmly will be much easier for you and your vet to handle than a dog who balks at being examined.

as broken bones, broken skin, or cancer may actually worsen after a massage session. The reasons: Massage can make an injury worse or increase circulation in a manner that promotes tumor growth.

To learn more about canine massage and other alternative therapies, check out *The Holistic Health Guide* by Doug Knueven, DVM (TFH).

Tellington T-Touch

Another type of hands-on therapy, Tellington T-Touch, utilizes finger and hand movements in circular patterns to effect positive changes to a dog's nervous system; adherents maintain that such changes in turn can relieve a wide range of physical and behavioral problems. Creator Linda Tellington-Jones is the author of several books about T-Touch and how to use it, and the official T-Touch website has a searchable database of certified practitioners at www.ttouch.com/pracDirectory.shtml.

Herbal

Despite the benefits that modern human and veterinary medicine bring, the ancient practice of using herbs to treat various ills still plays a big part in keeping people and animals feeling good. Humans use aloe vera to soothe sunburned skin or drink chamomile tea to settle an upset stomach. By the same token, herbs may help heal many canine ailments, such as constipation, skin irritation and injuries, infections, nausea, diarrhea, and urinary system problems.

Herbs are available in most health food stores and some high-end supermarkets. That said, you should check with an expert before giving your dog any herbs because an herb can interact adversely with medicines you're already giving your dog. To find a veterinarian who specializes in herbal veterinary medicine, log onto the Veterinary Botanical Medicine Association at www.vbma.org, and check out the website's searchable database. There you'll find veterinarians who have had postgraduate training in herbal medicine.

Homeopathy

Homeopathy is another type of therapy that can help your ailing Dachshund. This type of treatment is used to deal with complaints that range from eye inflammations to nail problems and a lot of other problems in between. The principle guiding homeopathy is that like cures like. Homeopathic vets employ this principle to give their canine patients very small—and very diluted—amounts of substances that would trigger symptoms that resemble those the dog already has if given in larger amounts. Homeopathic vets and adherents believe that dispensing such substances kick-starts the natural defenses in the dog's body, enabling the body to heal itself.

Homeopathic vets have a wide range of possible remedies to use in treating dogs. To learn more about this practice or to find a veterinary homeopathic practitioner, log onto the homepage of the Academy of Veterinary Homeopathy (AVH) at www.theavh.org.

EMERGENCY CARE

Sooner or later, you're likely to face a medical or other emergency that involves your Dachshund. These occurrences can be frightening and stressful—and such fear and stress may make it difficult for you to research what you need to do to help your Dachshund. For that reason, it's a good idea to uncover the information you need before any emergency occurs so that you can put your hands on it right away.

Medical Emergencies

Here is a list of the medical emergencies most likely to befall your Dachshund. If your dog experiences any of these symptoms, he needs immediate veterinary attention. His life could be at stake.

Your Dachsie may benefit from a chiropractor, who manipulates and adjusts the spine's position by using specific techniques and equipment.

Breathing Problems

A Dachshund who's having trouble breathing needs to see his vet immediately. Several problems can cause labored breathing, including pneumonia, bruising of the lungs, tumors near or on the lungs, or laryngeal paralysis. Labored breathing can also signal the onset of heart disease.

Change in Gum Color

Changes in your Dachshund's gum color—whether lighter or darker—require immediate veterinary attention. Such deviations from the normal pink gum color could signal the onset of shock, breathing problems, liver or gall bladder disease, severe infection, or blood poisoning.

Cold Exposure

If your Dachshund is shivering deeply, has cold limbs and/or rigid muscles, and is acting apathetically, he may have hypothermia. Bring him to his veterinarian immediately.

Heat Exposure

Extreme panting, profound lethargy, rapid or shallow breathing, and/or bloody vomiting are signs of heatstroke. If your Dachshund exhibits any of these symptoms after exposure to high temperatures, bring him to your vet at once. Heatstroke can be lethal if it's not treated quickly.

Persistent Vomiting

Vomiting that occurs several times over several hours—especially if the vomitus contains foreign material or is bloody—can mean that your Dachshund has swallowed a foreign object, ingested a toxic substance, or has problems with his pancreas or kidneys. Bring him to his vet immediately.

Retching

A dog who's trying to vomit but isn't succeeding needs to see his vet right away. He may be experiencing a blockage at the bottom of his esophagus.

Significant Bleeding

If your Dachshund is bleeding from anywhere on his body and the bleeding doesn't cease after 20 minutes of pressure bandaging, take him to your vet or emergency clinic right away. The same advice applies for pulsing or spurting blood, which may mean that an artery has been injured.

Sudden Collapse

If your Dachshund suddenly collapses—whether he loses consciousness or not—he needs immediate veterinary attention. Sudden collapses may signal a seizure or heart problem.

First Aid

Even though you're taking your sick or injured Dachshund to his vet or local clinic as soon as you can, you may need to stabilize his condition yourself before you and he head over to the animal hospital or clinic. Here's what to do to help your dog in some common emergency situations:

Bites

If your Dachshund has a fight with any other dog, check him carefully for bite wounds as soon as possible after separating the two combatants. If you find a bleeding wound, place a clean piece of cloth, gauze, or sanitary napkin on top of the wound and apply direct pressure. Then get him to his vet as soon as you can.

Bleeding

Placing a clean cloth, sanitary napkin, or piece of gauze directly over a bleeding wound can staunch the bleeding, thus permitting a clot to form. If the bleeding wound is on one of your dog's legs, elevate the limb, which will also slow the bleeding. Leave the cloth alone so that you don't reopen the wound, but bring him to your vet or emergency veterinary clinic as soon as possible.

Broken Bones

A Dachshund with a broken bone is in severe pain and is likely to bite anyone trying to help him. To protect yourself, muzzle him unless he's having trouble breathing. Then use direct pressure to staunch any bleeding. If the bone has broken the skin, cover the area with sterile gauze dressing; if you don't have any, use a sanitary napkin or clean cloth. Before taking your Dachshund to his vet, try to immobilize him on a large board or similar surface.

Frostbite

Dachshunds can develop frostbite if they're overexposed to cold temperatures. Symptoms include white skin and an abnormally cold feel to the body. If your dog exhibits such symptoms, bring him inside immediately and place warm wet towels on the affected areas. Then put in a call to your vet. If your dog's skin darkens, take him to your vet as quickly as possible.

Heatstroke

Heatstroke, which is also called hyperthermia, can result if your dog has been left in an area with insufficient shade or in a car where the outside temperature exceeds 70°F (21.1°C). Exercise in hot, humid weather can also cause this condition. Symptoms include bright red or purple gums, excessive drooling and/or panting, unsteadiness, and restlessness. Such a dog needs a vet's help, but it's crucial to cool him down first. Wet his ear flaps with cool water; place cool but not cold, wet towels on his groin, armpits, and back of his neck; and set up a fan so that its air flows directly over your dog. When he has stabilized, bring him to veterinarian.

Poisoning

If your dog has swallowed a poisonous substance, put in an immediate call to the ASPCA Animal Poison Control Center at 888-426-4435. The veterinary toxicologists who staff the Center will advise you and/or your vet as to the proper antidote. When you call, have your credit card ready because the Center charges a fee.

Disaster Preparedness

When Hurricane Katrina and its aftermath displaced countless pets in New Orleans and nearby localities, many people—including government officials—realized for the first time the necessity of including pets in disaster planning. That said, you shouldn't wait for a hurricane or other disaster to occur before hatching an escape or safety plan for yourself and your Dachshund. The US Department of Homeland Security suggests taking the following steps now and later to prepare for an emergency:

A Dachshund who's been exposed to excessive heat may suffer from heat exposure.

Know Where to Go

Because many emergency shelters can't accept pets, you need to determine in advance which motels and hotels in the area you plan to evacuate will allow you to bring your Dachshund. Another option is to check with out-of-town relatives or friends to see if they could take you and your dog in.

Write Down the Local Animal Shelter Phone Number

Write down the local animal shelter phone number, and include your local animal shelter's number in your list of emergency numbers. Shelter personnel might be able to provide information concerning pets during a disaster.

Bring Supplies

When you evacuate with your Dachshund, bring a few days' supply of his food, some bottled water, and medications. You should also bring his veterinary records (or at least records on his current immunizations), food dishes, and a first-aid kit. Consider packing such a kit now so that you won't have to worry about packing it if a disaster strikes.

Update Identification

Make sure that your Dachshund's identification tags and microchip information are up to date. If possible, attach the address and/or phone number of your evacuation site. If your pet gets lost, his tag and microchip are his ticket home. Make sure too that you have a current photo of your pet for identification purposes.

Getting Your Dog to the Vet

Unfortunately, getting a stricken Dachshund to the vet right away may be easier said than done. The reason is that your dog may be so frightened that he doesn't recognize you or what you're trying to do. Experts suggest that you do the following:

- **Stay calm.** If you're calm, your dog is more likely to be calm and cooperative.
- **Get a helper.** Having someone else around to help you with your dog—particularly to drive the two of you to your vet's or to an emergency clinic—can save time and stress. The helper can also phone the vet or clinic to let them know that you're coming.
- **Banish the audience.** Ask bystanders or family members to leave you and your assistant alone so that you can concentrate on helping your dog.
- **Minimize handling.** Handle your dog as little as possible, and when you do, make sure that you're gentle.
- **Protect yourself.** Your normally easygoing Dachshund may act out of character during this stressful time. For that reason, it's a good idea to put on some thick leather gloves or fireplace gloves before you try to handle your dog—and to muzzle him if necessary. That way, he'll be much less likely to bite you—or if he does, to inflict little or no injury.

Keep an eye on your dog if he's out playing in cold weather to prevent him from contracting frostbite.

Bring Restraints
Make sure that you have a secure crate, leash, and collar for your Dachshund so that you can keep him safe and secure during an emergency.

Get More Information
Check the websites of the Humane Society of the United States (HSUS) at www.hsus.org and the American Society for the Prevention of Cruelty to Animals (ASPCA) at www.aspca. org for more information on preparing for and coping with emergency situations.

CHAPTER 9

DACHSHUND TRAINING

Want to know a great way to help your Dachshund be happy? Train him. Really.

If you were to perform a Google search on the phrase "a trained dog is a happy dog," you'd come up with tens of thousands of hits. Clearly this phrase is pervasive in the world of dogs—and for a very good reason: It's true.

Now, the idea of a Dachshund being happier doing what humans want than what *he* wants to do might seem a little odd. How could a dog who does what's asked of him be happier than a dog who's never asked to do anything?

The answer to that question is that the Dachshund who's been schooled in basic good manners—if that schooling is done in a positive manner and takes advantage of his basic instincts—will probably enjoy far happier relationships with his people than the dog who doesn't receive such instruction. If your Dachshund comes when he's called, sits or lies down when asked, and remains in place when requested (to name just a few desirable behaviors), he'll be a dog whom people want to be with. He'll be a dog who can listen to, communicate with, and generally get along with people. He'll be far more welcome among human beings than his out-of-control

counterpart. The fact that humans enjoy his company means that he'll get to spend far more time with those humans than would be the case if he were socially clueless and cue-less. And because he, like all dogs, is a social being, the Dachshund who gets to spend a whole lot of time with people is a whole lot happier than one whose bad manners keep him from doing so.

Luckily, that Dachshund's people don't need to crack the whip or otherwise act like overbearing taskmasters to teach their dog what he needs to know to live happily in a human household. Training your dog in a positive, dog-friendly manner focuses on building a relationship, not on demanding obedience. Yes, you'll show your Dachshund what you want him to do and teach him how to respond appropriately. At the same time, though, you'll learn to listen to your dog, heed his signals, and work with him to obtain the results you want. The result is a win-win situation for both of you.

This chapter will show you how to create that win-win situation.

UNDERSTANDING INTERMEDIATE TRAINING

Both you and your Dachshund need to have mastered some training basics before you start be a factor during training. The fact of the matter is, you neither need to nor should try to physically coerce him into doing what you want him to do. The better course of action is to show him what you want him to do and reinforce him when he does what you ask. Bear in mind that we're talking about reinforcers that your dog really values—in other words, rewards that give him a big incentive to do what you're asking him to do.

For most Dachshunds, such incentives take the form of soft, tasty treats. Other reinforcers that can be effective include toys, like Nylabones, a quick play session, praise, and petting. No matter which reinforcer you choose, though, the bottom line is that you're looking to catch your dog doing something right—and when he does, you use that reinforcer to make sure that he knows without question that he's done the right thing. That way, he'll want to repeat the behavior.

Mark the Desired Behavior

Your Dachshund will know that he's done something right if you give him a clear, unmistakable signal immediately after he's done that something. Scientists and animal trainers have discovered that an extremely effective way to send that signal is by using a clicker: a small plastic box that has either a small button or metal strip on top. By pressing the button or metal strip, the device makes a clicking sound. Doing this immediately after your dog does what you've asked lets him know that he's done the right thing—and that a reinforcer such as a treat will follow very shortly. Chapter 4 contains an extensive discussion about how to use a clicker to maximum effect. However, if you choose not to use a clicker, selecting a word to mark the behavior—a great choice is an enthusiastic "Yes!"—can work too.

Training your dog in a positive, dog-friendly manner focuses on building a relationship, not on demanding obedience.

learning the moves in this chapter. For his part, your Dachshund should be able to respond to the cues listed in Chapter 4: paying attention when he hears his name, sitting and lying down when asked, coming when called, and walking politely with you when he's on leash.

For your part, you should:

Understand What Positive Training Means

Yes, you're a lot bigger than your Dachshund is, but that physical superiority shouldn't

Minimize Distractions

The best place to start teaching any new behavior to your Dachshund is in an environment that has no, or at least very few, distractions. That probably means holding initial lessons inside your house at a time when no other family members are around, the television's off, and there's nothing going on outside. Once your Dachshund masters the behavior in this quiet environment, you can start adding one distraction at a time while he perfects the behavior you're teaching him.

And we're not talking about just environmental distractions such as the dog in the yard next door or the squirrel scampering up a nearby tree. Sometimes a dog is his own worst distraction. For example, if your Dachshund has been alone for awhile, he'll probably be too busy greeting you and working off some pent-up energy to focus on learning new cues immediately after you return home. For that reason, postponing a training session until after he's calmed down and at least had a potty break (and you have a chance to catch your breath!) will help that session go better.

Train While He's Hungry

If you're using treats to train your Dachshund, conduct his lessons before mealtimes, when he's most likely to be hungry. His growling tummy will make him more eager to work so that he can score some of those treats.

Think Short and Sweet

Limit your training sessions to ten minutes each—or even less if his attention starts to wander before that—and always do your best to end any session with a behavior that your Dachshund already knows and does well. That way, the session will end with both of you feeling successful.

Want to Know More?

For a refresher course on basic training, revisit Chapter 4.

Phase Out Treats

News flash: You don't have to use treats forever to encourage your Dachshund to do what you ask. Once you're sure that he understands what you want him to do—in other words, he should perform the behavior the vast majority of the time that you ask him to do so—you can start cutting back on the treats you give to reward him for performing that behavior. Initially, give him a treat every other time, then cut back to every third or fourth time, and so on until you give him treats rarely. That said, don't eliminate treats completely. Giving him a goodie every now and then will keep him eager to work with you and to perform the behaviors that you're requesting.

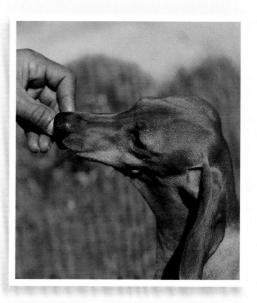

For most Dachshunds, incentives to follow cues take the form of soft, tasty treats.

INTERMEDIATE TRAINING CUES

Once your dog has mastered the basic cues in Chapter 4, he's ready to start learning some fancier moves.

Stay

The *stay* cue is a great multipurpose behavior to teach your Dachshund. Telling him to stay means that you're asking him to remain where he is. Once he understands this cue, you can apply it in many different ways. For example, when you feed your Dachshund his breakfast or dinner, you can first ask him to sit (as described in Chapter 4). Then before you place his bowl on the floor, you can ask him to stay and to remain in the *sit* until you release him. You'll never again have to deal with a dog who mows you down as he makes a beeline for his meal.

Another way in which the *stay* works well is if you have guests in your home. By having your Dachshund lie down at your feet and then stay in that position, he can be part of the festivities without making a pest of himself by bugging your guests.

As these examples show, the *stay* cue is often paired with either the *sit* or the *down*. That said, the cue works just as well if your Dachshund's standing up. For example, if your short-legged friend is standing next to you when you open your front door, telling him to stay can keep him from darting out that front door and into possible danger.

The *stay* maneuver is also important for your dog to learn if you plan to enter him in competitive obedience trials. These trials, as is explained in Chapter 11, test your dog's ability to perform increasingly complex behaviors in a competitive setting. To succeed at even a novice level, a dog must know how to stay when both sitting and lying down.

But don't expect your Dachshund to perform this cue under such challenging circumstances right away. As with any new behavior you teach, you need to begin in a low-distraction environment. He should also know how to perform a *sit* and *down* on cue; to teach both of those cues, check out Chapter 4.

How to Teach It

To teach the *stay*, proceed as follows:

1. Have a clicker in your hand and treats nearby. Then ask your dog to sit or lie down.
2. Tell your dog to stay, but elongate the single syllable so that you're actually saying "Staaaaaaay."
3. At the same time you say the cue, open the hand without the clicker. Place that hand at your dog's nose level, about 6 inches (15 cm) away from his nose.
4. Pull back your hand and take one step backward. Immediately afterward, return to your original position.
5. Click, say a word such as "Okay" or Free" to release him from the *stay*, and give your dog a treat. Make sure that you also praise him enthusiastically for having remained in place.
6. Repeat the previous five steps—but move back two steps this time.
7. Repeat the process, but with each repetition gradually increase the distance you

Want to Know More?

Some cues can help prevent problem behaviors in your dog, such as guarding food or toys or running off with unauthorized objects. To learn more about these very important cues and to teach them to your Dachshund, check out Chapter 4.

move away from your Dachshund, the distractions in his environment, and/or the length of time he must remain in place. When you can stand at the opposite end of the room or you're outdoors and your Dachshund can hold his *stay* for three minutes—or if he can hold the *stay* in the midst of regular household activity—you can start weaning him off the treats.

Stand

You may wonder why anyone needs to teach a dog to stand on cue. After all, your Dachshund already knows how to stand, and he spends quite a bit of time doing so. That being the case, why does he need to stand when you ask him to?

An answer to that question may become apparent when you bring your adult Dachshund to the walk-on scale at your vet's. If that scale is positioned against a wall, your dog will almost certainly feel that he must also position himself against the wall, which will result in a highly distorted reading on the scale. However, if your Dachshund knows how to stand on cue, you can use that cue to position him on the scale so that he's not leaning into the wall.

Another time to use this cue is if you want your Dachshund to pose for a picture. Moreover, knowing how to stand on cue can give your dog a head start if you're planning to show him in conformation. The reason: Every show dog must know how to strike a special standing pose called the stack.

How to Teach It

To teach your dog to stand on cue, do the following:

1. Ask your dog to sit.
2. Hold a treat about 6 inches (15 cm) from his face. Make sure that the treat is at nose level.
3. Give the cue word "Stand." At the same time, keep the treat at nose level but move

When teaching new cues, remember to begin in a low-distraction environment.

it away from your Dachshund's face. He will stand to follow the treat that you're moving away from him.

4. The minute he's on all fours, click (or use a marker word such as "Yes!") and give him the treat.
5. Repeat the previous five steps until your dog performs the *stand* reliably and consistently. When he does, start phasing out the treats. However, in a real-life situation, such as when your dog's being photographed or being weighed on the vet's scale, be prepared to use treats to lure him into position. The treats will help your

dog ignore the distractions posed by the photographer and her equipment or being at the vet's.

Place

This cue can make life easier for both you and your Dachshund—not to mention, at times, a whole lot safer. That's because any time you don't want him to be underfoot, you can simply say "Place" or another cue word, and your four-legged friend will take himself to a designated area where he'll stay until you release him.

Moreover, quite a few dogs learn of this cue in one form or another, even though their people haven't tried to teach it to them. I know of one dog whose people would say "Nighty-night" whenever they put their puppy into her crate. That puppy is now a senior citizen—but she still trots off to her crate whenever a human member of her household tells her "Nighty-night."

What if your Dachshund hasn't learned such a cue on his own? Not to worry—any dog of any age can learn it. Make sure, though, that he knows down and stay first.

How to Teach It

Here's what to do:

1. Put your dog on leash.
2. Say the word you've chosen for this behavior ("place," "bedtime," and "naptime" are all great choices). At the same time, lead your dog to the place you want him to retire to, such as his bed, his crate, or a cushion located somewhere else in the room.
3. When you reach the place, click (or say "Yes!") and treat.
4. Repeat the first three steps until your dog starts to head for his place on his own when you give the cue. At that point, take him to the place, then return to your starting point. Give the cue again; if he responds, click and treat. If not, repeat the first three steps.
5. When your dog consistently responds correctly to the cue, ask him to lie down in his place. Have him remain in that position for 15 seconds. Then click, treat, and give him a *release* cue such as "Okay."
6. Repeat, gradually increasing the time your dog remains in place to three minutes.
7. Don't push too far, too fast, or for too long. Limit your sessions teaching this or any other cue to ten minutes at a time, and end each session on a positive note. That means that for the last cue of a training session, ask him to perform a cue that he does consistently and well—and make sure that you click, treat, and praise when he does.

Touch

How would you like to be able to direct your

Dachshund to wherever you wanted him to go, just by holding your hand or an object at the place you have in mind? If you teach your Dachsie the *touch* cue, that's exactly what you'll be able to do. This cue consists of you asking your dog to touch his nose to your hand or to an object. Depending on where you place your hand or the object, he'll be there to do the touching and be exactly where you want him to be.

If you and your Dachshund plan to compete in dog sports such as competitive obedience or agility, the *touch* cue is a huge help. That's because many canine activities require your dog to put himself in exact places during exercises or on obstacles. The agility competitor who jumps off a teeter-totter before he reaches the bottom of the downward ramp won't do very well in competition; by using the touch cue, the owner can teach the dog exactly where he needs to be.

Even if your dog doesn't compete in sports, he may find performing the *touch* cue to be a lot of fun. When he's learned this cue, you can move your hand or an object between your legs, off to your right, off to your left, or almost anywhere else. Your dog will enjoy responding to these placement variations.

How to Teach It

Here's how to teach the touch cue to your Dachshund, no matter why you might want to apply it:

1. Rub a treat onto a long-handled utensil such as the bowl portion of a wooden spoon. The utensil will be easier than a hand for your Dachshund to reach.
2. Hold the utensil by the end of the handle in front of your dog's nose and no more than 1 foot (0.5m) away. Then say the cue word "touch."
3. Your dog will lean in toward the utensil to sniff the scent of the treat. When he does,

click and give him a real goodie.
4. Repeat, keeping the utensil in the same position each time. Once he responds consistently, try varying the position of the utensil—move it from side to side, and vary the height a little. However, don't lift the utensil so high that your Dachshund needs to jump or get up on his hind legs. Either effort could strain his long back and cause injury.

Dead

The *dead* cue is very helpful if you're attempting to groom your Dachshund and don't have access to a grooming table. You can simply sit down on the floor, have your dog perform a *down*, and then tell him "Dead." He should respond by rolling onto his side, ready to be brushed and otherwise pampered. In fact, if you pair this cue with grooming often enough, your Dachshund may assume this position as soon as he sees you pick up his brush!

How to Teach It

Teach your dog this cue as follows:

1. Ask him to lie down.
2. Hold a treat a couple of inches (cm) away from his nose—just close enough that he

Multi-Dog Tip

When your Dachshund has mastered a cue in an environment with few distractions, start practicing the behavior in the presence of your other dogs. The proximity of the other dogs will be a good training distraction for your Dachshund, and his canine siblings might decide to join in the lesson!

A well-mannered dog is a joy to be around.

can't grab the treat from you.

3. Move the hand with the treat away from your dog's nose at a two o'clock angle (if his left-paw side is facing away from you) or at a ten o'clock angle (if his right-paw side is facing away from you) and toward the floor.

4. As your hand reaches the floor, your dog should lie down on his side. When he does, click and treat.

5. Repeat until he is consistently lying on his side to follow the treat. Once he does, add the cue word, "dead," as you begin to move your hand.

This cue can also make a wonderful party trick. Once your Dachshund learns it, you can pose all kinds of provocative questions to your friends that he will be happy to answer. For example, if you're a fan of the Boston Red Sox, you can ask, "Max, would you rather the Yankees win this game or be dead?" and Max will flop over accordingly.

Push-Ups

Yes, your Dachshund can learn to perform doggy push-ups—and once he knows how, you'll be mighty glad you taught him how to do so. That's because doggy push-ups are great for siphoning off excess Dachshund energy in almost any situation. Is your dog barking up a storm at the leaf that's blowing in the wind just outside your window? No problem—just have him do five or ten push-ups and he'll mellow out enough to ignore any subsequent leaves—at least for a little while. Is he suffering from cabin fever from having been cooped up inside due to nasty weather? Help him regain his sanity by putting him through his push-up paces.

How to Teach It

Ideally, your dog will know how to sit on cue and how to lie down on cue before you teach the push-up. At the very least, you should be able to lure him into those positions with treats. Then do the following:

1. Use the treat to lure your dog into a sitting position.
2. Once he's sitting, use the treat to lure him into a *down* position.
3. As soon as he's down, lure him back into a sitting position. Click and treat.
4. Repeat this sequence as quickly as possible five to ten times.

At the end of your push-up session, your Dachshund should be panting at least a little—and feeling a lot mellower than he was before the session began.

Asking to Go Out

Almost all housetrained Dachshunds (and other dogs) do make an effort to tell their people when they need to potty. Some might take themselves to a door that leads to the backyard and gaze in that direction, perhaps hoping that those doors will magically open to allow them to take themselves to their bathrooms. Others lie down in front of those doors or scratch them. Still others stare at their people, hoping that they will decode the message they're trying to send. A desperate-to-go Dachshund may decide to give his people a verbal signal: a whine, a soft woof, or even an all-out, full-throated bark.

The wise human realizes that unless her Dachshund has a dog door that permits him to exit the house on his own, his access to this bathroom depends on his being able to tell his people that he needs that access. Then she shows him how he can get his message across.

How to Teach It

Here's what to do:

1. Get a set of sleigh bells or wind chimes and hang them from a doorknob so that they're with easy reach of your Dachshund's paw or nose. Both the chimes or bells will make a pleasant noise that can be heard throughout your house. Make sure that the chimes aren't sharp and that they're long enough to hang close to the floor, where your short-legged Dachshund can reach them easily.
2. Every time you take your dog for a potty break, ring the bells.
3. Watch your Dachshund to see when he shows an interest in the bells. When he does—even if he does nothing more than take a quick sniff—praise him, give him a treat, and take him to his outdoor bathroom. Do this every time he examines the bells, and he'll soon begin associate checking out the bells with being taken outside to do his business.

Eventually, your clever Dachshund will go beyond examining the bells to actually trying to manipulate them by tapping them with his paws or nose. When he does, take him out to his potty spot and give him a few extra treats.

Training Tidbit

The Dachshund's unique appearance presents an almost overwhelming temptation to his people: to teach him to sit up. But no matter how cute you think your dog would look sitting on his haunches and waving his stubby little front paws at you, resist that temptation. The reason? The Dachshund who's sitting up puts undue and unnecessary strain on his long back. Because Dachshunds are especially vulnerable to having back problems such as intervertebral disc disease (IDD), which is discussed in Chapter 8, any maneuvers that weaken or otherwise strain the back and spine should be avoided.

CHAPTER 10

DACHSHUND PROBLEM BEHAVIORS

There's no doubt about it: Dachshunds are terrific dogs, but terrific is not synonymous with perfect. In fact, no breed (nope, not even the Dachshund) is perfect, and every dog, no matter what his breed, has issues of one form or another. Some of these issues result from breed tendencies, others are unique to an individual dog's temperament or even physical condition, and still others result from human mistakes. But no matter what's causing an individual dog's problem behaviors, most of those problems can be managed and many can be totally resolved.

Even better is the fact that a Dachshund's owner doesn't have to try solving her dog's problem behaviors all by herself. Instead, she can get help from experts who have the knowledge and experience needed to solve almost any problem behavior that mars the relationship between a Dachshund and his human. Those specialists include:

Your veterinarian. Generally your veterinarian is the first expert you should consult when you need help to solve your Dachshund's problem behavior. The reason: Many such problems are symptomatic of physical ailments. For example, apparently unprovoked aggression may result from physical pain, deafness, seizures, or even a thyroid hormone reading that's on the low side of normal. Any good veterinarian understands that body and behavior are often interconnected, but if your veterinarian is a member of the American Veterinary Society of Animal Behavior (AVSAB), so much the better. This group's membership includes veterinarians and other scientists interested in understanding animal actions, and its website (www.avsabonline.org) includes a membership directory.

A good trainer. If a veterinary exam turns up no physical problems in your misbehaving Dachshund, your next step should be to consult a dog trainer who uses positive, dog-friendly methods when working with dogs. Many trainers not only conduct group classes but also offer one-on-one consultations to help owners with problem pooches. To find such a trainer, check out Chapter 4 of this book.

A behavioral consultant. The International Association of Animal Behavior Consultants (IAABC) is an organization made up of experts who perform one-on-one consultations for owners of dogs, cats, and other animals. The group's website, www.iaabc.org, has a

Some dogs aren't all that thrilled to be around other dogs and may express their discomfort by snapping, barking, lunging, or engaging in other similar behaviors.

searchable database where you can find either a Certified Animal Behavior Consultant (CABC) or a Certified Dog Behavior Consultant (CDBC) to help you solve your Dachshund's problem.

An applied animal behaviorist. An applied animal behaviorist is highly qualified to diagnose and treat complicated problem behaviors. However, she isn't allowed to prescribe any medications as part of a treatment plan unless she's also a veterinarian. To be credentialed as either a Certified Applied Animal Behaviorist (CAAB) or Associate Certified Applied Animal Behaviorist (ACAAB), a behavior pro must have at least a master's degree in a behavioral science that relates to animal behavior. Many of these behaviorists have doctoral degrees. To find a certified applied animal behaviorist, ask your vet for a referral or log onto the website of the Animal Behavior Society (ABS), which is the group that credentials these behavior pros.

The URL is http://www.animalbehavior.org/ABSAppliedBehavior/caab-directory.

A veterinary behaviorist. A veterinary behaviorist can be especially helpful if your dog's serious or complicated problem behavior has a physical origin because she can prescribe medications if necessary. The American College of Veterinary Behaviorists (ACVB) awards the certification suffix Dip ACVB to a veterinarian who has completed both an internship and residency at one of only eight U.S. veterinary schools, has written three case reports that have been reviewed by one or more other veterinary behaviorists, and has earned a passing grade on a two-day examination. Your regular vet needs to refer you to a veterinary behaviorist, but you can identify one by logging onto http://dacvb.org.

AGGRESSION

Aggression is the term used to characterize canine threats or attacks in a wide range of contexts. That's because dogs behave aggressively for many reasons—and often what looks like an offensive action may actually (at least from the dog's point of view) be a defensive reaction.

Like any other breed, Dachshunds are capable of behaving aggressively. The wise human being respects this capability and behaves accordingly. That doesn't make the dog's aggression okay, but solving an aggression problem requires that you and any behavioral professional you consult understand the environment in which the aggression occurs and the circumstances that trigger the behavior.

Here are some common circumstances in which aggressive actions or reactions occur among dogs:

Aggression around food or toys: Some dogs are so covetous of their toys, treats, or food that they will growl, snap at the air, or even attack individuals whom the affected dogs feel might be trying to remove those items. Behavioral professionals call this kind of behavior "resource guarding." Among dogs in the wild, resource guarding is a necessary survival strategy, but that's not the case for domestic dogs. In fact, a domestic dog's resource guarding can become dangerous not only to the dog but also to his people if carried to an extreme.

Aggression around other dogs: Dogs don't necessarily or always enjoy being around others of their kind, particularly as they age. A dog-averse canine may show his unease by barking, snapping, lunging, or engaging in other less-than-courteous behavior, especially if they think that the other dog has been less than courteous to them.

Aggression when touched: Some dogs don't like being touched, and many don't appreciate tactile contact if the body part being touched is painful or if the dog remembers a time when that was the case. A classic example is the dog who doesn't like having his feet touched if he's experienced a painful nail trim in the past.

Aggression around people: A dog may react in an aggressive fashion to certain people with whom he is unfamiliar or has had a negative experience. A shelter dog who experienced mistreatment by a woman may be unwilling to allow women in his new home to approach him, even if those women are kind to him. Other dogs might become unpredictably aggressive, even if they were fine earlier in life.

No matter what triggers a Dachshund's aggressive behavior, dealing with such behavior ultimately requires an expert's help. That said, an owner can take steps to create an atmosphere that's safer for the Dachshund, the household, and herself as treatment begins and progresses. Here are the steps you should take:

Call Your Vet

A Dachshund's aggression—especially if it has developed suddenly or is unpredictable—may have a physical cause. Among those physical triggers are pain, head trauma, infections, food allergies, toxin exposure, and hormone imbalances.

Avoid Aggression Triggers

Try to figure out what prompts your Dachshund to behave aggressively so that you can avoid those triggers in

Some dogs become very possessive of their food, treats, or toys.

To combat anxiety, try giving your Dachshund regular exercise and see whether it helps him become mellower.

the future. For example, if he's possessive about food and toys, don't try to take either away from him. And if he's not so keen about being around other dogs, bypass the local dog park and avoid contact with other dogs while you're taking him for a walk. For the sake of your safety—as well as that of your dog—do as much as you can to avoid putting your Dachshund into a situation in which an aggressive response might occur.

Supervise Children

Some experts believe that Dachshunds are especially intolerant of children who they feel have mistreated them, even if the child didn't mean to. If your Dachshund has had an unfortunate encounter with a child, protect him from such encounters in the future. Don't let him interact with kids without your direct and constant supervision, and emphasize to your own children the importance of not doing anything that could cause the dog to react in an aggressive manner.

Book a Consult

If your vet rules out physical causes of your dog's aggression, it's time to schedule a one-on-one behavioral consultation with a positive reinforcement dog trainer, an applied animal behaviorist, or a veterinary behaviorist. The behavioral pro you consult will assess your dog, and if possible, work with you to develop a training plan that will modify your dog's behavior. If your Dachshund behaves aggressively, don't take the matter lightly and don't delay getting treatment. The sooner you get help for him, the better your chances are of solving this very serious problem.

ANXIETY

If you acquired your Dachshund as a puppy from a reputable breeder and socialized him as described in Chapter 4, he's not likely to develop any deep-seated anxiety. That's because a truly well-socialized Dachshund can negotiate novel situations with aplomb and shake off most setbacks without any long-term damage. However, even a socialized, confident Dachshund may develop fear following a traumatic incident. For example, a dog who was attacked by other dogs may be skittish about being among his own kind after such a distressing event.

If your Dachshund is an adult whom you adopted from a shelter or rescue group, you obviously didn't have the opportunity to socialize him during those optimum first 12 to 14 weeks of his life. Such a dog may have one or more fear issues such as separation anxiety and/or thunderstorm anxiety. Such anxiety manifests itself in many ways: Some dogs become destructive, some drool, some pant excessively, and some bark frantically. Many fearful dogs tremble when confronted with the object of their fear and try to get as far away from that trigger as possible.

Fortunately, there's plenty you can do to help your Dachshund overcome his fears. Here are some ideas.

Build his confidence: Try to rebuild your Dachshund's overall self-confidence before you attempt to tackle his anxiety issues. Good ways to do that include teaching him new cues, playing with him consistently, and introducing him to new experiences that don't trigger reminders of whatever caused his anxiety.

Wear him out: Not only is a tired dog a good dog, but a tired dog may also be a less fearful dog. By giving your Dachsie some exercise that wears him out, he may actually be too tired to be apprehensive or frightened.

No sink or swim: Forcing your Dachshund to confront whatever is frightening him is exactly the wrong way to him overcome his fear. In other words, don't force him to ride in the car if auto jaunts scare him, and don't insist that he hang out with strange children if they give him the willies. All you'll do is increase his fear.

Car Anxiety

Although most Dachshunds adore taking car rides with their people, a few are less than enamored with this mode of transport. If your Dachshund fits the latter description, try the following tactics to turn him into a lover of auto travel:

Take a Breather

If your Dachshund's fear of the car is due to a traumatic event, such as his involvement in an auto accident, applying the old adage of getting right back on the bike or horse after you fall off may be counterproductive. Instead, wait a few weeks before you start subjecting him to car rehab.

Desensitize Him

After you take that time-out, start refamiliarizing your dog with the car—but begin very slowly and gradually in sessions

Want to Know More?

This chapter differentiates among behavior professionals and explains how to find them; Chapter 4 contains additional information on how to find a trainer.

A Dachshund who shows signs of anxiety when his owner is about to leave the house may suffer from separation anxiety.

that last no longer than five minutes each. Start by standing with your dog a few feet (m) away from the car and click and treat him for calm behavior. Next time, stand a little closer, again clicking and treating for calm behavior. Gradually decrease the distance between you and the car until you're both able to stand beside your car while he remains calm.

Now open the car door and place a treat on the door ledge. Praise him when he picks up the treat. At each subsequent session, move the treat farther and farther into the inside of the car until he's jumping into the car on his own.

Once your dog remains in the car calmly, go to the driver's seat and start the motor. Run the motor for a few seconds, then click and treat and end the session. Once your dog remains consistently calm with the motor running, move your car back and forth in the driveway, click and treat—and then again end the session. If he remains calm, go for the next step: driving the car around the block. Continue with this sequence until you are able to drive again with your dog seated calmly (and safely—make sure that he has a seat belt on or is otherwise secure) in the back seat.

If at any time during this process your dog hesitates or balks, heed his message: You're going too fast and he's not comfortable. Go back to your previous step, and make sure that he's calm and confident before attempting to progress.

Change the Association
The desensitization procedure outlined above involves the use of treats—but not just any treats will do here. The treats you employ need to be goodies that your dog drools over; in other words, they need to be so wonderful that they will override his negative association with the car. And if your dog's not big into treats, find something he does go crazy over, such as a favorite toy. In other words, figure out what really excites your Dachshund, and use that item to help him overcome his automotive antipathy.

Separation Anxiety
A Dachshund who shows signs of anxiety when his owner is about to leave the house and who barks and trashes that house within the first 30 minutes of his owner's departure may suffer from separation anxiety. Dogs who have had traumatic separations from owners, such as being surrendered to a shelter, may be at greater risk for developing this challenging problem behavior.

Some dogs are so upset over being separated from their people that they need medication before they can be helped. Such dogs need to see their veterinarians, who can prescribe medications specifically formulated to treat canine separation anxiety. However, their owners must realize that these meds are just a short-term measure. To truly solve this problem, they need to teach their dogs that being alone need not be traumatic.

If your Dachshund fits this description, you need to exercise patience and understanding. Time and consistent effort can diminish the problem considerably, but don't count on an easy or quick resolution. Here are some ideas on how to relieve separation anxiety:

Change Your Dog's Perceptions

Give your dog a special toy for when he spends time alone: a food puzzle such as a food-stuffed Nylabone (particularly when frozen ahead of time) is ideal. A special home-alone toy helps your dog in two ways: 1) The toy can change his perception of your leaving from something negative to something positive, and 2) the toy will keep him so busy that he'll forget to miss you.

Enrich His Environment

Try giving your dog some stimuli to help him forget that he's unhappy when left alone. For example, put him in a room with a window to your backyard so that he can watch birds and other wildlife there. Other options include turning a television on low, playing some music, or playing a recording of familiar household sounds.

Set a Calm, Independent Example

Keep your goodbyes and hellos low key and matter of fact. By keeping your cool, you'll help your Dachshund keep his.

Reward Calm, Independent Behavior

When you come home, greet your dog only when

he's calm. And when you are home, teach him that he'll be okay when you're not around. Try having him hold *sit* and *stay* cues for a minute or two, then leave the room. Gradually build up to five minutes. Another option: Give him his favorite chew toy or food-stuffed toy. Wait until he's fully engaged with it and then leave the room.

Thunderstorm Anxiety

Even the calmest Dachshund may feel unsettled by the rumblings and flashes that are part and parcel of thunderstorms. He may show that disquiet by panting excessively, whining, trembling, trying to hide under a bed or desk, or even being destructive in the house. To help your Dachshund weather the storm, try the following ideas:

Give Some Goodies
Find some treats that your Dachshund absolutely adores, and feed them to him during the storm. If he's willing to eat them, try stuffing them into an interactive toy, freezing it, and giving it to him the next time the rumbles start. The treats themselves may help him associate thunderstorms with getting treats, while the challenge of ferreting treats from the interactive toy might keep him so busy that he'll forget to be afraid during Mother Nature's sound and light show.

Try Some Pheromones
For many dogs, a spray or diffuser that contains dog-appeasing pheromone (DAP), which is similar to the pheromone released by nursing mother dogs, can help allay thunderstorm anxiety. These products are manufactured by Central Life Sciences; for more info, log onto www.petcomfortzone.com.

Wrap Him Up
For some dogs, a special garment called the Thundershirt (www.thundershirt.com/AboutUs.aspx) can ease thunderstorm stress, not to mention other forms of anxiety. Similarly, the Anxiety Wrap (www.anxietywrap.com) may also do the trick. A snug-

fitting T-shirt designed for wear by people could have a similar effect. No matter which remedy you choose, however, make sure that you acclimate your dog to the garment before you try to use it during a thunderstorm.

Stroke With a Dryer Sheet
Some experts believe that it's not the thunder and lightning that spook some dogs but the buildup of static electricity that goes along with thunderstorms. These experts suggest rubbing the dog with an unscented dryer sheet to reduce such static whenever thunderstorms appear in your local weather forecast.

See Your Vet
Some Dachshunds become so upset and panicky during thunderstorms that they need pharmaceutical help to get through them. If you've tried the previous suggestions but your dog still freaks out when he hears thunder, your veterinarian may be able to prescribe anti-anxiety medications to ease your Dachshund's fears.

BARKING
Alas, Dachshunds are known for being a little barky. But in addition to this breed-specific predilection, there are other reasons why your particular four-legged friend may be given to excessive vocalization and multiple ways in which to handle them.

Alleviate His Boredom
A Dachshund who's left out in the backyard alone for an extended period will probably get bored—and when that happens, he'll probably try to relieve that boredom by engaging in some extended barking. To solve this

To combat thunderphobia, find some treats that your Dachshund absolutely adores and feed them to him during the storm.

To alleviate excessive barking, don't leave your Dachshund out in the backyard alone for extended periods.

problem, just relieve his boredom. Play with him while he's outside, and teach him basic good manners (as described in Chapters 4 and 9) when he's with you in your house.

Relieve His Loneliness

Does your Dachshund make less-than-joyful noises during the night? Does he sleep all by himself in the laundry room or kitchen? Chances are, he's lonely. Try inviting him to spend the night with you in your bedroom. He's likely to be quieter, which means that you'll both get a better night's sleep. For daytime barking, check out the section "Anxiety" in this chapter.

Exercise Him

Even Dachshunds need a decent amount of exercise to keep their sanity. If your dog doesn't get exercise opportunities from you, he may well try to create such opportunities on his own. One way he may do that is to start barking at human passersby, a chipmunk who dares to cross your property, a falling leaf, or just about anything or anyone else you can imagine. If this behavior describes your Dachshund's vocalizations, give him more opportunities to move those little legs of his. Unlike larger sporting dogs like Labrador Retrievers or herding dogs like Border Collies, the Dachshund doesn't need to run like the wind for an hour a day to stay happy. In fact, a meandering walk for you will be a brisk walk for your Dachshund. At the end of that brisk walk, he should be panting—not to mention too tired to bark.

Short-Term Solutions

The previously mentioned strategies are long-term solutions, but what can you do about your barking Dachsie right now?

Teach an Alternate Cue

Begin by asking him to do something that's incompatible with barking, like having him lie down. If he complies, be sure to give him a tasty treat.

Teach *Quiet*

Another strategy is to teach him a *quiet* cue. Catch him barking—but as soon as he stops,

The Dachshund doesn't need to run like the wind for an hour a day to stay happy. In fact, a meandering walk for you will be a brisk walk for your Dachshund.

say "Quiet" and give him a treat. Repeat this sequence whenever possible, and soon he'll learn to associate not barking, or barking once and then quieting, with getting something tasty to eat.

What Not to Do

Stopping excessive barking also requires that you know what not to do. Those don'ts include:

Shout

Yelling at your barking Dachshund to be quiet will have the opposite effect. He'll think that you're barking too—and will respond by barking even more.

Use a Shock Collar

A collar that provides a mild electrical shock may stop your dog's barking temporarily, but it won't address the root cause of his particular barking issue. If you're using one, stop—and try to figure out another, more humane way to solve your dog's barking problem.

CHEWING AND DESTRUCTIVENESS

Like any other dog, the Dachshund is capable of considerable household destruction. One of the Dachshunds to whom this book is dedicated actually peeled wallpaper off a wall when she was a puppy. Other Dachshunds are less creative but commit just as much damage. These dogs' chewing, digging, and other demolition-dog tendencies can make life miserable for all concerned.

A Dachshund's chewing and destructiveness have many possible causes. Some go on destructive rampages because they panic when they're left alone. Others become chewing machines because they are bored, while others are teething puppies who bite on nearby objects to relieve discomfort in their gums. Still others engage in doggy vandalism because that's the only sure way they know to get attention from their otherwise neglectful people. To end your Dachshund's chewing and destructiveness, take the following steps:

Find Out Why

Your chances of ending your Dachshund's destructo dog rampages depend in large part on finding out what's causing those rampages in the first place. Ask yourself questions and study your Dachshund's behavior to try to determine what's triggering his indoor vandalism.

Don't Reprimand—Especially After the Fact

If you come home to find your place looking like a rock band's hotel room, don't scold your Dachshund. He'll have absolutely no idea why you're angry. He won't connect your unhappiness with the mess he's made. Even if he's sporting a hang-dog look when you walk into the room he's trashed, be assured that he's not feeling guilty. Instead, he's anticipating your being angry—for reasons he can't fathom.

Wear Him Out

Experienced trainers often tell their human clients that "A tired dog is a good dog"—and that's particularly true with respect to chewing and destructiveness. The Dachshund who gets a couple of brisk, energy-sapping half-hour walks each day (in addition to bathroom breaks, of course) is much less likely to demolish his owner's crib than one who's forced to live life as a couch potato.

Keep Him Busy

Every minute that your Dachshund is busy doing something interesting is a minute that

he can't spend destroying your home. Try stuffing a food-dispensing toy with food and treats, freezing it overnight, and giving it to your Dachshund before you leave the house or otherwise can't supervise him. The effort he makes to extract the treats will keep him from trashing your possessions—and after he finishes, his full tummy might prompt him to take a nap.

Remove Temptation

Study what exactly your Dachshund likes to chew or destroy, and try to limit his access to those items. Does he like to gnaw on shoes? Put those shoes into a closet and close the closet door. Does he like to run off with dirty socks? Stick those socks into the clothes hamper. You get the idea.

Consider Crating

If your Dachshund's trashing your house because he's bored and you need to leave the house for two or three hours, put him into his crate. However, do *not* crate him if you'll either be gone the entire day (crating a dog for eight hours or more is cruel) or if his destructiveness results from separation anxiety (because in such cases, crating will increase his panic.)

Try establishing a digging area to give your Dachshund space to practice one of his favorite activities.

Look for Teachable Moments

Keep a clicker and treats nearby, and watch to see whether he goes for something he shouldn't. If he does, tell him "Off!" (See Chapter 4.) As soon as he backs off, click and treat.

Pay Him Some Attention

If you're so busy that the only attention you pay your Dachshund is to get angry at him for destroying your stuff, he may decide that the only way to get some face time with you is to turn himself into a destructo dog. Give him—and yourself—some breaks. No matter how busy you are, taking a few minutes for a tug-of-war session, a quick game of fetch, or even just a mutual love fest will show him that there are other ways to gain attention from you besides getting into mischief.

DIGGING

Dachshunds, like all other dogs, love to dig. That's particularly true if a Dachshund is left all by himself in a backyard for hours on end. He'll engage in digging to relieve his boredom, and he couldn't care less about the painstaking landscaping that he ruins in the process.

Don't Let Him Get Lonely and Bored

If your Dachshund is digging because he's lonely and bored, take the time to give him plenty of physical exercise, to train him, and to just hang out with him. After all, didn't you get a Dachshund so that you could have some company?

Establish a Digging Area

If your Dachshund's digging isn't the result of social deprivation, your best strategy is to realize that he's a budding canine archaeologist and give him acceptable opportunities to practice his craft. Find an area of your yard that can withstand Dachshund excavations, and encourage your dog to dig there. Just get a few treats and toys, bury them in a few inches (cm) of soil, bring him to the area, and let him have at it. As he digs, praise him to smithereens. Change the buried items every couple of days.

Buy Him a Digging Area

Don't have anywhere in your yard that's suitable for digging? Buy your Dachsie a sandbox at your local toy store. Fill it with sand, bury some toys in the sand, and treat it the same way you'd treat an in-yard digging area.

JUMPING UP

Dachshund puppies are irresistible. That's why we love to pick them up: We adore lifting them into our arms, putting our faces to theirs, giving them kisses, and getting doggy kisses in return. The puppies appreciate this attention so much that they'll do just about anything to keep getting it. One of the things they do is jump.

Of course, a Dachshund can't jump very high. You don't have to worry about your short-legged friend being able to launch himself like a rocket up toward your face, as would be the case with a bigger dog who likes getting airborne. That said, a Jumping Jack Dachshund can certainly gain enough height to stain your trousers if his paws are muddy, rip your hosiery even if his nails are trimmed, and just be annoying even if his jumping doesn't do any damage. For those reasons, your dog's career as a one-pooch Dachshund Air Force needs to be a very short one—or better yet, not start in the first place.

No matter which strategy you employ, the key to ending a Dachshund's jumping is

consistency from both you and anyone he meets. Make sure that family members do not tolerate jumping and that they employ at least one of the steps outlined here to end the behavior. And if a household guest tells you she doesn't mind if your dog jumps on her, tell her that *you* mind and ask her not to interact with your dog until he has all four paws on the floor.

Here's how to deal with a jumpy Dachshund:

To deal with a jumpy Dachshund, don't give him any attention whatsoever; any kind of attention will actually encourage him to keep jumping up.

Walk Away

Yes, you read that correctly. Your Dachshund jumps up on you because he wants attention from you. By giving him that attention—even if that attention is to tell him not to jump—you reward his jumping and encourage him to do so again. Therefore, to discourage his airborne bids for attention, you need to withdraw that attention. The quickest way to do that is to turn around and walk away from him every single time he jumps. Do this consistently and eventually your Dachshund will learn that he'll get attention from you only when he keeps all four paws on the floor.

Divert Him

Another anti-jumping strategy is to have him do something that he can't do if he's jumping—like sitting. Assuming your Dachshund knows the *sit* cue (if he doesn't, check out Chapter 4), ask him to put his tush on the ground the next time he looks as though he's about to leap toward you. Praise and treat when he does so. Consistent repetition of this routine will soon prompt your Dachshund to sit instead of jump when he wants your attention.

Leash Up

If your Dachshund becomes a canine jumping bean when he greets people who enter your home, show him that greeting people while sitting is a more effective attention-getting strategy. Leash him up and tie the other end to a table leg or to a sturdy chair. Next pick up your clicker and a few treats and walk about 10 feet (3 m) away. Then turn and walk toward him; if he attempts to go airborne when you approach, turn and walk away. If he keeps all four on the floor, ask him to sit, then click and treat. Repeat until he sits when he sees you heading toward him.

LEASH PULLING

Dachshunds are little dogs, but they have big-dog attitudes and can be surprisingly strong. When they put their shoulders forward, they can pull their people along the sidewalk at a fast clip, especially if those people are human children. No human of any age should have to put up with a Dachshund-induced upper body workout. To break your short-legged friend's pulling habit, take one or more of the following steps:

Put Away the Retractable Leash

A retractable leash actually encourages your Dachshund to pull—and if he pulls hard enough or suddenly, he could yank the leash's inflexible handle right out of your hand. Moreover, retractable leashes are hard to see and can easily trip up pedestrians. Finally, using a retractable can make you a lawbreaker because many municipalities ban leashes that exceed 6 feet (2 m) in length. Instead of using a retractable leash, switch to a standard 6-foot (2-m) leash of leather, cotton, or nylon. Leather is relatively expensive but is easier on the hands and lasts longer than cotton or nylon.

Put Him in a Harness

Front-clip harnesses can go a long way toward teaching your Dachshund good on-leash walking manners. The harness exerts pressure on a dog's sides when he pulls, much as a horse feels pressure on his sides from a rider's

Multi-Dog Tip

Spay and neuter all of the dogs in your household to help prevent dog-to-dog aggression and conflicts.

legs. This pressure encourages either animal to slow down.

Bypass Bad Equipment

Just say no to coercive, discomfort-causing equipment such as choke collars, also known as slip collars or training collars, and prong collars. Both types of collars cause discomfort and even pain to dogs without being all that effective at curbing pulling. Head halters, also known as head collars, are more humane, but many dogs don't like them and will work to get them off their faces.

Show Him What You Want

Chapter 4 contains detailed instructions on how to teach your Dachshund to walk politely on leash and what to do if he acts up.

Be Patient

Refraining from leash pulling may be challenging for your determined little Dachshund. Plan to continue to remind him for most of his life that he'll get where he wants to go much faster by matching his pace to yours than if he acts as though he's in training for the Iditarod.

NIPPING

Like all other dogs, Dachshunds are oral creatures, especially during puppyhood. They use their mouths and teeth to explore the world around them through taste and touch. However, when their oral fixations come into contact with tender human skin, the results can be painful to the human.

Teach the *Off* and *Take It* Cues

To alleviate that pain, not to mention preventing its occurrence in the first place, teach your Dachshund the *off* and *take it* cues described in Chapter 4. Although these two

A harness can go a long way toward teaching your Dachshund good on-leash walking.

cues are intended to show your puppy not to pick up an off-limits object, they're also a great way to teach him that human skin is one of those items that he shouldn't be putting his teeth to. Proceed as follows:

1. Sit on the floor and face your Dachshund.
2. Place a treat in the palm of your hand.
3. Show him your palm and the treat.
4. When your dog moves toward the treat, shut your hand in a fist, say "Off," and keep your fist closed.
5. Repeat the word "off" each times he noses your hand.
6. After your dog noses your hand four or five times, open your fist so that he can see the treat and tell him to "take it.""

It's important to practice these two cues regularly, even if you think your puppy has them down pat. When you feel sure that he's mastered these cues, tell him "Off" if his teeth touch your skin. When he backs away, offer him a treat and tell him "Take it."

CHAPTER 11

DACHSHUND SPORTS AND ACTIVITIES

I get it: You love just chilling with your Dachshund. Having him curled at your feet while you're messing around on Facebook or stretched across your lap while you're watching your latest Netflix makes those already pleasurable activities that much nicer. But Dachshunds are much more than mere companions for quiet human activities; they like being involved in their own activities too. This chapter outlines some more active endeavors that you and your Dachshund can engage in together.

ACTIVITIES

Lots of organized dog sports—not to mention titles that recognize accomplishment in such sports—are available to you and your Dachshund. But of course, nothing requires the two of you to participate in any of them. You can have just as much fun simply engaging in everyday activities together. Here are some ideas for spending some low-key, high-quality time with your Dachshund.

Camping

Sharing time in the woods with your Dachshund can be a great experience because his keen interest in all that goes on around him can reignite your own appreciation of nature. However, plenty of prep is needed to make that great experience happen. As you and your Dachshund prepare to head into the wild, consider keeping the following suggestions in mind:

Confirm That Dogs Are Welcome

Although many private campgrounds welcome canine campers, campgrounds at state and national parks may not. Call ahead to make sure that dogs are permitted at the campground you're planning to visit.

Bring the Right Gear

Your dog's camping gear should include a supply of food to last the entire trip, plenty of water from home (don't let him drink from lakes or ponds, many of which contain harmful bacteria), bowls for food and water, a collar and leash, and a first-aid kit. Consider also bringing a brush so that you can keep your dog's coat untangled and remove any burs and dirt he might pick up during the trip.

Check IDs

Make sure that your dog's identification tags and microchip data are up to date—and don't

Camping with your Dachshund may be the perfect activity for the two of you.

remove his collar at all during the trip. That way you stand a better chance of finding him quickly if he gets lost.

Keep Your Dog Under Control
Even if you and your Dachshund are camping at a dog-friendly campground, other campers won't be happy if he barks and runs around a lot. Keep him on his leash, and keep him entertained so that he doesn't have to engage in barking to entertain himself.

Keep Your Dog With You
Bring your Dachshund into your tent every night—and never, ever leave him unattended at your campground. Taking these simple steps will limit his chances of getting lost, running away, or otherwise getting into trouble.

Clean Up
Pick up your dog's poop, and dispose of any leftover human or dog food that could attract wildlife or insects.

Check Your Dog Over
Check your dog for ticks, cuts, and bruises at least once a day while you're camping.

Walking
One of the joys of having a Dachshund is that a leisurely walk for you can be a brisk walk for him. In other words, you don't need to give yourself much of a workout to give him one. For that reason alone, it's a good idea to consider expanding your Dachshund's walks beyond mere potty breaks and take a real stroll with him at least once a day. Here are some ways to make those strolls fun for both of you:

Potty First

If you want your Dachshund to get some aerobic benefits out of your stroll, make sure that he potties before you get going. That way he'll be less likely to screech to a halt to anoint the street sign pole just as you and he are getting into a good walking groove.

Leave Distractions Behind

Give your stroll and your Dachshund your full attention. This isn't the time to be gabbing on your cell phone, chugging your morning cup of coffee, or listening to the tracks you just downloaded to your iPod. Such diversions not only cause you to miss some companionable time with your Dachshund but also render you less able to respond to unexpected events, such as encountering another dog. Picking up your dog's poop could also be challenging if you're juggling a drink, a phone, and/or an audio device.

Check the Temperature

Weather extremes require walking adjustments. If you don't enjoy walking in very cold or very warm temperatures, your Dachshund won't either. When the mercury either dips low or shoots high, don't exercise him excessively. By doing so, you'll avoid causing him not only discomfort but also more serious problems

Consider expanding your Dachshund's walks beyond mere potty breaks and take a real stroll with him at least once a day.

such as heat exhaustion and frostbite. And if the temperature isn't excessively cold but nevertheless chilly enough to require you to wear a winter coat, do your Smooth or Wirehaired Dachshund a favor and put him in a doggy sweater.

Attend to Surfaces

Avoid walking your Dachshund on asphalt during warm weather; the surface temperature of the asphalt can burn his tender paw pads. And during the winter, try not to walk him on salted or de-iced sidewalks, which can also injure those paw pads. If you can't avoid snow-treated surfaces, wipe his feet with a damp cloth when you return from your walk.

Want to Know More?

Taking a walk is no fun if an out-of-control Dachshund is at the other end of the leash. Check out Chapters 4 and 10 for pointers on how to teach your dog to walk nicely with you when he's on the leash and how to deal with a Dachshund who insists on channeling his inner sled dog.

CANINE GOOD CITIZEN® PROGRAM

Organized dog sports and activities generally involve tests that require your dog (and you as well at times) to perform in front of human evaluators. For many Dachshunds and their people, training for these tests and earning titles for passing them are enjoyable activities; for others, test-taking anxiety overrides any fun to be had from test-taking prep and post-test glory. If you're not sure which category you and your Dachshund fit into, consider training for the relatively easy stress-free test offered by the American Kennel Club (AKC): the Canine Good Citizen (CGC) program.

In 1989, the AKC launched an initiative designed to publicly reward dogs who show good manners in public. This initiative, the CGC program, also recognizes responsible behavior by dog owners. Training your Dachshund to pass the CGC lays an excellent foundation for further training in some of the dog sports discussed in this chapter. And by passing the CGC test, your dog may gain entrance into places where dogs aren't normally allowed, such as certain hotels. Finally, working to pass the CGC can strengthen the bond between you and your Dachshund.

You and your Dachshund need not take classes from a CGC Evaluator. In fact, you don't have to take any classes at all, although classes or other expert instruction can be very helpful. In any case, only an AKC CGC Evaluator—whom you can find by searching the AKC's evaluator database at www.akc.org/events/cgc/cgc_bystate.cfm—can administer the ten-component CGC test. Those components are:

1. **Accepting a friendly stranger.** Passing this component shows that your dog will permit a friendly stranger to approach and speak with his handler in an everyday situation.

Dachshunds are multitalented dogs who can excel in a wide variety of activities.

2. **Sitting politely for petting.** This component is designed to show that the dog will permit a friendly stranger to touch him when he's out in public with his handler.

3. **Accepting grooming, exhibiting good health.** By completing this component successfully, the dog shows that he welcomes being examined and groomed by a stranger, and the owner is being responsible in caring for the dog and safeguarding the health of the animal.

4. **Walking on a loose lead.** Successful completion of this component shows that the handler has control over the dog while the dog is on leash.

5. **Walking through a crowd.** This component is designed to demonstrate that the leashed dog is under control in public places and can move politely through pedestrian traffic.

6. **Sitting and lying down on cue and staying in place.** The purpose of this component is to show that the dog will respond correctly to his handler's cues to sit and lie down, and will stay in place until the handler releases him.

7. **Coming when called.** Successful completion of this component shows that the dog will go to the handler when called to do so.

8. **Reacting to another dog.** Passing this component demonstrates that the dog can behave politely around other dogs.

9. **Reacting to distractions.** This component is designed to show that the dog will remain calm and confident when faced with common distractions.

10. **Accepting supervised separation.** Successful completion of this component shows that the dog will maintain his training and good manners when his

By the Numbers

Don't perform strenuous sports such as agility with your Dachshund until he's a minimum of one year old. Engaging in such activities before that time can cause excessive stress to his developing bones and joints. Wait until he's passed his first birthday and then introduce those activities gradually.

handler leaves him with another person.

To learn more about the CGC program, log onto the AKC website at www.akc.org/events/cgc/.

SPORTS

This multitalented breed can excel in a wide variety of activities, from agility to conformation to competitive obedience. This section provides listings of sports and activities in which Dachshunds are especially talented and describes how to find out more about them.

Agility

Does your Dachshund like to race around the yard? If you're racing ahead of him, will he follow you no matter how much you twist and turn? If so, he could be a great candidate for agility, a very popular canine sport. The Dachshund Club of America (DCA) has a great web page on agility that also includes information on special considerations for Dachshunds at www.dachshund-dca.org/agility.html.

In agility, a human handler guides her dog through a timed obstacle course that includes tunnels, teeter-totters, hurdles, weave poles, A-frames, and balance beams. While almost any breed can learn this sport, you might find it difficult to teach your Dachshund agility moves on your own. Fortunately, plenty of professional dog trainers hold classes for agility beginners of all breeds.

For more information about canine agility, log onto these websites: the AKC (www.akc.org); the North American Dog Agility Council (www.nadac.com); and the United States Dog Agility Association (www.usdaa.com).

Conformation

Have you ever watched the National Dog Show, the AKC Eukanuba Dog Show, or the Westminster Kennel Club Dog Show on television? Then you've seen a conformation competition. These events aim to determine how closely dogs conform to the standards of their respective breeds. (See Chapter 1 for a description of the Dachshund breed standard.) The dogs who win ribbons are those whose bodies and temperaments adhere most closely to their breeds' standards.

In a multi-breed competition, the dog who wins Best in Show is the animal that judges have decided conforms most closely to the standard for his breed not only among dogs of his breed but also the other breed winners in his AKC group. (Dachshunds belong to the Hound Group.)

If you want to know whether your Dachshund has the makings of a successful show dog, ask a reputable breeder for her opinion. You can start by consulting your

In agility, a human handler guides the dog through a timed obstacle course that includes tunnels, teeter-totters, hurdles, weave poles, A-frames, and balance beams.

dog's breeder and/or checking the listings on the DCA's website. Either way, the breeder will examine your dog closely and will give you an expert opinion on whether he conforms enough to the breed standard to succeed in the show ring. If the breeder gives you a thumbs-up, go to a few shows without your dog so that you can see for yourself what happens at these events.

If you like what you see, take the next step: enrolling your Dachshund and yourself in a dog-handling class. You can find such classes at your local all-breed kennel club or local Dachshund club. To find such groups, check out the AKC's website at www.akc.org and the websites of regional and local Dachshund clubs. Meanwhile, start learning about the show world by subscribing to a show magazine. A good starter is the AKC Gazette; to subscribe, go to the website at www.akc.org/pubs/gazette.

Do take note of the fact that only intact (unneutered males, unspayed females) dogs are eligible to enter AKC conformation. The reason: One of the traditional purposes of dog shows is to exhibit good breeding stock—and of course, altered dogs can't breed. However, if your dog has been spayed or neutered, she or he can still compete in other AKC events.

Earthdog

Earthdog tests capitalize on your Dachshund's roots and instincts by measuring his ability to deal with an underground hunting situation.

The first such test is an instinct test called "Introduction to Quarry." After placing a caged rat (the quarry) in a dark underground den, evaluators test a dog's willingness to follow a scent to the entrance of the den; willingness to enter the den; and willingness to work the quarry by barking, digging, growling, lunging, biting at the protective bars or any other work

that the judge feels displays a desire to get to the quarry. After passing this initial test, you can challenge your Dachshund to progressively more challenging tasks to earn the Junior Earthdog, Senior Earthdog, Master Earthdog, and Endurance Earthdog titles.

More information on earthdog events is available from the AKC at www.akc.org/events/earthdog/index.cfm.

Field Trials

Many of today's Dachshunds are still able to perform the tasks for which they were bred many years ago. Some owners choose to tap into these instincts through participating in earthdog events, while others opt for competing in field trials.

In Dachshund field trials, braces of dogs (two Dachshunds are released together on the same rabbit scent) are given the opportunity to track rabbits by following a scent. These exercises are somewhat similar to the field trials conducted for another hound, the Beagle.

For more information about field trials for Dachshunds, consult the AKC at www.akc.org/events/field_trials/dachshunds.

Obedience

This activity measures a dog's ability to respond appropriately to cues ranging from coming when called to discriminating among objects. In an obedience trial, a judge scores a dog for each cue he performs. If he scores at least 150 out of a possible 200 points in a single trial, he earns a "leg" toward an obedience title. After earning three such legs, he earns his first title: Companion Dog, or CD. If a dog earns additional legs, he racks up more titles until he reaches the pinnacles of the sport: Obedience Trial Champion (OTCh) and maybe even National Obedience Champion (NOC). The latter accolade is earned by

In a rally event, signs at multiple stations tell your dog to perform various obedience-style maneuvers.

just one dog each year at the AKC National Obedience Invitational.

More information about the world of competitive obedience is available from the AKC at www.akc.org/events/obedience.

Rally Obedience

Some people believe that canine agility requires too much human agility, while others find that competitive obedience is dull. For folks from both of these groups, there's a happy-medium sport called rally obedience.

Rally obedience requires you and your Dachshund to complete a 10- to 20-station course designed by the event judge. Each station has a sign that tells you what you and your dog need to do. At one station, you might need to ask him to lie down; at another, you and he may need to walk a figure-8 pattern; at another, you and he may need to walk in a pattern that's called out by the judge. The judge will score you and your dog on how well the two of you perform the tasks specified at each station.

The AKC and the Association of Pet Dog Trainers (APDT) both sponsor rally obedience programs. To learn more about the AKC Rally® program, log onto www.akc.org/events/rally; for details about the APDT program, go to the organization's website, which is www.apdt.com.

Tracking

Like field trials, tracking also involves following a scent, but instead of following the scent of a rabbit, the Dachshund follows the scent of a person. The goal is to use the scented track to locate one or more articles left by the person who laid the track. The dog wears a long leash, and the owner/handler follows him. Dachshunds are especially well suited to tracking because, as hounds, they have keenly sensitive noses.

Depending on the level of the test, the track is between 440 and 1,000 yards (402.5 and 914.5 m) long, been laid between 30 minutes and 5 hours earlier, and includes three to eight directional changes. The track may also have obstacles, such as creeks or roads to cross, and can have areas with no vegetation, such as parking lots. Tracking tests are held in fields of grass or in urban areas, such as industrial parks or college campuses.

For more information on tracking, consult either the DCA's website at www.dachshund-dca.org/tracking.html or the AKC at www.akc.org/events/tracking.

THERAPY WORK

For years, researchers have studied and documented the benefits of the human–animal bond. All too often, though, those who have the greatest need for those benefits don't have access to them. These individuals may be patients in hospitals, nursing homes, and other health care facilities; they may be children who need an extra injection of confidence to succeed in reading and other challenging activities; they may be people who are grieving over the loss of a loved one or grappling with other difficult personal issues; or they may simply be lonely college students who are away from home for the first time.

For all of these individuals, specially trained therapy dogs can help. Some of these dogs work in libraries, lying down next to children and listening to them read aloud. Others provide some much-needed unconditional love and cheer to hospital patients. Still others provide similar services to the elderly in nursing homes and assisted living facilities, while others extend a loving paw to those who have experienced a death in the family, are themselves dying, are coping with a traumatic experience, or are seeking mental health treatment.

Although many Dachshunds have feisty, independent personalities, a well-socialized Dachsie can make an excellent therapy dog. In addition to such socialization, however, a Dachshund also needs training to be controllable by a handler and to cope with the challenging and novel situations that therapy work might entail.

Among the many organizations that are involved in animal-facilitated therapy, three stand out for providing excellent training to aspiring human-canine-therapy teams. They are the Delta Society (www.deltasociety.org), Therapy Dogs International (www.tdi-dog.org), and Love on a Leash (www.loveonaleash.org).

TRAVELING WITH YOUR DACHSHUND

Traveling with your Dachshund can be very enjoyable—provided you do a little planning beforehand and put your dog's welfare first. Below are suggestions for keeping the two of you safe, happy, and healthy whenever you hit the road.

By Car

Car trips with dogs can be a lot of fun—but to be safe, prior planning is crucial. Here are some tips to ensure the welfare of both you and your dog while driving:

Keep Him in Back

All dogs, Dachshunds definitely included, belong in the backs of cars. As much as you might want to keep your canine companion in the front seat next to you, having him there

Multi-Dog Tip

If you have a second Dachshund, consider teaching both of them to work in "Brace Obedience." This American Kennel Club (AKC) event, open to dogs who can perform Novice-level obedience exercises, involves having two dogs performing obedience exercises in unison, often literally attached to each other with a short lead—the brace—connecting their collars. For more information, log onto the AKC's competitive obedience website at www.akc.org/events/obedience.

Traveling with your Dachshund can be fun if you plan carefully and keep his welfare in mind at all times.

could put him in jeopardy. If you have an accident and the passenger air bag deploys, the impact could severely injure or even kill your dog. Even if you don't have an accident, he could try to climb into your lap, distracting you while driving.

Crate if Possible

Don't let your Dachshund have free reign in the backseat. If you have an accident or even stop suddenly, he could become seriously injured or even thrown out of the car—and he could injure you as well. Putting him in his crate will go a long way toward ensuring his safety. If your car is small, simply put the crate on the backseat and strap it in; for larger vehicles, place the crate in the cargo bed in a way that will keep it from moving around.

Buckle Up

If you'd rather not crate your Dachshund, secure him on the backseat with a seat belt. Make sure, though, that the belt you choose does not contain plastic clasps, which can shatter if a crash occurs. Instead, opt for a clasp-less belt that's made of the same material as seat belts for human passengers. Several such belts are available at www.ruffrider.com. You may also want to consider getting him a booster seat if you want him to be able to see out your car window. Plenty of pet supply stores sell such seats, and they can work in tandem with your car's seat belts.

Stop Often

If you're on a long trip, stop at least every two hours so that your Dachshund can stretch his legs and take a potty break.

Bring the Right Gear

Canine automotive gear should include plastic bags to pick up your dog's poop, bottled water, and a dish to pour the water into so that your canine traveling companion can quench his thirst.

Have His Back

To reduce the strain that jumping would put on your Dachshund's back, lift him in and out of the car. Make sure, though, that you have him leashed in case he bolts before you're able to secure him on his seat.

Don't Leave Him Alone

Don't leave your Dachshund alone in an automobile. During the summer months, the car's interior can heat up to dangerously high temperatures; during the winter, the interior can become dangerously cold very quickly. And even in good weather, a Dachshund who's alone in a car is in danger of being stolen.

Help Your Queasy Canine

If your Dachshund drools, vomits, or shows other signs of carsickness, don't feed him less than two hours before you depart. Allow fresh air to circulate by opening the windows a little. If those measures are ineffective, ask your vet about whether to give your dog some Dramamine an hour before your departure. She can tell you how much to give.

Ginger snaps or ginger root tablets found at health food stores are an excellent natural remedy to alleviate carsickness.

By Plane

Flying with a Dachshund—or for that matter, any dog but the very smallest—can be complicated. That's because commercial airlines don't allow a dog to fly in a passenger cabin with his person unless he can be enclosed in a carrier that fits under the seat in front of the person. Miniature and many standard Dachshunds can fit under the seat, fortunately, but some standards may not.

Consequently, transporting a standard Dachshund by air means placing him in a crate and checking him as baggage. The U.S. Department of Agriculture's (USDA) Animal and Plant Health Inspection Service (APHIS) has a downloadable fact sheet at www.aphis. usda.gov/publications/animal_welfare/ content/printable_version/fs_awpetravel.pdf that gives travelers the scoop on how to ship animals via the friendly skies.

However, transporting your Dachshund by air can be a challenge even if you follow all of the USDA's regulations. That's because most airlines won't put pets in the baggage compartment during the summer because those compartments would become dangerously hot while the plane awaits takeoff or arrives at the gate after landing. Some airlines won't ship pets even in moderate weather—and those that do might charge some very high fees. Moreover, even if you can transport your Dachshund in

If your dog gets carsick, ginger snaps may help settle his stomach.

the cabin, many airlines allow only one or two animals per flight—which means that if you don't book your flight early, your chances of nabbing a spot for your dog drop dramatically. In addition, you need to pay for a ticket for your Dachshund, even though he technically does not occupy a seat.

One way to transport your Dachshund by air is to book him on a carrier that's dedicated to transporting pets in the cabin, not the baggage hold. One such carrier is Pet Airways, reachable online at http://petairways.com. Bear in mind, however, that you will not be able to accompany your Dachshund on his trip.

In short, flying with your Dachshund will probably be both complicated and costly.

Training Tidbit

As you introduce your Dachshund to various activities, keep in mind that he is a unique individual—and that his idea of a good time may differ greatly from yours. For example, the fact that Dachshunds dominate in earthdog events doesn't mean that your particular Dachshund will be equally dominant or will even enjoy this activity. Your dog should enjoy what he's doing. Look for signs of enjoyment, such as relaxed tail wagging, a soft, happy expression, and eagerness to work. If he shows a droopy or stiff tail and reluctance to participate in whatever he's doing, he's not having fun. In such instances, you should respect his wishes and try another activity.

To reduce stress for both yourself and your dog—not to mention the hit to your bank account—consider finding another way for the two of you to reach your destination. If that's not possible, leave your dog at home—either by boarding him at a kennel, having him stay with a friend, or having a pet sitter come to your home.

Lodging for You and Your Dachshund

You shouldn't have much trouble finding Dachshund-friendly accommodations. Many facilities that once excluded dogs now realize that being dog-friendly boosts profits and leads to repeat business. Consequently, motels, hotels, and even bed-and-breakfasts are increasingly welcoming Dachshunds and other dogs.

To find these pet-friendly lodgings, start by checking out print and online offerings targeted to the dog-owning traveler. Among the best websites are Fido Friendly (www.fidofriendly.com); Pets on the Go (www.petsonthego.com); and Dog Friendly (www.dogfriendly.com). Great books include the American Automobile Association's (AAA) *Traveling with Your Pet*, 11th Edition and *Vacationing with Your Pet* by Eileen Barish (Pet Friendly Publications).

After you've picked a place to stay, start making plans. Your action agenda should include:

- **Phoning or e-mailing ahead.** Telephone or e-mail the hotel you're considering to be sure that it still welcomes pets. Find out too whether the facility requires a pet deposit or other additional fee, and ask about special rules that pet-owning guests must follow.
- **Packing appropriately.** Include your dog's crate, collar and leash, dog food, immunization record, and plastic bags in your luggage.

- **Bringing something from home.** When your Dachshund's in a place he hasn't been before, a couple of comforts from home can help him relax. Bring one or two favorite toys and a T-shirt with your scent on it. The T-shirt could be of considerable comfort if you have to leave him alone in his crate.

If You Can't Take Your Dachshund With You

Sometimes bringing your Dachshund with you isn't the best sort of vacation for you or for him. If you're flying (especially during the summer) or going to any destination where you'll be touring around and leaving him alone all day, your best bet is to leave him behind while you hit the road. Of course, you need to arrange for someone else to care for him while you're gone. Here are some caregiving options:

A Friend or Family Member

If you can count an experienced dog lover among your friends or family, consider asking whether she'll either come and stay with your Dachshund while you're gone or if she's willing to care for him at her home. This option is particularly good if you'll be away for more than a day or two. Make sure, though, that she has the information she needs to care for your Dachshund properly—and if she has other dogs, make sure that they get along with your dog.

Your Breeder

Consider contacting your Dachshund's breeder and asking her if she'd like to have your dog stay with her while you're gone. She may enjoy spending time with her "baby."

A Professional Pet Sitter

If you're going to be away for only a couple of days, you might consider hiring a professional pet sitter to come to your home two or three times a day to walk, feed, and play with your Dachshund. Make sure that the pet sitter you employ is licensed, bonded, and insured and that she meets your dog before your trip so that the two can feel comfortable together. To find a professional pet sitter, log onto Pet Sitters' International (PSI) at www.petsit.com/locate/ or the National Association of Professional Pet Sitters (NAPPS) website at www.petsitters.org/index.cfm?section=Find&content=findsitter.

A Boarding Kennel

If you can't bring your Dachshund with you, can't find a friend or family member to take care of him, or will be away for too long for a pet-sitting pro to be a practical option, find a good boarding kennel. Your vet, groomer or dog's trainer may have ideas. But before you make a reservation, visit the kennel to make sure that it's clean, escape-proof, and has someone on the premises 24/7 (many don't). Be sure, too, that the kennel staff knows and understands dogs and pays sufficient attention to the dogs who are staying with them.

PART III

SENIOR YEARS

CHAPTER 12

FINDING YOUR SENIOR DACHSHUND

In our youth-obsessed culture, the benefits of aging are all too often overlooked. That's unfortunate because age can enhance so many aspects of life. For example, a pot roast or beef stew always tastes better as leftovers than when it's freshly prepared and served. Age also improves fine wines. And for many people, the older a Dachshund gets, the better he becomes.

Think about it. The out-of-control puppy, the whack-a-doodle adolescent, and the highly individualistic young adult dog all give way to a more sedate and often more affectionate nature by the time a Dachshund turns ten years of age—and signs of aging may become apparent a couple of years before that time.

Those pluses may be obvious to those who have had the privilege of living with Dachshunds since they were puppies. But if you're thinking about welcoming a senior Dachshund into your home for the first time, you may have a hard time figuring out how anything can outweigh the possible disadvantage of perhaps having only a few years together with him. This chapter will help you figure out why adopting a senior Dachshund offers plenty of advantages over adopting his younger counterpart.

WHY ADOPTING A SENIOR IS A GOOD IDEA

There are often more senior Dachshunds available for adoption than there are people who want to adopt them. Prospective adopters often hesitate to take on an older dog because they're afraid that the dog won't live for very long. Not only are such adopters afraid of bonding with an older dog only to lose him, but they also understandably are cautious about adopting a dog who, due to his age, may accumulate medical expenses rather quickly.

Such fears are understandable but not entirely valid. Life doesn't offer any guarantees—including how long a dog might live. For every dog who becomes a canine Methuselah, there's at least one other dog

By the Numbers

A Dachshund is considered to be a senior citizen at about ten years of age—but with good luck and good health he can live well into his teens.

Age can enhance so many aspects of life—especially when it comes to a senior Dachshund.

who died prematurely, maybe even during puppyhood. The average Dachshund lives from 12 to 14 years, but many live quite a bit longer.

Still not convinced? Here are some more pluses that come when one adopts a senior Dachshund:

He's Probably Housetrained

Older dogs do need to potty more often than younger ones, but at least they know when and where they should do it. In other words, by adopting a senior Dachshund you'll almost certainly bypass the hassles associated with housetraining.

He Won't Trash Your Stuff

The mature Dachshund has years of experience living in human households, so he probably knows that he shouldn't destroy or otherwise mess with your possessions.

What You See Is What You Get

Puppies—even purebred Dachshund puppies— are a little bit of a mystery. A person can't know for sure if a new little Dachshund will grow up to be undersized or oversized or know exactly how intense the puppy's coat color will be when he reaches adulthood. Temperament's not always predictable either; the puppy who was a shy little darling may grow up to be Mr. I'm-Large-and-in-Charge, especially if he doesn't have appropriate training. By contrast, a senior Dachshund is exactly who he appears to be.

He Minds His Manners

Even if he hasn't had all that much training, a senior Dachshund isn't likely to indulge in puppy-like antics. He's way too dignified to jump up on people, and digging through trash cans or wiggling into a bottom kitchen cabinet may be too much of an effort for him.

Training Tidbit

He Costs Less

Generally, adopting a senior dog costs considerably less than adopting a younger one and much less than buying a puppy from a reputable breeder. For example, in early 2010, the fee for adopting a Dachshund from Dachshund Rescue of Houston (Texas) was $250 for a dog through age nine but only $150 for a dog who was ten or older. Such discounts for senior dogs don't mean that they are inferior in any way to youngsters—they simply reflect the fact that many people bypass the joys of adopting an older Dachshund in favor of one who's younger. Meanwhile, a reputable breeder might be selling a puppy for anywhere between $900 and $1,500, depending on the area of the country and the size and variety of the puppies being sold. Do the math, and you'll see that senior Dachshunds are cheaper but no less valuable than their younger counterparts.

He Likes Being With You

Puppies, adolescents, and young adult Dachshunds certainly love their people, but they have additional priorities. After all, there's a whole world out there for them to explore! Consequently, if you let a younger Dachshund off leash in an unprotected area, he may decide to take off on an exploratory expedition. And youthful Dachshunds are surprisingly speedy despite their short little legs; they can give their humans a run for their money. Contrast such behavior with that of the older Dachshund, who not only doesn't possess such speed but also probably isn't at all unhappy about having lost it. He's no longer beset with wanderlust; instead, his idea of a good time is hanging out with you.

He Gives You a Rest

The sock-eating, laundry-stealing, furniture-leg-chewing, drywall-destroying Dachshund puppy

One advantage of adopting a senior Dachsie is that he likely has already been taught good manners.

Generally, adopting a senior dog costs considerably less than adopting a younger one and much less than buying a puppy from a reputable breeder.

or young adult keeps his people way too busy dealing with such antics. But for the senior Dachshund, such troublemaking is beneath his dignity—and the more dignity he has, the more rest you get.

He Knows When to Leave You Alone

Yes, an older Dachsie will probably hang around with you more than his younger counterpart does—but that doesn't mean that the older one is going to pester you. He just needs to know where you are—and when he does, he'll be just fine with whatever you're doing. For example, if you're watching your favorite television show, your senior Dachshund will probably give your leg a nudge in hopes that you'll pick him up and put him either on your lap or next to you. By contrast, the juvenile Dachsie may make television watching impossible by pestering you for attention or barking at some event that's important to him but not to you.

Multi-Dog Tip

Do your best to make sure that the senior Dachshund you want to adopt will get along well with the other dogs in your family.

He Appreciates You

Dachshund puppies, adolescent Dachshunds, and even young adult Dachsies are all cuteness personified. However, that cuteness may not always translate to out-and-out affection toward their people; instead they expect us to be entertained by watching them exhibit their total joy in living and their frequently playful behavior. They often don't seem to be all that bonded to their people (although regular positive training sessions can help build such a bond). By contrast, the older Dachshund has gained wisdom as he's matured, not to mention the experience of having been relinquished if you adopt him from a shelter or rescue group. In his wisdom, he knows that he lucked out when you adopted him. Consequently, he'll really appreciate an extra cuddle, treat, or other form of positive attention. In fact, many people who've adopted their dogs from shelters or rescue groups—not to mention those who work or volunteer for such organizations—are convinced that all adopted dogs know how lucky they are and appreciate getting a second chance to have a first-class life.

Senior Dachshunds tend to be calmer than their younger counterparts.

He Teaches You What Really Matters

Crazy, active young Dachshunds are all about having a good time. Just watching a Dachsie run in his inimitable fashion can put a smile on even the grumpiest person's face. That said, young dogs don't bring peace to the lives of their people. There's too much mischief for a young dog to get into (and for their person to get them out of) to expect much in the way of serenity. That reward—the peace that comes from simply spending time with your dog without having to do anything—is much more likely to occur with an older Dachshund. Living with a Dachsie is a great way to remember that in the end, it's not where you go—it's who you travel with.

Want to Know More?

If you decide you'd rather adopt a younger adult, see Chapter 5 for more details.

CHAPTER 13

CARE OF YOUR DACHSHUND SENIOR

Caring for your Dachshund when he's a senior citizen may not differ greatly from the way you cared for him when he was younger. Any Dachshund of any age needs good food, good grooming, good health care, and good training to be at his best. However, you may need to fine-tune the ways you perform those tasks as he ages. This chapter describes some of those adjustments.

WHEN DOES A DACHSHUND BECOME A SENIOR?

On average, Dachshunds begin to show signs of aging when they reach their eighth or ninth birthdays and reach true seniorhood by around the age of ten. While some of that variation can be attributed to just plain chance, other factors that affect the rate at which a Dachshund ages are well within his owner's control.

For example, an overweight Dachshund is likely to age more quickly and have a shorter life span than a Dachshund who is fit and trim. Keeping your short-legged friend lean and giving him plenty of exercise could add months or even years to his life span—especially if the food he eats is the highest-quality food you can afford.

Good dental health is also an important component to maintaining health and extending your Dachshund's life. The reason: an infection from dental disease can spread to the dog's vital organs. And even if that doesn't happen, bad teeth and painful gums greatly diminish a dog's quality of life.

In any case, reaching a double-digit age does not automatically mean that an individual Dachshund has become a senior citizen. Just as with people, dogs show signs of entering their golden years that don't always mesh completely with chronology. Those signs include the following:

Slowing Down

A senior dog generally doesn't move as quickly as he did when he was younger. He needs more time to go up and down stairs, get up from a nap, or just get around in general. And during a walk, it takes him less time and distance to get tired than was the case when he was younger.

Whitening Up

As a Dachshund ages, he starts sprouting white hair on his face, particularly on his muzzle and around his eyes. His coat may also become

Good dental care is an important component to maintaining health and extending your Dachshund's life.

thinner and his skin drier than was the case during his youth.

Having Accidents

Just as many humans find their bladder control diminishing as they age, so also do more than a few Dachshunds. If the Dachshund in question is a spayed female, the cause is likely to be a shortage of estrogen, which can be corrected. Other aging Dachshunds of either sex may forget their bathroom manners because they've developed canine cognitive dysfunction syndrome (CDS), which is similar to Alzheimer's disease in humans.

Taking Their Lumps

Senior dogs, including Dachshunds, often develop soft spongy lumps on their bodies that are usually benign fatty tumors—but don't assume any lumps your Dachshund develops are of this variety. Get them checked.

Appearing to Ignore You

An aging Dachshund who doesn't respond to his name or to a familiar cue isn't necessarily ignoring you or otherwise exhibiting what dog owners jokingly call "selective deafness." He may truly be going deaf—which happens fairly often among senior dogs.

Becoming Disoriented

Some senior Dachshunds appear to be lost even when they're in familiar places. Such disorientation can be a sign of CDS.

Becoming Fearful

Age may cause your senior Dachshund to become apprehensive or even frightened of occurrences that didn't bother him in his youth. If your short-legged friend used to be impervious to thunderstorms, loud noises, or other startling occurrences but now whines, trembles, or becomes clingy, age could be the reason.

FEEDING YOUR SENIOR DACHSHUND

The fact that your Dachshund has entered his golden years doesn't automatically mean that you need to change what he eats. If he's doing fine on his current diet, there's no reason to stop feeding him that fare. But if your Dachshund develops health problems—whether or not those problems are age related—a change of diet might help because certain conditions often respond well to dietary adjustments. Those conditions include:

• heart and kidney problems, which may be

eased with a low-sodium, low-phosphorus regimen

- cancer, which can respond to a diet that aims to feed the body while starving the tumor
- dental disease, which can respond well to a diet designed to reduce the buildup of plaque and tartar on the teeth

However, before you make any changes in your senior Dachshund's diet, consult your veterinarian. Your vet can help you identify foods that optimize your dog's health and can also suggest helpful dietary supplements. For example, she might suggest adding fatty acid capsules to your dog's meals to improve his skin and coat quality and to strengthen his immune system.

How to Feed Your Senior Dachshund

No matter what changes—if any—you make to your senior Dachshund's diet, it's a good idea to at least consider fine-tuning the way you feed him. That's because a dog's dining needs and preferences may change as he ages. The wise owner takes those possible changes into account and accommodates them as much as possible. Here are some tips to consider:

Be Consistent

Your senior Dachshund will not welcome a sudden change in routine. Feed him twice and walk him at least three times daily at the same times each day.

Watch for Appetite Loss

A Dachshund who develops a sudden loss of appetite may be sick. Contact your vet if he refuses to eat for more than two meals.

By the Numbers

On average, a Dachshund shows signs of seniorhood when he reaches his eighth or ninth birthday. There's plenty of room within that variation, though. Some Dachshunds show signs of aging when they turn seven, while others—especially Miniature Dachshunds—may behave like puppies until they're well past the age of nine.

Pamper the Picky Eater

If your Dachshund picks at his food and a checkup shows that nothing's amiss, try jazzing up his daily fare a little bit. One way to do that is to add warm water to dry food to make a gravy. Another option: adding a little fresh lean meat such as white-meat chicken to any meal. Fresh fruits and veggies can give a meal some added zip too.

Bow to His Dining Preferences

Some dogs prefer to dine in solitude, while others prefer having company. Pay attention to how your Dachshund behaves while he eats— for example, whether he stops eating when you leave the room—and use those observations to decide whether changes are needed.

Don't Mess With the Food Bowl

Even if your senior Dachshund appears to be easygoing if people

Feed your mature Dachshund twice a day at approximately the same times each day.

hover around while he eats, don't surprise him while he's eating his breakfast or dinner. Many dogs lose some of their hearing as they age and may react with a growl, snap, or even a bite if approached from behind. Hang around while your Dachshund eats if that's what he seems to want—but leave him and his food dish alone while he eats.

Minimize Stress

Do everything you can to keep your senior Dachsie's dining experiences stress free. Good nutrition is essential to maintaining his good health. If he tosses his cookies after meals because those mealtimes are stressful, he won't benefit from the good nutrition you're trying to give him.

GROOMING YOUR SENIOR DACHSHUND

A dog's advancing age doesn't relieve you of your obligation to groom him. Dachshunds of any age—including seniors—need their people to attend to their coats, ears, feet, teeth, and other body parts. That said, a grooming session with an older Dachshund is much less likely to turn into a wrestling match than with a younger one. The senior dog is calmer, knows what to expect, and generally enjoys the attention. Generally, a senior Dachshund's grooming routine can be the same as for his younger counterpart. To keep him comfortable, you need to make only a few small adjustments. Here's what those adjustments should include:

Secure Your Bathtub

If you bathe your Dachshund in your bathtub at home, put a bathmat in the bottom of the tub so that he doesn't slip.

Let Him Take It Lying Down

Brushing will be more comfortable for your Dachshund if you allow him to lie down on his side during the procedure. Use the *dead* cue to help him assume this position; Chapter 9 explains how to teach it.

Check Him Over

Use the time you spend grooming your Dachshund to also give him a little checkup. As you brush him, watch for lumps or bumps under the skin—and if you find a new one, call your veterinarian. (Don't worry—it probably isn't cancer, but checking with your vet is a good way to make sure that that's not the case.) When you clean his ears, peer inside to see if there's any discharge, and give them a sniff (yes, really) to see if they smell yeasty or otherwise offensive. Note too whether he's had any significant hair loss and whether he has bad breath. Any of these conditions may signify the onset of a serious health problem—but by noticing that problem early, the chances of resolving it successfully multiply considerably.

Savor the Experience

Life with a well-loved senior Dachshund is a uniquely sweet experience, and there's no better time to savor that experience than when you groom him. Let your gentle strokes and loving attention provide some quality time together for the two of you, as well as a brief respite from the stresses of day-to-day living.

CARING FOR YOUR SENIOR DACHSHUND'S HEALTH

Older Dachshunds are similar to older people in that they tend to have more health issues

Want to Know More?

For detailed information on how to groom your Dachshund, see Chapter 6.

Grooming your senior Dachshund will enhance the special bond the two of you share.

than their younger counterparts do. With both species, living longer takes its toll on the body—and the longer that body lives, the greater the chances that illness will strike. But don't worry—more often than not, good veterinary care (plus TLC from you) can put right whatever's gone wrong.

Preventive Care

The best way to fight senior dog illnesses is to catch them early, and preventive care is crucial to such an effort. You can provide some preventive care yourself. For example, check your dog regularly for bumps, lumps, and other possible signs of health problems, and watch for appetite changes that may also signal that something's amiss. You can also safeguard his health by keeping his physique sleek, giving

him exercise opportunities, and feeding him the best food you can afford. But you also need a partner to help safeguard your Dachsie's health. That partner should be your vet.

Your partnership with your vet will be most effective if you continue to take your Dachshund in for regular wellness checkups, as well as whenever he shows any signs of being sick. Until your Dachsie reaches his eighth or ninth birthday, such checkups need occur only once a year. Once he hits either one of those milestones, however, you should step up those exams to twice a year. The twice-yearly checkup can help your vet find signs of trouble even earlier than with an annual physical—and the odds of successful treatment (or at least management) improve the earlier such trouble is found.

During the wellness exam, the vet will take your Dachshund's temperature, check his respiration and pulse, and peer into his eyes and ears for redness, inflammation, discharge, or other signs of infection. She'll also run her hands over your dog's body and feel around his abdomen for tenderness, lumps, or swollen areas; check his skin for rashes, flakiness, and excessive oiliness or dryness; and peer at his teeth and gums to check for plaque, tartar, inflammation, and redness. The vet will probably also want to see a urine sample to check for urinary tract problems and signs of illness that affect the urine. She may also want to draw a blood sample to check for the presence of a wide variety of illnesses ranging from diabetes to hypothyroidism (insufficient production of hormones from the thyroid gland).

Wellness exams aren't cheap; you should expect a dent to your bank balance of several hundred dollars. However, you can save some money by taking advantage of yearly "Senior Pet" or "Geriatric Pet" promotions that many vets offer. These promotions may include discounts on laboratory tests or the entire senior pet examination.

In any case, you should consider that fee an upfront investment in helping deal with future problems in a more cost-effective way later.

Common Senior Dog Illnesses

Some conditions are more likely to strike senior Dachshunds than their younger counterparts. Those maladies include:

Arthritis

Arthritis results when a dog's cartilage deteriorates as he ages, causing the bones

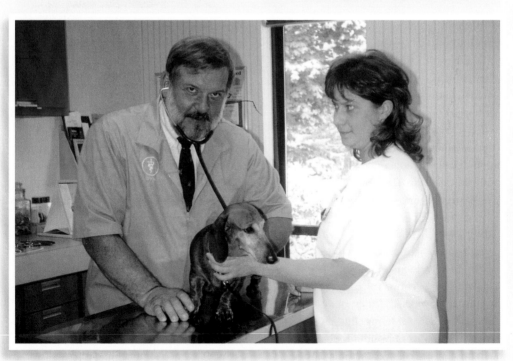

Many veterinary practices offer yearly promotions that involve senior pets.

that form a joint to rub up against each other instead of gliding smoothly over each other like they're supposed to. Making matters worse is that the fluid that normally lubricates the joint is diminished, resulting in inflammation. The result is pain at the joint, sometimes severe, and perhaps mobility problems.

Dogs who are older, overweight, have congenital joint abnormalities such as hip or elbow dysplasia, previous injuries, or have recovered from Lyme disease are especially prone to arthritis. Bigger dogs are also more likely to become arthritic than smaller dogs are, but even smaller dogs like Dachshunds can still acquire this painful condition.

The arthritic Dachshund may have mobility problems, especially in the morning, on stairs, when lying down, or when getting up from lying down. He may not want to exercise and may favor one leg over the other if only one leg is affected. But these symptoms can also herald the presence of other diseases, and arthritis itself can be a by-product of other conditions such as Lyme disease and hip dysplasia. That's why you should consult your vet if you suspect that your Dachshund has arthritis. She can see whether his symptoms have an underlying cause.

Many arthritis treatments are available, including glucosamine and chondroitin supplements and acupuncture. (See Chapter 8 for more information.) Your vet may also suggest that you try giving your dog nonsteroidal anti-inflammatory drugs (NSAIDs). NSAIDS can be very helpful but require a vet's supervision.

If your Dachshund is too heavy, your vet is also likely to prescribe a weight-loss regimen to reduce the stress that the excess weight puts on his joints. She may also suggest some gentle exercise for your dog, even though he may not want to try. Such exercise can help keep his joint stiffness from worsening.

Training Tidbit

Senior Dachshunds enjoy being rewarded with treats as much as younger Dachsies do. However, because the older Dachshund has a slower metabolism, those treats are more likely to cause him to put on excess poundage. To keep his physique sleek, either feed much smaller servings of the treats you currently give him, or switch to less fattening fare such as apples, bananas, carrots, and frozen green beans.

If your dog's arthritis is very severe, the vet may suggest that he undergo surgery, such as a hip replacement. Such surgery can restore mobility and relieve pain.

Canine Cognitive Dysfunction Syndrome (CDS)

Just as some aging humans fall victim to Alzheimer's disease, some aging dogs fall victim to canine cognitive dysfunction syndrome (CDS). Both conditions are believed to result when proteins form deposits of plaque on the brain.

CDS symptoms include behavioral changes such as new fears or phobias; a sudden onset of separation anxiety—especially if such anxiety occurs at night; housetraining lapses; confusion and disorientation; failure to recognize familiar people; changes in sleep cycle; uncharacteristic aggressiveness; diminished interest in people; unexplained vocalizing; forgetting how to navigate stairs or around obstacles; and failure to respond to known cues or directions.

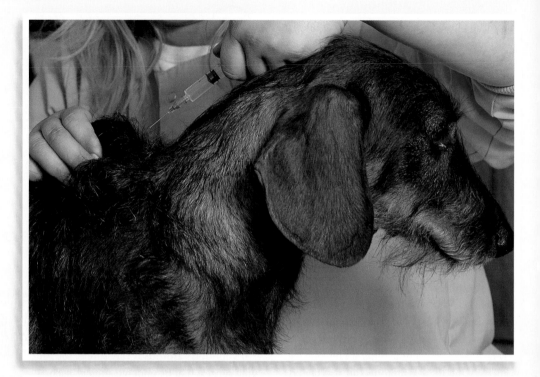

Once your Dachsie becomes a senior, he should visit the vet twice a year for preventive care.

To confirm a CDS diagnosis, a vet will perform a variety of tests, such as a neurological examination, blood tests, a urinalysis, and perhaps imaging of the brain to rule out other conditions.

CDS can't be cured, but some symptom-controlling options are available. One is Anipryl, a drug approved by the U.S. Food and Drug Administration (FDA) specifically to reduce CDS symptoms. Another comes from Hills Pet Foods: Prescription Diet Canine b/d, which the company says can combat the effects of aging on a dog's brain. A veterinarian must prescribe either product.

Cataracts

Cataracts occur when too much water enters the lens of the eye, resulting in a clouding of the lens. In fact, the primary symptom of cataracts is a whitish cloudiness to one or both eyes and possibly signs of vision loss. This cloudiness is not the same as the blue-gray color on the eyes that almost all older dogs develop. That condition, which is called nuclear sclerosis, has little effect on a dog's vision.

Only a veterinarian or veterinary ophthalmologist can confirm a diagnosis of cataracts. Blood work may be needed to rule out the possibility that the cataracts result from an underlying condition such as diabetes.

The only cure for cataracts is surgery to remove the affected lens, but in many cases—such as a frail senior dog or a dog with diabetes—such surgery isn't advisable. For such dogs, treatment of the inflammation cataracts may cause may be a better option. However, healthy older dogs whose owners can commit to weeks of postoperative care and restriction of their dogs' activities can do well with such surgery. That said, many cataracts are best left alone, especially if they're small and not interfering with the dog's vision.

Cushing's Disease

This common condition among older dogs, also known as hyperadrenocorticism, results when a dog's adrenal glands produce too much cortisone. Cushing's results from one of the following scenarios: if a dog has been given steroids over a long period to treat another health problem; if the dog has a small, usually noncancerous tumor on his pituitary gland; or if the dog has a tumor on the adrenal glands themselves. Of these three scenarios, the pituitary gland tumor is the most common.

Symptoms include increased appetite, water consumption and/or urination, a swollen belly, unexplained weight gain, weakening of the legs, hair loss on both sides of the body, and darkened, thinning skin. Behavioral changes associated with Cushing's include lethargy, excessive panting, nighttime restlessness, and seeking cool surfaces on which to lie down.

The symptoms of Cushing's are similar to those of other diseases, so a veterinarian must conduct several tests before arriving at a diagnosis. Those tests will probably start with the drawing of a blood sample to determine what your dog's white blood cell, liver enzyme, and cholesterol levels are. If those readings are higher than normal, additional testing is likely to confirm the diagnosis.

The cause of the disease determines the course of treatment. If a pituitary gland tumor is the cause, the veterinarian will prescribe a drug to reduce the level of cortisol in the blood. If an adrenal gland tumor is the culprit, the vet may remove the tumor surgically. If steroid medication is the cause, the vet will stop using the steroid and look for another way to treat the condition that prompted the steroid regimen.

Vestibular Syndrome

A senior Dachshund who looks as though he's had a few drinks too many could be suffering from vestibular syndrome. An affected dog may tilt his head, lose his balance, lean to one side, refuse to eat or drink, and vomit. Some affected dogs may try to walk straight ahead but end up walking diagonally. To confirm the diagnosis, a vet's physical exam is usually all that's needed.

Vestibular syndrome generally looks a lot worse than it actually is. The vet's treatment

Using positive reinforcement training is just as important for an older Dachshund as it is for a puppy.

plan will concentrate on keeping the affected dog comfortable. She may also insert fluids through a tube into an area under your dog's skin to combat any dehydration that may result from his refusal to eat or drink. The dog's body gradually absorbs the fluids. Plenty of rest also helps. The symptoms usually take a few days to disappear.

TRAINING YOUR SENIOR DACHSHUND

You certainly *can* teach an old dog new tricks—and doing so is a very good idea. That's because learning something new sharpens your senior Dachshund's mind and improves his quality of life. However, you should tailor your training technique to both the physical and mental capabilities of your particular mature Dachshund. Here's how to do so:

Stay Positive

Using positive reinforcement training is just as important for an older Dachshund as it is for a puppy. Keep your lessons upbeat and happy: Instead of focusing on what your dog does wrong, catch him doing something right—and when he does, reward him in the form of a tasty tidbit, verbal praise, a short play session, or any combination thereof.

Be Realistic

An older Dachshund may not be able to perform the same physical feats that were possible when he was younger. For example,

A senior dog's attention span is often shorter than when he was a young adult, so adjust your training sessions accordingly.

rally obedience may be better for the senior dog than agility, which is much more strenuous; searching for a hidden toy or treat may be easier on your dog than attempting to chase down errant squirrels or rabbits. To give your dog a great mental challenge that won't tax him physically, consider preparing him to pass the American Kennel Club's (AKC) Canine Good Citizen test, which is described in Chapter 11.

Teach Hand Signals

Consider teaching hand signals to your dog now if he's beginning to show signs of hearing loss. Such signals will enable him to respond to your cues even if he can't hear you. For example, when you ask him to lie down, pair the verbal cue with moving your palm downward; pair a verbal sit cue with placing your hand on your chest. And clap your hands when you ask him to come; the vibration from the clapping can be perceived even by hard-of-hearing dogs.

Keep Sessions Short

A senior dog's attention is likely to wander more quickly than his younger counterpart's. This means that you should shorten your training sessions and end a session as quickly as possible if your dog seems uninterested in continuing. And even if he does continue to seem engaged, end a session after ten minutes.

Multi-Dog Tip

If you welcome a new puppy into your family, make sure that your senior Dachshund doesn't feel neglected or have any reason to feel that his place in the household has changed. He needs to know that you still love him best. The new puppy, who's already had to share human attention with his mother and littermates, won't mind sharing your love.

No Sitting Up

Yes, a Dachshund sitting up looks incredibly cute—but he is also seriously straining his hips and back. Please stop giving him this cue now if you haven't done so already.

End on a Good Note

No matter what your dog's age is, it's important to end a training session by giving him a cue that you know he'll do easily and do well. Give him lots of positive feedback—a tasty treat, a play session, verbal praise, and/or petting—when he responds as requested. Even if the session didn't go all that well, you'll both end it feeling proud of what you've achieved.

CHAPTER 14

END-OF-LIFE ISSUES

No book is long enough to contain an entire list of the joys that come from living with a Dachshund. A big-dog personality in a little-dog package, a unique combination of dignity with a sense of humor, and a wonderful blend of independence with inquisitiveness are just a few of the traits that generate fierce loyalty to the breed among Dachsie devotees. Unfortunately, though, there's one minus counteracting all the pluses of living with these dogs—or, for that matter, any dog.

The minus is that you'll probably outlive your Dachshund. The happiness you're currently experiencing in day-to-day life with your short-legged little dog will, in time, give way to sadness when he's no longer sharing that day-to-day life with you. But you can take the edge off that future sadness by living life to the fullest with your Dachshund now and by planning ahead to reduce, if not eliminate, the pain you and he will experience as his life ends.

WHEN IS IT TIME?

For the owners of many Dachshunds, the question "When is it time?" is really two different questions. One question is when

it's time to end aggressive treatment for a terminal condition. The other is when it's time to euthanize. Here are some thoughts about how to answer each.

Deciding to End Treatment

Veterinary science has come up with some amazing ways to extend the lives of dogs whose diagnoses would have been automatic death sentences just a generation ago. A wheelchair can provide mobility to a dog who has lost the use of his hind legs (which is a special issue with Dachshunds). A dog with heart disease can be given new drugs that can give him an additional year of life—and a high-quality life at that. And for the dog who draws a cancer diagnosis, surgery, radiation, and chemotherapy can not only prolong life but also maintain the quality of that life.

But the fact that veterinary science offers such options doesn't mean that one or more of those options are the right choice for any dog at any time. For example, an owner may consult with her veterinarian and decide that it's time to end aggressive treatment of her dog's illness and focus instead on keeping him pain-free for the rest of his life. Such decisions can be difficult to make. To help

By planning ahead, you can make the end of your Dachshund's life as painless as possible for both of you.

you deal with this decision, ask yourself the following questions:

- Has your dog's quality of life improved since he began treatment?
- Is his quality of life likely to improve, if it hasn't already?
- Does your veterinarian favor continuing treatment—and if so, why?
- Do you think that continuing treatment will be good for your dog?
- Are you able—emotionally, physically, and/or financially—to continue treatment?

If the answer to any of these questions is no, you might want to consider whether the time has come to end aggressive treatment of your Dachshund's illness.

Hospice Care

If you've decided that ending aggressive treatment is appropriate for your Dachshund, you may still be able to keep him comfortable, happy, and content for a while. You can do that by giving him hospice care. With hospice, you shift your focus from treating a condition to providing your dog with a safe, comfortable, and caring end-of-life experience. Such care can be good for your Dachshund because he no longer has to endure arduous treatments. Hospice care for your dog can also be good for you because providing him with such care gives you time to come to terms with his impending death and to say goodbye.

However, the benefits of hospice care don't happen all by themselves. To maximize those benefits and minimize the stresses, you need to prepare beforehand. Here are some steps you can take:

Consult With Your Vet

If you're wondering whether your Dachshund is a candidate for hospice care—and what such care might involve—ask your vet. For some dogs, hospice care means extensive nursing, while for others, a few prescription medicines and everyday TLC are sufficient. With your vet's help, you can make the right decisions regarding hospice care for your Dachsie.

Do Some Reading

Because the veterinary profession is paying

By the Numbers

The average life span of a Dachshund is 12 to 14 years of age.

more attention to the idea of hospice care for pets than was once the case, resources for prospective hospice-providing owners are more readily available. Check out the American Association of Human-Animal Bond Veterinarians' (AAH-ABV) hospice web page (http://aahabv.org/index.php?option=com_content&view=article&id=71&Itemid=930); the Nikki Hospice Foundation for Pets (www.pethospice.org); and the American Animal Hospital Association's (AAHA) hospice page (www.healthypet.com/library_view.aspx?ID=9&sid=1).

Know What You're Getting Into

There's no one-size-fits-all method of hospice care; the level of care that's needed varies from dog to dog. In some cases, providing hospice care for a dog could involve providing fluids intravenously, giving regular injections, and/or preparing special food. In other cases, such care might entail little more than giving the dog some medicine. Either way, though, the end result is likely to be either eventual euthanasia or death from natural causes. Ask yourself whether you are up for the financial and emotional costs of providing such care—and in addition, whether you have the time to do so.

Deciding When to Euthanize

Whether you provide hospice care or not, at some point you may need to decide whether the time has come to end your Dachshund's life in a compassionate, humane manner.

With hospice, you shift your focus from treating a condition to providing your dog with a safe, comfortable, and caring end-of-life experience.

The effort you invested training your Dachshund when he was younger can pay off big time now. The reason: Training is a great way to build the human–canine bond—which in turn means that your Dachshund will be able to tell you he's ready to say good-bye in a way that you'll understand.

However, determining when that time has occurred can be incredibly difficult for two reasons. First, you love your dog and don't want to lose him. Second, your dog doesn't have the words to tell you that he's ready to go. That said, your emotional pain and your dog's inability to converse in English don't preclude your being able to figure out when it's time to euthanize. Answer the following questions as honestly as you can; those answers will help you make the right decision at the right time.

How Is My Dog Doing?

A Dachshund who's still eating, interacting with you, and otherwise engaged with the world around him may want and be able to stick around a little longer. By contrast, an apathetic dog who's refusing to eat, eating very little, refusing to interact with his people, or showing other signs of clear misery may well be ready to call it a day.

How Am I Doing?

Is hospice care for your Dachshund draining your bank account? Is his prognosis poor? Is providing hospice care proving to be much more stressful than you anticipated? An affirmative answer to any of those questions may signal that it's time to consider euthanasia. Don't feel guilty if this situation describes you and your dog. You need to consider the needs not only of your Dachshund but also those of the rest of your family and yourself to do the best you can by each.

How Does the Rest of My Family Feel?

The decision to euthanize a dog should be made jointly by all of the adults in a family. If you're thinking that it's time to end your dog's life, see what the other adults (and near-adults) in the household think. By sharing your feelings and listening to what they have to say, you can give each other the support needed to either go ahead and euthanize or delay the procedure for a little bit longer.

DEALING WITH EUTHANASIA

Euthanizing a dog is always difficult and painful no matter how many times you've had to do so before. However, you can lessen the stress and pain you and your family will experience if you do everything you can before and during the procedure to make sure that your dog has a good death and that you and your family aren't traumatized. To ensure both outcomes, consider taking the following steps:

Decide Where

Some people prefer to have their pets euthanized at home so that the animal will be in familiar surroundings. If you want a home euthanasia for your Dachshund, ask your vet if she's willing to make house calls. (Not every vet will provide this service.) If she can't or won't do so, ask if she can recommend a vet who can. On the other hand, some people choose to have their pets euthanized at a veterinary clinic so that they don't associate a place in their homes with where their pets have died. Either choice is perfectly valid; the choice is entirely yours.

Book and Pay Ahead

No matter where you have your dog euthanized, it's a good idea to book an appointment and pay ahead of time. If the procedure will take place at your vet's office, try to book the last appointment of the day so that your vet can give you and your Dachshund her full attention and not have to rush off to her next appointment. And by paying ahead of time, you'll save yourself the stress of having to deal with financial matters just after you've had to say goodbye to your dog.

Minimize Stress

If you're having your Dachshund euthanized at the vet's and he has been nervous there in the past, ask for a prescription for a tranquilizer or other medicine to help your dog relax. Pick the prescription up from the clinic ahead of time and give it to your dog as directed. Giving such medicine beforehand will minimize both your Dachshund's stress and yours.

Ask for Privacy

In cases of euthanasia, most clinics allow owners to bring their dogs into the clinic through an employee-only entrance and proceed directly to an exam room. That way the owners don't need to face other people and their pets before the procedure takes place.

An apathetic dog who's refusing to eat, eating very little, refusing to interact with his people, or shows other signs of clear misery may be ready to go.

Be honest with your child about what's happening regarding the death of the family dog.

Don't Drive Alone

If you're having your Dachshund euthanized at a clinic, have someone else drive you there and back home. You're likely to be too distracted to drive safely, which could pose a danger not only to you but also to other motorists.

Bring the Comforts of Home

If your dog is being euthanized at the vet's, bring his bed with you so that he can be more comfortable and have some familiar smells with him during the procedure.

Consider Staying

If your vet approves, consider staying with your Dachshund during the procedure. The familiar presence of you and other family members can be of tremendous comfort to him and can give you and your family a welcome feeling of closure. Be very cautious, though, about having children younger than school age present during the procedure; seeing the death of their dog might prove to be too intense or frightening for them.

DEALING WITH GRIEF

In the days immediately before and after your Dachshund's passing, you will undoubtedly be full of sorrow. That's as it should be—your love for your dog is what fuels your sadness now. That's why it's important during this time to not try to rid yourself of grief but to cope with it and help the other members of your family—human and nonhuman alike—do the same.

Coping With Your Own Grief

The death of your Dachshund is the death of a family member, and it's appropriate for you to grieve deeply. Give yourself permission to acknowledge and grieve your loss, but also take care of yourself. Here are some suggestions to help you deal with the immediate aftermath of your Dachshund's passing.

Take a Break

Take a day or two off from work so that you have the time and space you need to cope with your dog's death.

Keep Your Routine

You probably won't feel like doing so, but make an effort to keep to your normal routine, especially eating and exercising regularly.

Expect Delayed Reactions

Don't worry if you feel relieved that your Dachshund has died, especially if he'd been sick for a long time. That said, your relief may give way to deep sadness and grief weeks or even months later. All of these feelings are totally normal.

Ask for Help

If your grief is so profound that you're having trouble performing day-to-day activities, a pet loss support group may be helpful. Consult your vet and local animal shelter, which may have contact information for such groups.

Explaining Pet Loss to Children

When a child is about to experience a painful event, such as the death of a cherished dog, a parent's first instinct is often to limit the child's pain as much as possible. However, such efforts may not be what's best for her. Experts in child development generally recommend that parents tell their children the truth about what

is happening to their pet. Here are some ways to help your child deal with a dog's impending death and the aftermath.

Be Direct

Tell your child that your Dachshund is dying or will die soon. And beware of using euphemisms that aren't meant to be taken literally. Such expressions can backfire. For example, if you say you've "put our dog to sleep" after your Dachshund is euthanized, your child may become afraid to go to sleep.

Tell the Truth

Don't tell your child that your Dachshund ran away or was given to someone else to take care of. Sooner or later, she'll find out what really happened, and the realization that you lied could cause serious repercussions in your relationship. It's far better to tell the truth now and help your child through the resulting pain than to attempt to reduce that pain by lying, only to cause both of you far greater pain later on.

Show That You're Sad

Don't be afraid to let your child see that you're sad over the loss of your Dachshund. If she

Multi-Dog Tip

If at all possible, try to arrange for your other dogs to see your Dachshund's body after euthanasia takes place. Death is understood by dogs and other animals, and being able to see for themselves that your Dachshund has died will help your surviving dogs accept his passing.

If other animals reside in your home, the absence of your Dachshund can trigger an emotional reaction.

sees you cry occasionally or hears you say how much you miss the dog, she'll feel freer to grieve for your Dachshund too.

Tell Other Caregivers

If your child is 12 years of age or younger, tell her teacher about your dog's death. The teacher can comfort your child if need be, keep an eye on her behavior, and report to you on how she's doing.

Helping Other Pets

If other animals such as dogs and cats reside in your home, they'll probably realize that your recently deceased Dachshund is missing. That absence can trigger an emotional reaction that affects both the physical health and emotional behavior of the animals left behind. A grieving animal may lose his appetite, forget his bathroom manners, or simply act lethargic. To help him, take the following steps:

Resume Routines Quickly

Experts note that a dog or cat is often less upset by the absence of another animal than by the change in routine that absence may cause. Returning as soon as possible to that routine can help your remaining pets get back to normal more quickly.

Tempt His Taste Buds

If your pet is refusing to eat, tempt his taste buds a little. By adding a couple of treats or aromatic pieces of lean meat to his meal, sprinkling dry food with warm water to make a gravy, or warming the meal up in the microwave can reignite his interest in food.

Get Moving

A great way for both you and your pet to chase away the blues is to get some exercise. Try taking a brisk walk with your dog, or take a few minutes to play with your cat and an interactive toy.

Consult Your Vet

Sometimes what appears to be feline or canine grieving is really a sign that an animal is ill. A dog or cat who hasn't eaten for two days, a cat who doesn't urinate for several hours (or who misses the litter box when he pees), or a housetrained dog who starts having lapses all need a vet's attention. The vet also needs to see a dog or cat who acts lethargic or is vocalizing in a manner that indicates discomfort for more than two weeks.

Want to Know More?

If you've decided to add a new dog to your home, see Chapter 2: Finding and Prepping for Your Dachshund Puppy, Chapter 5: Finding Your Dachshund Adult, or Chapter 12: Finding Your Dachshund Senior for some pointers.

At this time, when your grief is sharpest, it can be hard to realize that your pain will not last forever. Time can go a long way toward healing your wounds. A time will come when the sorrow that you and your family feel over your Dachshund's death will give way to happy memories of the time you all spent together.

50 FUN FACTS EVERY DACHSHUND OWNER SHOULD KNOW

1. Dachshunds are among the most popular dog breeds in the United States. In 2009, the most recent year for which such information was available when this book was being written, the breed ranked 8th among 164 breeds in American Kennel Club (AKC) registrations.

2. The Dachshund was the fifth most popular dog in Austin, Texas, in 2009, the most recent year for which such information was available when this book was being written.

3. The name "Dachshund" combines two German words: *Dachs* and *hund*, which together mean "badger dog."

4. Two other names for the breed are "erdhundle" (earth dog) and "teckel."

5. The first Dachshunds had either the very short coats of the Smooth Dachshund or the long, Irish Setter-like coat of the Longhaired Dachshund.

6. Descriptions of the Wirehaired Dachshund first appear in the early 1800s.

7. Queen Victoria's consort, Prince Albert, gave several Smooth Dachshunds to her in England around 1840, thus introducing the breed to Great Britain.

8. The first British dog show to feature Dachshunds was held in 1859.

9. The Dachshund is a member of the Hound Group of the AKC.

10. The breed's popularity plummeted during World War I as a result of anti-German propaganda. Dachshund clubs in England shut down, Dachshund owners were branded traitors, and some dogs were stoned to death. The AKC renamed the breed "Badger Dog" during this period in an effort to give the breed a more neutral-sounding name, but it didn't fool anyone—only 26 dogs were registered in 1914.

11. An important muse of artist Pablo Picasso was a Dachshund named Lump.

12. Another famous artist, Andy Warhol, lived with two Dachshunds named Archer and Amos in the 1970s.

13. Newspaper magnate William Randolph Hearst eulogized his beloved Dachshund, Helen, in a newspaper column after the dog died in 1942.

14. Dachshunds come in two sizes: standard and miniature. The miniature Dachshund is less than 11 pounds (5 kg); a standard Dachshund weighs between 16 and 32 pounds (7.5 and 14.5 kg).

15. A Dachshund who weighs between 11 and 20 pounds (5 and 9 kg) is not called a substandard.

16. The Dachshund's life expectancy is 12 to 14 years.

17. A pet-quality Dachshund puppy may cost anywhere between $900 and $1,500 (as of early 2010).

18. The Dachshund's propensity for barking makes him a less-than-ideal apartment dog.

19. Caution should be exercised when Dachshunds are in the company of children. Many experts believe that this breed is less tolerant of children's mishandling than other breeds are.

20. Although the breed is among the most popular in the United States, no Dachshund has ever won Best in Show at the Westminster Kennel Club dog show.

21. Dachshunds have won the Hound Group competition at Westminster eight times. Smooth Dachshunds won in 1938, 1951, 1968, and 1969. (In the latter two years, the same dog won.) Wirehaired Dachshunds won in 1952 and 1997, and a Longhaired Dachshund won in 1998.

22. No Dachshund has ever lived in the White House.

23. The Dachshund is featured in *Wiener Dog Art*, a collection of cartoons by Gary Larson, creator of the beloved comic strip The Far Side.

24. Oscar, the dog featured in the comic strip *Liberty Meadows*, was a Dachshund.

25. E.B. White, author of *Charlotte's Web*, was a longtime Dachshund owner. He once said of his dogs that "I would rather train a striped zebra to balance an Indian club than induce a Dachshund to heed my slightest command." That said, the Dachshund's natural independence does not preclude the need to teach him basic good manners.

26. The mascot for the 1972 Summer Olympics in Munich, Germany, was a multi-colored painting of a Dachshund called Waldi.

27. Although Dachshund racing is a popular form of entertainment, the Dachshund Club of America

(DCA) opposes such events. Among the reasons: concerns that Dachshunds are being used to draw crowds to Greyhound tracks to see Greyhound racing, and the potential of such races to injure Dachshunds, particularly their backs.

28. The mascot of General Claire Chennault's World War II Flying Tigers was the General's Dachshund, Joe.

29. Dachshunds are not born with those long, elegant snouts. Puppies are initially snub nosed, but the snouts gradually lengthen.

30. The Dachshund is the only breed that is certified to hunt both above- and belowground.

31. Dachshunds can and do compete in conformation, earthdog, field trials, tracking, agility, obedience competition, and rally obedience.

32. The DCA offers a Versatility Championship (VC) to Dachshunds who have either earned championships in conformation, field, and obedience events or who have earned a total of 18 points from conformation and three to five of the other events in which Dachshund may compete. Such dogs must also earn an AKC Canine Good Citizen certificate.

33. Three famous Dachshunds are actually cartoon characters: Paddlefoot, who was featured in the animated *Clutch Cargo* series of the 1960s; Itchy, featured in the animated movie *All Dogs Go to Heaven*; and Dinah, the canine girlfriend of Pluto, Mickey Mouse's dog.

34. Dachshunds have a reputation for being somewhat challenging to housetrain, but consistency and patience can go a long way in teaching most of their bathroom basics.

35. Dachshunds should never be asked to sit up on their haunches because the position can strain their backs.

36. Dachshunds are active hunting dogs, not lapdogs.

37. Because the Dachshund has such short little legs, a leisurely stroll for you can be a brisk walk for him. Hence, the breed is ideal for people who are not all that active.

38. Two World War II generals on opposing sides—America's George S. Patton and Germany's Erwin Rommel—owned Dachshunds.

39. The Dachshund's unique looks make him an unforgettable character in films and television. Dachshunds have been characters in films such as *Raising Helen, Mon Oncle,* and *Hitch* and in television shows such as *The Suite Life of Zach and Cody* and *That 70's Show.*

40. The DCA was formed in 1895.

41. The first Dachshund was registered in the United States in 1879.

42. Dachshund puppies are generally ready to go home with their permanent owners at around 10 to 12 weeks of age.

43. A Dachshund has achieved his full adult growth by about one year of age.

44. Dachshund puppies need three meals a day until they're 16 weeks of age.

45. A Dachshund should have one wellness exam each year until he's eight to nine years of age, after which he should have two such exams annually.

46. Dachshunds are teenagers from six months to about one year of age; as such, they need even closer supervision than normal.

47. A Dachshund is considered a senior citizen at around ten years of age, but with luck and good care can live into his teens. One Dachshund, Senta, who belonged to German Kaiser Wilhelm II, died in 1927 at the age of 20.

48. The myth that the role of Dorothy's dog in *The Wizard of Oz* was supposed to have been actress Margaret Hamilton's Dachshund Otto is just that—a myth. The name of the dog in the novel was Toto, and the movie stayed true to the book by casting a terrier-type dog in the role and giving him the same name.

49. Some common health issues for Dachshunds include intervertebral disc disease (IDD), patellar luxation, eye problems, and hair loss.

50. Among the celebrities who own or have owned Dachshunds are actor Kevin Smith, former Secretary of Defense Donald Rumsfeld, and artist David Hockney.

ASSOCIATIONS AND ORGANIZATIONS

Breed Clubs

American Kennel Club (AKC)
5580 Centerview Drive
Raleigh, NC 27606
Telephone: (919) 233-9767
Fax: (919) 233-3627
E-Mail: info@akc.org
www.akc.org

Canadian Kennel Club (CKC)
89 Skyway Avenue, Suite 100
Etobicoke, Ontario M9W 6R4
Telephone: (416) 675-5511
Fax: (416) 675-6506
E-Mail: information@ckc.ca
www.ckc.ca

The Dachshund Club of
America, Inc. (DCA)
www.dachshund-dca.org

Dachshund Club UK
www.dachshundclub.co.uk

Federation Cynologique
Internationale (FCI)
Secretariat General de la FCI
Place Albert 1er, 13
B – 6530 Thuin
Belqique
www.fci.be

The Kennel Club
1 Clarges Street
London
W1J 8AB
Telephone: 0870 606 6750
Fax: 0207 518 1058
www.the-kennel-club.org.uk

United Kennel Club (UKC)
100 E. Kilgore Road
Kalamazoo, MI 49002-5584
Telephone: (269) 343-9020
Fax: (269) 343-7037
E-Mail: pbickell@ukcdogs.com
www.ukcdogs.com

Pet Sitters

National Association of
Professional Pet Sitters
15000 Commerce Parkway, Suite
C
Mt. Laurel, New Jersey 08054
Telephone: (856) 439-0324
Fax: (856) 439-0525
E-Mail: napps@ahint.com
www.petsitters.org

Pet Sitters International
201 East King Street
King, NC 27021-9161
Telephone: (336) 983-9222
Fax: (336) 983-5266
E-Mail: info@petsit.com
www.petsit.com

Rescue Organizations and Animal Welfare Groups

American Humane Association
(AHA)
63 Inverness Drive East
Englewood, CO 80112
Telephone: (303) 792-9900
Fax: 792-5333
www.americanhumane.org

American Society for the
Prevention of Cruelty to Animals
(ASPCA)
424 E. 92nd Street
New York, NY 10128-6804
Telephone: (212) 876-7700
www.aspca.org

The Humane Society of the
United States (HSUS)
2100 L Street, NW
Washington DC 20037
Telephone: (202) 452-1100
www.hsus.org

Royal Society for the Prevention
of Cruelty to Animals (RSPCA)
RSPCA Enquiries Service
Wilberforce Way, Southwater,
Horsham, West Sussex RH13
9RS
United Kingdom
Telephone: 0870 3335 999
Fax: 0870 7530 284
www.rspca.org.uk

Sports

International Agility Link (IAL)
Global Administrator: Steve
Drinkwater
E-Mail: yunde@powerup.au
www.agilityclick.com/~ial

The World Canine Freestyle
Organization, Inc.
P.O. Box 350122
Brooklyn, NY 11235
Telephone: (718) 332-8336
Fax: (718) 646-2686
E-Mail: WCFODOGS@aol.com
www.worldcaninefreestyle.org

Therapy

Delta Society
875 124th Ave, NE, Suite 101
Bellevue, WA 98005
Telephone: (425) 679-5500
Fax: (425) 679-5539
E-Mail: info@DeltaSociety.org
www.deltasociety.org

Therapy Dogs Inc.
P.O. Box 20227
Cheyenne WY 82003
Telephone: (877) 843-7364
Fax: (307) 638-2079
E-Mail: therapydogsinc@
qwestoffice.net
www.therapydogs.com

Therapy Dogs International
(TDI)
88 Bartley Road
Flanders, NJ 07836
Telephone: (973) 252-9800
Fax: (973) 252-7171
E-Mail: tdi@gti.net
www.tdi-dog.org

Training

Association of Pet Dog Trainers
(APDT)
150 Executive Center Drive Box
35
Greenville, SC 29615
Telephone: (800) PET-DOGS
Fax: (864) 331-0767
E-Mail: information@apdt.com
www.apdt.com

International Association of
Animal Behavior Consultants
(IAABC)
565 Callery Road
Cranberry Township, PA 16066
E-Mail: info@iaabc.org
www.iaabc.org

Veterinary and Health Resources

Academy of Veterinary
Homeopathy (AVH)
P.O. Box 9280
Wilmington, DE 19809
Telephone: (866) 652-1590
Fax: (866) 652-1590
www.theavh.org

American Academy of Veterinary
Acupuncture (AAVA)
P.O. Box 1058
Glastonbury, CT 06033
Telephone: (860) 632-9911
Fax: (860) 659-8772
www.aava.org

American Animal Hospital
Association (AAHA)
12575 W. Bayaud Ave.
Lakewood, CO 80228
Telephone: (303) 986-2800
Fax: (303) 986-1700
E-Mail: info@aahanet.org
www.aahanet.org/index.cfm

American College of Veterinary
Internal Medicine (ACVIM)
1997 Wadsworth Blvd., Suite A
Lakewood, CO 80214-5293
Telephone: (800) 245-9081
Fax: (303) 231-0880
Email: ACVIM@ACVIM.org
www.acvim.org

American College of Veterinary
Ophthalmologists (ACVO)
P.O. Box 1311
Meridian, ID 83860
Telephone: (208) 466-7624
Fax: (208) 466-7693
E-Mail: office09@acvo.com
www.acvo.com

American Holistic Veterinary
Medical Association (AHVMA)
2218 Old Emmorton Road
Bel Air, MD 21015
Telephone: (410) 569-0795
Fax: (410) 569-2346
E-Mail: office@ahvma.org
www.ahvma.org

American Veterinary Medical
Association (AVMA)
1931 North Meacham Road,
Suite 100
Schaumburg, IL 60173-4360
Telephone: (847) 925-8070
Fax: (847) 925-1329
E-Mail: avmainfo@avma.org
www.avma.org

ASPCA Animal Poison Control
Center
Telephone: (888) 426-4435
www.aspca.org

British Veterinary Association
(BVA)
7 Mansfield Street
London
W1G 9NQ
Telephone: 0207 636 6541
Fax: 0207 908 6349
E-Mail: bvahq@bva.co.uk
www.bva.co.uk

Canine Eye Registration
Foundation (CERF)
VMDB/CERF
1717 Philo Rd
P O Box 3007
Urbana, IL 61803-3007
Telephone: (217) 693-4800
Fax: (217) 693-4801
E-Mail: CERF@vmbd.org
www.vmdb.org

Orthopedic Foundation for
Animals (OFA)
2300 NE Nifong Blvd
Columbus, Missouri 65201-3856
Telephone: (573) 442-0418
Fax: (573) 875-5073
Email: ofa@offa.org
www.offa.org

US Food and Drug
Administration Center for
Veterinary Medicine (CVM)
7519 Standish Place
HFV-12
Rockville, MD 20855-0001
Telephone: (240) 276-9300 or
(888) INFO-FDA
http://www.fda.gov/cvm

PUBLICATIONS

Books

Anderson, Teoti. The
  Super Simple Guide to
  Housetraining. Neptune City:
  TFH Publications, 2004.

Anne, Jonna, with Mary Straus.
  The Healthy Dog Cookbook:
  50 Nutritious and Delicious
  Recipes Your Dog Will Love.
  UK: Ivy Press Limited, 2008.

Boneham, Sheila Webster, Ph.D.
  Dachshunds. Neptune City:
  TFH Publications and
  Discovery Communications,
  Inc., 2007.

Dainty, Suellen. 50 Games to
  Play With Your Dog. UK: Ivy
  Press Limited, 2007.

Ewing, Susan M. The
  Dachshund. Neptune City:
  TFH Publications, 2005.

Morgan, Diane. The Complete
  Guide to Dog Care. Neptune
  City: TFH Publications and
  Discovery Communications,
  Inc., 2011.

Magazines

AKC Family Dog
American Kennel Club
260 Madison Avenue
New York, NY 10016
Telephone: (800) 490-5675
E-Mail: familydog@akc.org
www.akc.org/pubs/familydog

AKC Gazette
American Kennel Club
260 Madison Avenue
New York, NY 10016
Telephone: (800) 533-7323
E-Mail: gazette@akc.org
www.akc.org/pubs/gazette

Dog & Kennel
Pet Publishing, Inc.
7-L Dundas Circle
Greensboro, NC 27407
Telephone: (336) 292-4272
Fax: (336) 292-4272
E-Mail: info@petpublishing.com
www.dogandkennel.com

Dogs Monthly
Ascot House
High Street, Ascot,
Berkshire SL5 7JG
United Kingdom
Telephone: 0870 730 8433
Fax: 0870 730 8431
E-Mail: admin@rtc-associates.
freeserve.co.uk
www.corsini.co.uk/dogsmonthly

Websites

Nylabone
www.nylabone.com

TFH Publications, Inc.
www.tfh.com

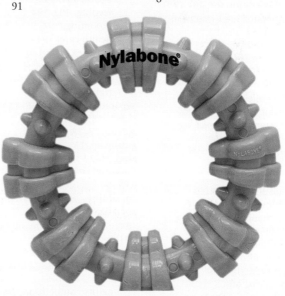

PHOTO CREDITS

6493866629 (Shutterstock): 155; absolut (Shutterstock): 205, 207; Bragin Alexey (Shutterstock): 109; Aaron Amat (Shutterstock): 130; Utekhina Anna (Shutterstock): 50; Alexander Bark (Shutterstock): 21; Dan Briški (Shutterstock): 170, 199; Coral Coolahan (Shutterstock): 124; ericlefrancais (Shutterstock): 110; Dewayne Flowers (Shutterstock): 57, 127, 137, 204; Jean M. Fogle@jeanmfogle.com: 176; BW Folsom (Shutterstock): 112; jarvis gray (Shutterstock): spine; Groomee (Shutterstock): 141; Hannamariah (Shutterstock): 16, 65 (dog), 144; Mark Herreid (Shutterstock): 152, 174; In-Finity (Shutterstock): 116; Kirsanov (Shutterstock): 87; Liliya Kulian-ionak (Shutterstock):106, 123; Chris leachman (Shutterstock): 179; maxstockphoto (Shutterstock): 172; Losevsky Pavel (Shutterstock): 178; Lobke Peers (Shutterstock): 6; Steven Pepple (Shutter-stock): 208; South 12th Photography (Shutterstock): 51; Carsten Reisinger (Shutterstock): 40; Nata Sdobnikova (Shutterstock): 26; Shutterstock: 131, 160; Alexey Stiop (Shutterstock): 44; tiptoee (Shutterstock): 126; April Turner (Shutterstock): 193; Vaida (Shutterstock): 118; Svetlana Valoueva (Shutterstock): back cover, 168; vgm (Shutterstock): 92; Aaron Willcox (Shutterstock): 210; woody-graphs (Shutterstock): 139, 167; Lisa F. Young (Shutterstock): 89

author photo: PawPrints Photography

All other photos courtesy of Isabelle Francais and TFH archives

DEDICATION
To Casey, Lola, and Mimi—all great Dachshunds

ACKNOWLEDGMENTS
I'm just one of many people who've put this book into your hands. I'd like to thank those people, especially:

Stephanie Fornino, who asked me to take on this project;

Wayne Hunthausen, DVM, who critiqued the medical portions of the manuscript;

the many dog professionals from whom I've learned so much about canine care, health, and training;

my parents, Robert and Estelle McCullough, who introduced me to the joys of life with Dachshunds;

my patient, good-humored husband, Stan Chappell; daughter, Julie Chappell; and Golden Retriever, Allie.

ABOUT THE AUTHOR
Susan McCullough writes about dog behavior and health for media outlets all over the United States and is also the author of several dog care books, including DogLife *Golden Retriever*. She has won six Maxwell Awards from the Dog Writers Association of America (DWAA) for her work. Susan and her Golden Retriever, Allie, live with their family in Bradenton, Florida.

VETERINARY ADVISOR
Wayne Hunthausen, DVM, consulting veterinary editor and pet behavior consultant, is the director of Animal Behavior Consultations in the Kansas City area and currently serves on the Practitioner Board for *Veterinary Medicine* and the Behavior Advisory Board for *Veterinary Forum*.

BREEDER ADVISOR
Vicki Spencer has trained and raised standard Smooth Dachshunds for more than 20 years under the Lorindol Kennel name. She has bred and shown many dual champions (conformation and field) and has earned earthdog and obedience titles. Vicki is a Canine Good Citizen (CGC) evaluator, has been an obedience instructor for more than 30 years, has taught puppy and conformation classes for more than 20 years, and visits schools, nursing homes, and hospitals with her Dachshunds. She is also an American Kennel Club (AKC) field trial judge and a breeder referrer and archivist for the Dachshund Club of America (DCA).

JOIN NOW
Club Nylabone
www.nylabone.com
Coupons!
Articles!
Exciting
Features!

He **Plays** Hard.
He **Chews** Hard.

He's a **Nylabone**® Dog!
Your #1 choice for healthy chews & treats.